Old Hippie on a Bike

From Russia to England at seventy-two after a stroke

Alan Deakins

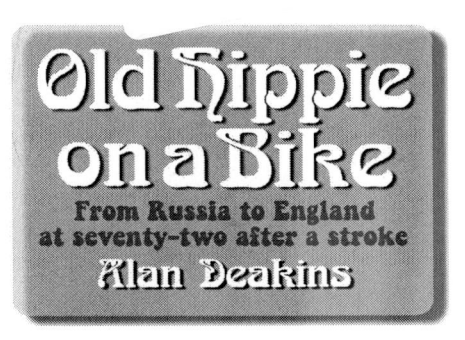

Copyright© 2019 Alan Deakins

All rights reserved. No part of this book may be reproduced, distributed or transmitted in any form or by any means, except for brief extracts for the purpose of review, without my permission.

Cover design: © Alan Deakins

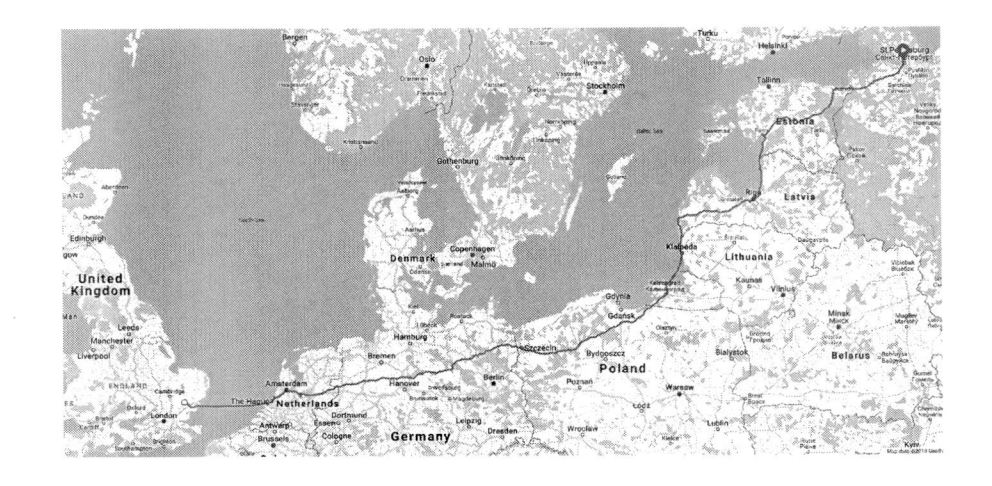

FOR

Marnie
Joseph
Zack and Annie
Charlotte and Evelyn

You are my nucleus

Bo
I wish you silence

CONTENTS

INTRODUCTION

CHAPTER 1. HAPPY BIRTHDAY
CHAPTER 2. STANDING ON MY HEAD
CHAPTER 3. WHAT IF...?
Chapter 4. DECISION MADE. NOW WHAT?
DAY 1. SUDBURY – ST PETERSBURG
DAY 2. ST PETERSBURG
DAY 3. ST PETERSBURG – GLUKHOVO
DAY 4. GLUKHOVO – GURLOVO
DAY 5. GURLOVO – NARVA, ESTONIA
DAY 6. NARVA – JOVHI
DAY 7. JOHVI – MUSTVEE
DAY 8. MUSTVEE – JOGEVA
DAY 9. JOGEVA – SUURE-JAANI
DAY 10. SUURE-JAANI – PARNU
DAY 11. PARNU – REST
DAY 12. PARNU – SALACGRIVA, LATVIA
DAY 13. SALACGRIVA – LAKE DZIRNEZERS
DAY 14. LAKE DZIRNEZERS – LAKE KLIGU EZERS
DAY 15. LAKE KLIGU EZERS – SKRUNDA
DAY 16. SKRUNDA - LIEPAJA
DAY 17. LIEPAJA – KLAIPEDA, LITHUANIA
DAY 18. KLAIPEDA – NIDA
DAY 19. NIDA – PRIBREZHNYY, KALININGRAD
DAY 20. PRIBREZHNYY – ELBLAG, POLAND
DAY 21. ELBLAG – STAROGARD
DAY 22. STAROGARD – CZLUCHOW
DAY 23. CZLUCHOW – WALCZ
DAY 24. WALCZ - STARGARD
DAY 25. STARGARD – SZCZECIN

DAY 26. SZCZECIN – LÖCKNITZ, GERMANY
DAY 27. LÖCKNITZ – NEUBRANDENBURG
DAY 28. NEUBRANDENBURG - USERIN
DAY 29. USERIN – REST DAY
DAY 30. USERIN – PERLEBERG
DAY 31. PERLEBERG – GARTOW
DAY 32. GARTOW – BAD BODENTEICH
DAY 33. BAD BODENTEICH – WINSEN AN DER ALLER
DAY 34. WINSEN AN DER ALLER – REHDEN
DAY 35. FERIENHOF IN REHDEN – REST
DAY 36. REHDEN – LINGEN
DAY 37. LINGEN – ALMELO, HOLLAND
DAY 38. ALMELO – ZWEEWOLDE
DAY 39. ZWEEWOLDE – HARWICH, ENGLAND
DAY 40. HARWICH - SUDBURY
DAY 41. SUDBURY – BURY ST EDMUNDS

AT THE END OF IT ALL…

CYCLING ON A BUDGET – OR NOT

TWO PENNIES WORTH

THE SAMARITANS

INTRODUCTION

I am a reluctant cyclist.

I didn't start out to be a cyclist. It just happened due to changes in my life. I became a septuagenarian, I retired and I had a stroke in a very short time period.

The combination of these circumstances thrust me onto a bike.

Cycling isn't the first activity I would turn to for fun or enjoyment. It isn't a passion with me, yet I feel compelled to ride. Perhaps it makes me feel better…inside and out. Perhaps it is my 'poke in the eye' to ageing. Perhaps it is just the need to feel the road moving under me. Perhaps.

There is one definite reason why I continued cycling: adventure. I am irresistibly drawn to the bend in the road. What will happen next? What will I see? Who will I meet? How will it affect me? It has become an addiction.

When I first began thinking of a long bike tour, I needed more justification for the journey other than just to scratch an itch. Fortunately, I had a real passion to link it to…The Samaritans. I have been a Samaritan listener for over three years, and it too is an adventure. We are there for people who feel suicidal or who can't cope in their lives. Listening without judgement is extraordinarily powerful. It can change lives and sometimes save lives. It is a privilege to be a Samaritan. It is challenging, and far more rewarding than anything I ever did as a film-maker.

Each Samaritans branch is a charity in its own right and has to find the money to operate. I hoped that my ride would raise funds for my branch, Samaritans of Bury St Edmunds and West Suffolk.

That's why I chose to ride from St Petersburg to my Samaritans Branch in Bury St Edmunds.

My ride across Russia and northern Europe was just shy of three thousand kilometres. It is by no means a record-breaker in any category. Older people than me have ridden far greater distances across more continents than I did. So what makes my journey so special? I suppose what seemed to capture peoples' imaginations was the fact that I had a stroke, I was riding completely on my own without any support, and of course, in some minds, I was considered positively ancient. Will the old bloke make it…?

As far as I was concerned, I was just an ordinary guy, with time on his hands who took on a fairly challenging ride in aid of his favourite charity, which is why I toyed with the idea that *The Diary of a Nobody on a Bike* was a more apt title for this book.

This is basically a journal, rather than a diary, or travelogue, or a how-to book. I wrote very little in the way of historical significances of places I travelled through or sights I had seen.

My interest in the terrain was more or less limited to the difficulty of cycling it. Also, I had little concern with my age or the effects of my stroke. I was happy as long as everything worked without too much difficulty or pain. So, I'm afraid I didn't write much in that regard.

What made this journey unique was the fact that it was experienced through my personal filters that developed over seventy-two years. My impressions were uppermost in my mind in writing this book. My experiences, the things that I saw and people I met affected me greatly, and that's what I wanted to write about.

This is not to say that this book is totally bereft of any practical advice. Riding on a budget, meant I had to find gear that would do the job at bargain prices. I include winners and losers in what I chose.

I also include thoughts on long-distance cycling gleaned from my experiences that some may find helpful.

Lastly, I hope that I am able to communicate more than mere experiences. My desire is to express how it felt to be heartened, defeated, inspired, exhausted, moved, frightened, lost, lifted, lonely, loved. What happened inside me. In my head. In my seventy-two-year old heart.

Because that really is where my journey took place.

February 2019

CHAPTER 1
HAPPY BIRTHDAY
MAY 2016

'A sextagenarian! At his age?'
-Gracie Allen

'There it is. That's it.'

'What? That little dot?'

'It's tiny. A TIA. You're lucky.'

I was standing next to the Consultant Doctor in the Stroke Ward at West Suffolk Hospital staring into a monitor displaying the inside of my head in the minutest detail. We are looking at an MRI scan of my brain.

At 70, this was the first time I have been hospitalised for anything in my adult life. A stroke is a pernicious event. One second you are healthy, the next you experience a malfunction. Your body doesn't respond to what you have told it to do.

In my case, it was on the morning of my seventieth birthday. I woke up, came down to the kitchen, as usual, turned my coffee machine on, and opened the cupboard to get a cup. Instead of grasping the cup cleanly, my knuckles hit the shelf…I missed the mark by three centimetres or so. No big deal…I reached again and the same thing. 'Odd…' I thought.

I stretched my left arm, gave it a few swings, grabbed the cup and thought nothing more of it.

After all, it was a special day...we were all going out to lunch to celebrate my birthday. Both boys, Joseph and Zack and Annie (Zack's partner) would arrive soon. Marnie had booked a table at a local pub. Nice. Nothing fancy, just a relaxed day with family.

During lunch, I noticed that my left hand was not quite as nimble as I'm used to when using my fork. Nothing alarming...just annoying more than anything. And on our walk after lunch, my left leg seemed a bit weak...which I put down to tiredness. I had done a night shift at the Samaritans, and I attributed my slight off-colour feeling to lack of sleep.

That evening, I told Marnie I was turning in early to make up for my lost sleep. I slept soundly. Very soundly. And I felt rested when I came down to the kitchen, turned the coffee machine on and reached for a cup. Bang, my knuckle hit the edge of the shelf again.

'OK,' I thought. 'Maybe there is something wrong.' But why? I didn't feel particularly bad. Even if it was my imagination or the product of a hypochondriac's mind, I felt I should have it checked out. Marnie was out walking the dog. I didn't want to be alarmist...what if it was nothing? I thought a nonchalant call to her would be best.

'Hi...my left hand is feeling a bit funny. I think I'll pop up to A&E...'

'What do you mean funny?'

'I dunno...it doesn't do exactly what I tell it to. So I'm going to drive up and...'

'I'm heading back...'

'No, really it's probably nothing. It's been like this since yesterday. It's not getting worse. I'll be OK. Really...'

Old Hippie on a Bike

'I can be back in a half an hour…'

'I kind of want to go now. Really…I'm OK. I can drive. Really…'

By then, I was doing my best to convince myself. Really.

The 18-mile, early Sunday morning drive from Sudbury to the West Suffolk Hospital in Bury St Edmunds was easy. I felt confident driving, and I knew just about every curve, every pothole, every nuance of this road intimately. I ferried my younger son, Joseph, countless times up and down this route over the years to primary, middle and upper schools, then 6th form college, and lastly when he became a Samaritan.

Being a Samaritan was such an incredible thing to do for someone so young. I was in awe of him. It was his dedication, at age nineteen, to be there for people who needed emotional support that inspired me to want to be a Samaritan also.

'Yes,' I thought. 'When I retire.'

So there I was. Retired. A Samaritan. Travelling this oh-so-familiar road. Worried. I had a feeling it was a stroke. It was either that or my hypochondria was kicking in.

The Accident and Emergency room was virtually empty when I arrived, just a few people waiting to be called either into triage or for treatment. Two young men were staring intently into a computer screen as I approached the reception desk.

One of them glanced up. 'Can I help…?'

'Uhm…my left side feels a bit strange.'

The second young man was still looking into the screen. 'Maybe if I close this window.'

'No…I don't think that will help. Check the menu.'

'Where's that?'

'Up there on the left...see those three lines?'

'Excuse me...I just told you my left side feels strange. Could I possibly be having a stroke? Could you possibly attend to that later...?'

'Oh...right. Sorry. Are you able to take a seat? I'll call the stroke team.'

Before I completed the dozen or so steps to the nearest seat, the doors burst open and two people emerged, introduced themselves as part of the Stroke Team and immediately took me into the ward. From then on, it was the National Health Service at its best. The dedicated professionals on the Stroke Team were marvellous. I was given a battery of tests, comforted, kept informed and generally put at ease that everything possible was being done.

Yes, the tests indicated that I had had a stroke. A mild one, but a stroke nonetheless. A Consultant would be with me shortly to assess the findings and prescribe what would happen next.

I called home with the news, and within the hour, Marnie, Joseph, Zack and Annie were brought in to see me. Seeing them eased my apprehension somewhat. But it was disconcerting to have people I loved gathered around me because I was the one who was ill. I put on a brave face, assuring them that I was OK. I even acted healthy, perhaps over- exaggerating my fitness.

I'm the father, the strong one in this family. It wasn't easy to accept that at that moment, I wasn't.

The Consultant arrived, and after examining me and the test results decided that even though I seemed well enough to go home and return tomorrow for an MRI scan, it was best for me to be admitted into the hospital for observation before the scan. Damn. I wanted to go home.

The Stroke Ward was certainly an eye-opener. I met men suffering the consequences of stroke in varying degrees. A young man, John, across from me, was just 32. He was mostly mobile with a decided limp but his right arm was for the most part paralysed. There was an old boy next to him who I would guess was well into his 80's, completely bedridden, and completely non-corpus mentis. He lay there wide-eyed moaning without respite. I was convinced he had no idea where he was, or why he was there. The nurses were wonderful to him. They treated him with gentleness and respect. Clearly, he hadn't much time left, but he still clung tenaciously on to life.

There was the chap at the end who also was severely affected. He had his mental faculties as far as I could surmise, but very little control over his physical state. He couldn't really move, and his only communication was with garbled words and sounds. He lay on his left side, for the most part, staring at the corridor waiting for his wife. When she arrived, he would emit a happy sound, and she would sit very close and whisper to him for the entirety of the visiting hours.

Another chap at the end of the bay, next to the corridor, had it particularly tough. He wasn't mobile at all, but he had full use of his right arm and limited use of his left. He couldn't walk, but at least he could eat, and read his newspaper. He told me he had no family to speak of. So although he was chatty and amiable outside of visiting hours, when the ward was full of visitors, he sat alone in his wheelchair next to his bed. I remember one time glancing over to see him in his chair struggling with a bedpan while trying to cover his dignity. It was a sad sight. And it made me think how each of us lives a life that is, for the most part, unplanned, and we try as best we can in the circumstances we find ourselves in.

As my teacher once told me: 'Life can be good...but it is seldom, if ever, fair.'

The bed next to me was empty, and I liked it that way. I relished the space. But my smug satisfaction soon ended when a man was wheeled in to claim it. He was in his 80's, deeply tanned with unusual golden wavy hair. He seemed a caricature of an Essex born Benidorm retiree. In fact, that is exactly what he was. His equally tanned wife and family gathered around his bed as he held court. According to him, he was fine, nothing wrong; he was the paragon of health, and he'd be out in the morning. For all intents and purposes, he looked and acted fine. Perhaps when the lights go out, he will sleep. In fact, we will all sleep.

Just as I was dozing off, I was woken; a light shined in each eye and my blood pressure taken. I was told this would happen every two hours during the night. This obviously would be a major obstacle in any effort on my part to sleep. Worse still, the bronzed senior Adonis next to me was to have this same routine done to him every hour, which woke me up also. After the third time, I decided drastic action was needed. I snuck past the nurses' station and padded down to the TV lounge at the end of the corridor. There were two reclining chairs. One was occupied by a slumbering male nurse. I curled up in the other and soon succumbed to blessed sleep.

I was deep into a dream when I felt a shaking of my body. It took some time for me to realise this was real.

'Alan...I've been looking all over for you. I thought you escaped.'

'Impossible to sleep in there.'

'I understand,' she said as she shined her torch into each eye again, and took my blood pressure. 'You don't have to go back. You can stay here.'

'Thanks. Can we also stop this routine? I'm fine. Really.'

'OK. I promise.'

Two hours later she was back with her torch.

'You said you weren't going to do this again...'

She gently replied, 'I lied.'

The next morning, because I was mobile, I could shower on my own. It was heaven, albeit a bit of a struggle. I had to admit to myself that my left side was slightly uncoordinated. Even so, I managed and was clean, fresh and ready for my MRI scan.

I had an MRI a few years earlier for a bulging disc in my lower back, so I knew what to expect. Still, being slightly claustrophobic, it is daunting being slid into the tunnel.

'OK...fifteen minutes,' I told myself. 'You can stand on your head for fifteen minutes.'

I can't remember where that expression came from, but it was a much-used saying in our family. If the boys complained that a four-hour car journey was too long, the reply would be: 'You can stand on your head for four hours.' Or, 'I have to wait two more weeks until Summer Break' would be met with: 'You can stand on your head for two weeks.' We would all accept this explanation, and somehow, it would make the wait bearable.

So, I stood on my head for fifteen minutes. With the MRI over, I was back in the ward looking forward to going home. I phoned Marnie to tell her that I would be signed out soon.

I was ready to leave. I had enough. Enough of being prodded and poked. Enough of being woken every two hours. Enough of lights being shined in my eyes. Enough, I'm sorry to say, of the moaning old boy across from me. Enough of illness around me. Enough of the illness in me. I was desperate to escape.

The joy of my impending release from it all was shattered when a nurse informed me that the Consultant would not be

Alan Deakins

signing my release. His instructions were for me to have a session with the Physiotherapy Department and stay another night for further observation. He would then see me with my MRI results the next afternoon. I was stunned. I wasn't prepared for the effect that this news would have on me.

I walked out into a courtyard adjoining the ward. I sat on a bench facing away from the windows. I could feel the tears running down my cheeks. I didn't know why. I don't know how long I sat there.

'Alan.' A nurse sat beside me.

'I'm not ready to go back in…'

'I'm not here to take you back. I came to see how you are.'

'I'm so disappointed…'

And I was. Disappointed at not going home was really low on my list. I was disappointed in myself, my condition, in my vulnerability, in my attitude to it all…and of course, in my mortality. It all hit me at once.

She sat with me for quite some time, a generous gesture considering the demands this environment placed on her. It was an unselfish kindness, and it reminded me of the power of listening. It reminded me of the Samaritans.

A Samaritan, when on the phone, just listens. He or she won't impose their views, nor offer advice, nor judge. It is a simple concept. To be heard with respect and acceptance has the power to change a life. That nurse could make a terrific Samaritan.

I called Marnie to tell her that I was to be there for another day. She could hear the disappointment in my voice, and she gave me the perfect response.

'You can stand on your head for a day.'

'A hospital is no place to be sick.'
-Samuel Goldwyn

I've seen MRI scans in television documentaries and medical dramas. Seeing one in real life would be about the same if it had belonged to another person. But viewing my own brain objectively as a subject to be studied, was disconcerting.

Perhaps it is because we see ourselves as entities...living breathing cognitive emotional spiritual beings capable of abstract thought and analytical reasoning. So to be presented with an image that says, 'I am really a machine,' is an affront to my perception of myself.

The fact is, our being alive on this planet is dependent on the machine we live in. If the machine is functioning well, we go about our lives without worry about it. (Except we are prone to obsess over our machine's appearance, which keeps all sorts of businesses thriving. Clothing. Hairdressers. Plastic Surgeons. Tattooists, tanning salons, dieticians, jewellers...etc.)

On the practical side, if our machine malfunctions, we are thrown into all sorts of problems of how we deal with our quality of life, and the hard decisions we face to keep going. If our machine stops working altogether, we are no longer alive on this planet.

None of this was going through my mind while staring at my brain with the Consultant. I just felt strange. Inside out. My brain was layered like filo pastry.

'You're lucky.'

'Am I?'

'It is very small. Looks like it happened from an old injury. Did

Alan Deakins

you ever bump your head?'

'Too many to recount here.'

When I was five, I decided to swing by my legs on a fence bar. I was too young to calculate how close the cement base was to the bar. I remember seeing stars when my head connected with it. That incident required two stitches on the side of my head. Then there was the time I fell while climbing up the stone chimney breast in our house, that resulted in three stitches in the back of my head. Or the three car accidents I was in. I was diagnosed as concussed in one of them. Or the most recent time when a dog ran out in front of my bike sending me over the handlebars...the first thing to hit the rock hard ground was my head. Fortunately, I was wearing a helmet, but I did have a headache for hours afterwards.

'Your blood pressure is slightly high, nothing to be alarmed about...I'll attribute that to the fact that you are 70, so I'm going to prescribe something to bring it down. Your cholesterol is normal so we'll leave that as it is...oh...and you can't drive for a month.'

'What? But I'm OK...'

'It's the law. One month...then get your GP's OK to drive again...'

I could hear Marnie and the boys in my mind, 'You can stand on your head for a month.'

'OK,' I said. 'I've got a bike...'

CHAPTER 2
STANDING ON MY HEAD

'If I can bicycle, I bicycle.'
'David Attenborough

Yes. I had a bike. It was not as though I was a cycling enthusiast. Far from it.

I had recently bought a bike on eBay.

Before that, I hadn't been on a bike since the boys were young. Some 25 years ago. I bought a Peugeot hybrid bike to accompany them on local cycle trips around our village on the rural roads of Suffolk. I even convinced myself that it would be good for losing weight and staying healthy with cardiovascular exercising. This commendable effort lasted for a few months, consisting of my cycling three miles (five kilometres) to the next village and back. It was, in my opinion, a strenuous endeavour. I would be totally out of breath, and my legs feeling rubbery when I returned home. Still, I thought, 'You're getting healthy.'

As with any regime we force upon ourselves for our own good, this was doomed to failure. I soon found more important (and less strenuous) activities to occupy my time, and feeling justified, I hung the Peugeot on the wall of my workroom, with the specific promise to myself that I would get back on it when I had the time. Soon. Very soon.

Fifteen years later, Zack was helping me with a clear out. It was a task he relished. He was and still is, an orderly person.

Alan Deakins

Even as a very young boy, he hated anything out of place. His room was always neat and tidy.

He pulled the old Peugeot from the wall, by now it was an irreparable rusting heap.

'When's the last time you were on this...?'

'I dunno...a few years ago.'

'I haven't seen you on it since I was 12.'

'It hasn't been that long. I might want to get back on it...'

'It's been too long...it's going in the skip.'

His axiom, for as long as I can remember, was: if you haven't used an item in the past year, it has to go. It's clutter. Either throw it out or sell it.

Given the state of it, and Zack's stare...I knew its fate.

'You won't miss it.' He unceremoniously carried it out to the skip and chucked it in.

He was right, I didn't miss it. And I probably would have lived without another bike for the rest of my life if it hadn't been for two things. Joseph had moved to London and had taken up cycling for recreation and to commute to Homerton Hospital where he was a Clinical Psychologist.

Also, Marnie and I had moved from our home of two and a half decades in a rural village into Sudbury, a small town on the Essex/Suffolk border. The boys had long since left the nest, and downsizing from a large house with two acres of land seemed a logical step.

It was a novelty to have all the amenities we needed on our doorstep. For the first time in twenty-five years, we didn't have to hop in a car every time we needed a pint of milk.

Meanwhile, Joseph obsessed on what bicycle to buy. He would

send me links to various bikes on eBay. What did I think of this one or that one? He finally settled on a vintage lightweight road racer. One weekend, he rode it from London to visit us. I was impressed with his ride of over sixty miles in roughly five hours. A superhuman feat in my mind. But I was equally impressed with his bike.

It sat there in our courtyard, red and gleaming in the sun. I'm a sucker for machines, and I was instantly attracted to it. And a thought began forming in my mind: 'Perhaps a bike would be useful for my getting around town.'

The practicality of it made sense and completely justified my getting a gleaming desirable machine. 'Poop. Poop,' Said the Toad. (The Wind in the Willows was favourite reading at bedtime when the boys were little.)

I began scouring eBay. Not being very au fait with the current bicycle scene, I relied on my 1990 sense of what would be a proper bike. I also thought that an older bike would be cheaper. If this idea turned out to be a total disaster, at least I wouldn't have a lot of money sunk into it. Being newly retired, and on a fixed income, this had to be a primary consideration.

I finally settled on a rather natty 1990's Raleigh Pioneer. It had a turquoise frame with silver mudguards. Nice. It appealed to me. I won the auction for the princely sum of £49. Woohoo! I excitedly drove to Clacton on a rainy Saturday morning to collect it, but being so long off a bike, I made one mistake that had two consequences. I didn't consider its size.

First, the gentleman who answered the door was considerably taller than me, about Zack's height: 6'3" (190cm). I'm about 5'11" (180cm). I didn't think too much of it until he took me into his garage to show me the bike. It was tall…very tall. I had already committed to buying it, so I thought all I needed to do was lower the saddle as far as possible and it would be OK. Besides, it was gleaming.

Secondly, I drove there in my Alfa Romeo GT. Although it was a hatchback, it was woefully small for the task of transporting a bike. After removing both wheels, reclining the passenger seat, and moving the driver's seat as far forward as possible, we managed to squeeze it in. The drive home was a lesson in contortionism: my legs in a squatting position with my knees on either side of the steering wheel which was only a few centimetres from my chest, operating the pedals mostly with my toes. Nonetheless, I managed to get my prize home.

Just a short distance from our house (about two hundred metres) is a lovely trail known as the Valley Walk which connects Sudbury with Long Melford about two miles away. It is a disused railway line that fell victim to the Beeching Axe in 1965. Now it is a much-used park for walking and cycling. What better place to try out my new gleaming machine?

I lowered the saddle and set off. It was a big bike, my toes of one leg could barely touch the ground when I stopped. Still, I enthusiastically rode about two miles along the trail. It was also a heavy bike, and I was out of breath. When I finally made it back home, I managed to crush two vulnerable bits of my lower anatomy (my 'Niagara Falls' in Cockney Rhyming Slang) on the high crossbar.

I hobbled around the house with a pain in my groin, on two rubbery legs, with my feet flopping rather than stepping as I walked. (I must have looked like John Cleese with a hernia doing his silly walk.) All the while, I was thinking maybe this cycling malarkey is better left to fit youngsters like my younger son.

I was utterly out of shape. I knew it. And the only way to get the best out of my £49 investment was to ride again...and again. Which I dutifully, if unenthusiastically, did.

I bought two inexpensive pannier bags so I could do the shopping, which worked fine until I tried to transport six bottles of wine in one of them. Not surprisingly, its mountings broke due to the weight. It didn't put me off…I continued to ride.

I rode the four-mile round trip on the Valley Walk every day until my legs weren't wobbly at the end. I began to take longer excursions, five miles, then ten miles. It took a couple of months, but my muscles were getting acclimatised to riding, and my head followed. I couldn't say I was falling in love with cycling…it was something I more or less felt compelled to do. I began to appreciate that this was now more than a passing fancy, and I would continue to ride every day. Maybe I stopped thinking this was good for me. Whatever, I started enjoying my rides a bit. Just a bit.

Once I reached this point, I knew the Raleigh's days were numbered. It was too heavy for a start. And after bashing my "Niagara's" on the crossbar more times than I cared to remember, I had enough.

I began searching eBay once again. It wasn't long before I discovered a new entry on a Wednesday afternoon. It was a 'buy it now' listing of a Dawes Sonoran Hybrid bike for £80. It was silver with silver mudguards. By this time, I knew that looks mattered less than the bike itself, but I had to admit it was handsome. It seemed the right size, and it had a frame designed with a low crossbar. I was sold. I immediately clicked on the buy-it-now button. Within a few minutes, the seller responded that it was ready for collection.

That afternoon, I drove to Saxmundham in Marnie's Fiat Idea, a car more suited to transporting a bike. I liked the Dawes straight away. It was gleaming. It was lighter than the Raleigh. I could straddle the crossbar with both feet flat on the ground. It handled well on my test ride. It also had two powerful Ultrafire lights mounted on the handlebar included. We bundled it into the car, and I drove home a happy man.

Alan Deakins

For the next few months, I set about adapting the Dawes to my liking. I purchased a rear rack, handlebar bag and several saddles. A saddle is a very personal thing. Your bottom has to get along with it. If it doesn't, it will make riding a misery for you. I tried several of the foam padded saddles, which were fine at first, but horrible after constant riding. I tried new designs, even one that claimed to be good for my prostate with no success. I was riding frequently and changing saddles frequently.

In spite of my posterior, I was liking cycling. I don't know why. Every day, it took an effort to overcome my inertia to get on it and go. I rode well into the autumn, and most of the winter if the roads were clear. Some days were so bitterly cold, that my hands would ache. These were times that challenged my desire to ride. Why was I putting myself through this? I didn't have an answer. I wasn't really enjoying the cold, but I still rode even if for a few miles.

Spring came, and my Dawes and I were well suited to each other. I was satisfied with it. I knew it intimately. I knew two things to expect when I got on it. One was a compliant ride from the bike, the other was a pain in the ass from the saddle. I still hadn't figured out that side of my riding experience.

I had steered clear of Brooks saddles because they were too expensive, and being leather, they aren't considered weatherproof. But since I had tried just about every other option, and just about every long distance cyclist recommends them, I bought a black carved Brooks Flyer. The Flyer had springs, and being carved meant that it had a hole cut into the seat where the soft bit between my legs would be. This saddle was a revelation. It transformed my ride. For the first time, I was comfortable.

I could now enjoy my ten-mile run every day in comfort. Even though I was finally content with my bike, I still didn't consider myself a cyclist.

I certainly wasn't in the lycra brigade. I had no intentions of becoming a MAMIL (Middle Age Man In Lycra). Or an old man in lycra in my case. The fact was, I still really considered myself a petrol head.

I had a love affair with cars as long as I can remember. My mother would recall my standing behind the front seat of our Buick (no seatbelts in those days), naming all the oncoming cars. It tickled her.

'What car is that, Alan?'

'Packard.'

And that one...?

'Studebaker.'

'What about that one...?'

'Chevy.'

I was never wrong. I knew my cars. When my father brought a new car home, I would spend hours sitting behind the wheel. I marvelled at the 3D logo in the middle of the steering wheel and all the gleaming chrome on the dashboard, and I would travel the world in my Dad's new car parked in the drive of our house.

My first car was a 1930 Model A Ford four-door sedan. I bought it a week before I was 16 for $300. It was the coolest thing on four wheels that I'd ever seen. I passed my driving test two days after my birthday. I remember the thrill of setting off down the road in it, totally on my own, feeling a million dollars. How I loved that car.

I was never one for thinking a car as merely a way to get from A to B. To me a car was...adventure. A beautiful thing to own. Over the years, I would own many interesting cars: Volkswagen Beetle convertible, '57 Chevy convertible, 1950 MGTD,

1952 Jaguar XK120, two Morris Minor convertibles, several Alfa Romeos, a 1965 Mini which Marnie and I drove to Trondheim and back over the Norwegian Alps when we first arrived in Europe in 1979.

Zack and Joseph became petrol heads also. We attended several Grand Prix events at Silverstone and Belgium. We spent many hours together working on their first cars.

When the boys left home, I bought a first edition silver Mercedes SLK, which I still have.

So really, all my life I've been primarily a car enthusiast, except for a brief stint in 1967 with a Triumph Bonneville motorcycle, which I rode across America. When I arrived in San Francisco, I sold it and bought a 1958 MGA roadster. I haven't been on a motorcycle since.

Indeed, I was a car man through and through.

But that changed on my 70th birthday when I couldn't get a cup down off the shelf.

CHAPTER 3
WHAT IF...?

'Dreaming is a form of planning.'
-Gloria Steinem

Life was bound to change after my stroke, at least for the month I couldn't drive. I felt OK physically. The only thing I noticed was my handwriting had changed a bit, and I wasn't as dexterous with chopsticks. And I walked a bit flat-footed with my left foot. Other than that, I was getting on fine.

But I felt lost without my car. Unfortunately, I had no choice. I could either have someone drive me about, or I could cycle. I chose the bike. It became my primary mode of transport. I rode every day for shopping. I also cycled extended distances, pushing myself occasionally. Not that I was a power cyclist. My average speed was 8 to 10 mph. It was good, my strength returned quite quickly. In fact, I felt more confident on my bike than on my feet. It induced me to ride more often.

Because of my inability to drive, there was one activity that I couldn't do, and that was my shifts at the Samaritans, which was in Bury St. Edmunds. Cycling the forty-mile round trip in a day was inconceivable to me. Up until then, the longest I'd ridden was eighteen miles.

I loved being a Samaritan. I missed not being on the phone. I missed the comradery of my fellow Samaritans. I missed my post-shift drink. I usually did the 19.30 to 23.00 shift on Saturday nights, then stopped at Zack's restaurant, 1921 Angel Hill, for a small glass of wine and a chat with him as he was finishing the last few orders. These were perfect nights for me.

I began thinking maybe I could do the trip to the Samaritans, so I decided to give it a try; not to do a shift but to gauge if I was capable of such a distance in one day. I set off on a Saturday morning and completed the journey in a little over four hours. It wasn't as tiring as I anticipated, but it convinced me that it wasn't practical to do a four-hour shift on top of a four-hour ride. This was hardly a long distance bike tour, but it did plant a seed in my mind.

Surprisingly, a series of what-if's started floating around in my head. What if I actually did a bike tour? What if I could physically cope?

As I gained strength in my legs, and my sense of coordination returned, I began to feel more confident in my body. It seemed to respond well to my daily rides. Perhaps I had a long distance trip in me. But was I too old?

More questions began to evolve. What would it be like? Do I have the courage? How many miles could I average a day? Why do I want to do it in the first place?

Back in the early '80s, I worked in a London advertising agency. One of my fellow Art Directors in the creative department was Geoff Allum, who rowed the Atlantic Ocean when he was 18. I admired his direct, no-nonsense attitude.

Marnie once asked him, 'Why did you decide to do it?'

He responded simply, 'I thought I would become rich and famous.'

I wasn't under any illusion that a modest bike tour would bestow fame and fortune upon me, but I had to admit to myself that it would be a cool thing to do.

Cool was nice but hardly incentive enough for me to take it seriously until I saw a posting on Facebook from a friend seeking sponsorship for her participation in Women V Cancer Ride the Night. That gave me an idea. What if I did a charity ride to raise funds for Samaritans? And with that, my daydream was evolving into a remote possibility.

All I needed was a journey. Where could I go? What would capture peoples' imaginations? My first thought was to ride to the Arctic Circle across the Norwegian Alps. I soon gave up that idea as too challenging for a septuagenarian. A journey that did interest me, however, would start in Russia, and take in the Baltic countries. The route appealed to me for two reasons: it would be relatively flat, and I would be travelling through countries new to me.

Soon I was frequenting Google maps. I sketched a preliminary route out, then I would drag the little yellow man from his moorings in the lower right onto a given road to get a visual sense of what would be in store for me. I travelled most of the roads from St. Petersburg to Holland in this way (with the exception of Germany where this feature is disabled in Google maps).

The month soon passed, and I was back behind the wheel of my Mercedes and back to being a Samaritan. Life would have settled back to normal if it wasn't for my riding on my imaginary journey. It solidified more and more in my mind, but still, it remained in my mind. I said nothing about it to anyone, including Marnie. I didn't want it to be thought of as yet another one of my hare-brained fantasies that comes to nothing.

It might have stayed in my mind, or dropped out completely because I began to lose interest in getting on my bike. Riding was increasingly a struggle. A dull ache was slowly affecting my legs, arms and hips. It was so gradual, that first, I didn't notice that my cycling was decreasing, or that I was suffering from anything that couldn't be attributed to advanced years. But soon, it was impossible to ignore the pain, and I knew it wasn't my age, there was something definitely wrong with me. I knew I had to see a doctor, but for some reason, my last visit sprang to mind, when I sought approval to drive again. It was the first time I had any medical attention since I was released from the hospital a month earlier with 30 days' supply of medicine.

'Your clopidogrel and perindopril doses are fine...on top of that, I'm prescribing statins, which you will be on for the rest of your life.'

I didn't like the thought of a life sentence, but I also remembered the Consultant at the hospital telling me that my cholesterol level was where it should be.

'Why? My cholesterol level is normal.'

'We can get it lower than that.'

I wondered then why it had to be lower than normal, but like most people of my generation, I acquiesced. The doctor knows best. So now, a few weeks later, my aching joints induced me to book another appointment. Before I picked up the phone, however, I decided to consult Doctor Google.

Searching the internet for an understanding of medical conditions can either be beneficial or detrimental. We either gain insights, or we run the risk of becoming paranoid hypochondriacs. Of course, Doctor Google should not be the definitive answer, especially when it comes to diagnosing symptoms. A person could be ecstatic because their search leads them to believe their condition is minor, which might not be true. Or on the other hand, someone could be thrust into the depths of despair because their search points to some horrible disease, which also might not be the case. In my instance, I wasn't looking for the cause of my joint pain, I already had my suspicion. I merely wanted to know the side effects of statins since it was the only change in my medication since my stroke.

I discovered that one of the most common side effects of statins is muscle pain. I researched further, and I found that there isn't a consensus among the medical community on the benefits of statins. Some sites likened them to Gillette razor blades…once you start shaving you need blades for the rest of your life…much the same as the doctor told me about statins. I then looked into why many doctors don't take them, followed by the statistics of their effectiveness of preventing heart attacks and strokes. At the end of it all, I was convinced that I was not convinced.

I decided not to talk to the doctor, stop taking statins for a month and assess how I felt. After all, I was sent home from the hospital without them, and I survived a month, so another statin free month was worth the risk to me. It didn't take long for the results. The pain began to subside. Well before the end of the month, it was completely gone, so I started riding. I still had to fight my daily inertia to get on my bike, which is to be expected of a reluctant cyclist. Still, I was back riding…and dreaming about a tour once again.

I dreamed. I thought. I ruminated. I contemplated. I imagined. I visualised. Basically, the idea remained in the ethers for various reasons. I hadn't fully made up my mind. I thought I might not be capable (physically and financially) to pull it off. I had fears and doubts. Also, I knew that talking about an idea that is in incubation dissipates the energy that created it in the first place.

The 'what-ifs' revisited. What if I got lost? What if my bike breaks in the middle of nowhere? What if I can't cope with being alone for so long? What if I had another stroke? What if I was robbed? What if I were injured, or run over? But there was one overriding question that finally convinced me to unwrap my idea and present it to the world.

'What if I didn't do it?'

Alan Deakins

I was on late night shift with Gordon, the Samaritans Branch Director. (There are always two Samaritans on each listening shift. We're not only there to offer emotional support to our callers, but we are also there to support each other.) Even though it is non-stop calls, we manage to find a few minutes for tea and chat. This was my second or third shift since my return.

'It's nice to have you back. We missed you.'

'I missed you guys!'

'How are you feeling? Any problems...?'

'Yes. I'm shit with chopsticks. Oh, and my left foot is a bit floppy sometimes. Other than that, I'm 98% back to normal.'

'Are you OK with that?'

'I think so. I feel all right. I'm back on the bike, so that's cool. Which brings me neatly to something I want to talk to you about.'

'Go on.'

I told him that I had a mad idea, I wanted to ride my bike from St Petersburg to Bury St Edmunds to raise money for our branch. I haven't said anything to anybody, because at this stage, I didn't know if I could afford it or was physically capable of it.

His enthusiastic response and was all I needed.

CHAPTER 4
DECISION MADE. NOW WHAT?

*'Give me six hours to chop down a tree
and I will spend the first four hours sharpening the axe.'
-Abraham Lincoln*

I got home at around 06.00. I made a coffee and waited for Marnie to wake. I had decided to actually do it, if she approved, or course.

'I've been thinking of doing a bicycle trip.'

'Oh...? How long?'

'St Petersburg to Bury St Edmunds...for Samaritans...what do you think?'

'I think you should see a doctor.'

She could have said 'psychiatrist', but I knew what she meant. 'Get checked out...after all, you did have a stroke.'

The doctor was accommodating, but to be fair, there wasn't much he could do in a short visit.

'I can check your heart and blood pressure if you like.'

I was OK in those two departments.

'How are you planning to do the trip?'

'I thought a couple of hours in the morning...then a long lunch...and a couple of hours in the afternoon.'

Alan Deakins

'I'm jealous. I can't think of any medical reason why you shouldn't.'

That's what I wanted to hear. As far as I was concerned, the trip was on, and now there was so much to do. I immediately called Gordon to break the news, and a team of Samaritans set about to register our branch as a charity on a fundraising website. Once that was done, I would create the contents to promote the ride.

I had spent most of my adult life promoting something or other for other people, either as an advertising creative or as a filmmaker; promoting my ride shouldn't be too difficult. I needed something that instantly told people about me. I listed what would be different about my endeavour:

1. I was seventy-two.
2. I had suffered a stroke.
3. I would be riding a bicycle three thousand kilometres (eighteen hundred miles) from St Petersburg to Bury St Edmunds.
4. I would be riding solo without any support.
5. I would be camping all the way.
6. I would be riding to raise funds for my branch of the Samaritans.
7. I was nuts.

There was no label of phrase that would convey all of that, but surely there was something that would capture peoples' imaginations enough to want to know more. 'Alan Deakins rides a bike' was dull as dishwater. 'Charity marathon bike ride'... who cares. 'From Russia with love' was about as trite as trite could be.

I finally settled on 'Old Man on a Bike' because that was what I was. Unfortunately, after I Googled it, I found that Don Petterson had already written a book, 'Old Man on a Bicycle', about his ride across America. Damn.

I mentioned my dilemma to Joseph over a glass or two of wine on one of his visits.

'Why not Old Hippie on a Bike? Let's face it, Dad, you never stopped being a hippie.'

It was inspired. I Googled it, and nothing came up, so I immediately opened a Facebook page: 'Old Hippie On A Bike.'

A couple days later, Gordon informed me that we were now registered as a charity on BT's MyDonate.com site. BT runs this site as a community service, and takes no commission, unlike JustGiving which charges for their service. I quickly created a page on this site as Old Hippie on a Bike and within a couple of days, when I Googled, Old Hippie on a Bike the search came up with my Facebook page and my MyDonate page, so the handle seemed to be exclusively mine.

I then spent the next three months researching, planning, buying, experimenting, testing, preparing, packing and worrying.

I had cards printed up to distribute to local shops, and gave many to my fellow Samaritans to also distribute. The local papers picked up the story and soon, Old Hippie on a Bike was capturing people's imaginations.

All was coming together, except for one thing, I hadn't budgeted for the trip. In fact, I really didn't have the funds. I did have a few generous friends, and two generous sons, who helped. I figured if I wild camped all the way, I could just about make it without going into overdraft.

One expense I hadn't counted on was my Russian visa. Because I would be passing through Kaliningrad (a Russian territory between Lithuania and Poland) I needed a double entry visa costing £90. Ouch.

At the same time, I had to acquire camping and travelling gear. I went to a few car boot sales, with no luck, and with time ticking away, I turned to eBay. I couldn't afford the best bike gear, but I managed to find decent pannier bags, a bargain tent, a used sleeping bag and quilt. I bought a miniature camping gas stove and basic mess kit on Amazon. I also managed to find end of line merino wool t-shirts. The rest of my clothing was found in charity shops. Finally, I found a foldable chair on eBay that should come in handy while camping, as I didn't think my old body would take kindly to sitting on the ground.

I packed everything up into four bags. My Panasonic stills camera, two GoPro cameras, iPad and Kindle in the front bag, which would be easily detachable. The two panniers contained my clothes, rain gear, sleeping bag, quilt, stove, mess kit, first aid kit and various plastic containers for coffee and other dried food. Finally, I packed my tent, air mattress and chair in a waterproof bag that would ride between the panniers on the back.

The entire kit weighed in at eighteen kilos, which I considered fairly light. I fully packed the bike and took it out on several runs. I found that once I was rolling, the weight didn't seem to be much of a burden. I soon got used to cycling with it and felt confident that I could cope with it, and survive comfortably enough on the trip.

I wrote to British Airways, explaining the nature of my journey, the ethos of the Samaritans and how it was aligned with that of BA in as much as both organisations had the wellbeing of people as our primary concern, and that any assistance that they could possibly provide would be greatly appreciated. They responded that indeed they had great respect for the Samaritans, but as a matter of policy, they couldn't offer free flights, but they would be happy to allow one extra bag gratis, which I appreciated very much.

I had signed up to a cycling app called 'RideWithGPS'. I mapped out a route and was able to download it to my iPhone, so I could follow the route while I was offline by use of the phone's GPS. It seemed a good system, and I felt confident that I had ample navigational power. As a back-up, however, I bought paper maps of the Baltics.

Finding a window for my ride was important. There were two events I didn't want to miss coming up. First, Suffolk Open Studios was planned for 9 and 10 June, where the public was invited to our home to view, and hopefully, buy Marnie's paintings and ceramics. Secondly, Zack and Annie were expecting their second daughter in mid-August. I reckoned if I departed on 16 June, I would have sixty days to complete my ride. I booked my flight to St Petersburg for the 09.15 flight on 16 June. I had butterflies in my stomach when I clicked on the pay now button. Job done. I was going. I was really going.

I contacted the St Petersburg Cycle Club to see if they could offer any assistance or advice. I received a nice polite response that they would be happy to find a room that would take me and my bike, but because of the World Cup, it would cost €100-120. That was well outside my budget, so I decided to check AirBnB, where I found a small room in a flat in the centre of St Petersburg, shared by five people. I messaged them, explaining my trip (with a link to my Old Hippie on a Bike Facebook page), and if it would be possible, would there be room to unpack and assemble my bike? The next day, I received an enthusiastic message saying I would be most welcomed, that they were all cyclists, one more bike would be no problem and they looked forward to meeting me. I immediately sent my thanks and booked the room for two nights at £13 per night. It was all coming together.

All during this time, I cycled about ten to fifteen miles a day. I knew I would have to at least double that when I was truly on the road, but at least I satisfied myself that I was doing some modicum of training.

The weekend of Suffolk Studios was a busy time. I framed Marnie's paintings, and she had the brilliant idea to have them dotted around the garden since the weather was forecast to be fine and dry. This idea was particularly good, because we found from experience, that half of the visitors came to view her art, and the other half came to snoop around the garden. I thought the display looked fantastic. She sold a couple of paintings and several pieces of her ceramics.

Our next door neighbour, Jude is also an artist, and she and John were participating in the Open Studios as well. Aside from selling her work, they had a cake stall in aid of the Samaritans. We all met up Sunday evening for drinks and Jude and John presented me with £75 takings from the cake sale. How touching and generous. All in all, it was a great weekend.

On Monday before I was to leave, I stopped into my local Halfords and asked if they could donate a bicycle box for my trip. They kindly unpacked a bike there and then, and gave me the box. I took it home, disassembled my bike, carefully wrapped all the bits in bubble wrap, and put it into the box along with my tent, mattress, chair and various bits I couldn't fit into my panniers. It took the better part of two days to achieve this seemingly simple task.

Everything else was packed into my two panniers, then wrapped together using an entire roll of cling film, making them into one bag. The two wrapped panniers and the large bike box constituted two bags. Perfect. I was ready to go.

One bike. Ready. Two Panniers. Ready. One Old Hippie. ???

The final event on the agenda was a *bon voyage* party on Saturday afternoon. The entire neighbourhood turned up, and we had drinks and laughs in the sunshine. I was most grateful to see them all and to have them as friends. Marnie and I considered ourselves to be fortunate to have moved into the centre of Sudbury from a small village and be instantly welcomed so warmly by our neighbours. It is a close-knit community, and I felt good knowing that if Marnie had any problem while I was gone, someone would be there for her.

And that was it, the end of months of dreaming, planning and preparing. All was packed. I was ready as I could be. I had no idea what laid ahead.

I did not sleep well that night.

DAY 1
SUDBURY – ST PETERSBURG
16 June 2018

'My favourite thing is to go where I've never been.'
-Diane Arbus

Short ride there. Long ride home.

My flight was at 09.15 from Heathrow, about a two-hour drive from Sudbury. The boys insisted that they would drive me there. Joseph travelled up from London the night before, and Zack would come to collect us at 05.00.

I was aware of the imposition that this caused both of them. Zack's restaurant was always fully booked on Saturdays, and on top of that, he and the kitchen staff scrubbed the whole kitchen after the shift, which meant he would have worked until 02.00 at least. I knew at best, he would arrive with no more than two and a half hours sleep.

Old Hippie on a Bike

'Listen you guys, I think I should get a taxi, this is too much for you.'

'Are you joking? How many times did you drive us to the airport on our travels?'

'No way are we going to let you go off on your own.'

End of argument. I was extremely moved; they are such great guys. I love what they've grown into. I love that we love one another. I love that they are best friends with each other. I love that they want to see us, be with us, share their ups and downs with us.

Marnie is a very independent person. She has more courage than I have. She was not afraid to explore the world. When she was eighteen, she flew to London and hitch-hiked across Europe on her own…an incredibe journey for a lone young American woman in 1970. She is amazing, and I have no doubt that the boys inherited their sense of adventure from her.

The bike box fitted easily in the back of Zack's BMW estate. The ride to Heathrow was easy; the M25 was traffic free, as expected that time of the morning. I had driven this road thousands of times, for work, for travel, to ferry Joseph to University, but today, I was in the hands of my sons. I was their charge. They were looking after me.

We arrived in plenty of time. The boys unloaded everything and loaded it all onto a trolley for me. We hugged. Strong comfortable embraces. I could feel myself welling up. Not out of apprehension for the trip, but for the love I had for them.

They headed back to their lives that they've carved for themselves, and I headed off into the new life that I would live from there on.

The flight to St Petersburg is only three hours and thirty minutes, a small amount of time really. The window seat was especially welcomed because I would see St Petersburg as we landed. I tried reading my Kindle during the flight but gave up, there were too many thoughts and apprehensions floating around in my head.

I soon surrendered to the fact that there was no turning back. Like it or not, I would find myself in Russia soon enough, and I would have to deal with it. This thought eased my angst somewhat. Besides, I've landed in dozens of airports all around the world as a filmmaker over the years, so I knew the drill upon landing. Disembark, go through immigration, collect your bags…then…well, this is where it could get sticky, depending on what country I landed in, and who I was travelling with.

If I were alone, I would have two bags at most, and I would saunter through the customs green lane. If I were with a film crew, we would have a convoy of trolleys loaded with various silver boxes of camera equipment, a 'must inspect' sight to any customs official.

I wasn't sure about today. I would have one piece, which was my two pannier bags wrapped together (which looked very odd indeed), and an extremely large box containing my bike straddled across the trolley. Would it be 'must inspect'? Never mind, I'll deal with whatever happens.

As we descended over the Gulf of Finland, I caught a brief view of St Petersburg as we banked into our approach to the airport. A nervous twinge of excitement rose in my stomach. This is it.

Smooth landing, short walk to immigration. There wasn't a huge throng of people in the arrivals hall like in some airports I've been to. I've waited for hours in countries such as China and Brazil, so this looked relatively easy. The immigration officer was thorough, checking every page in my passport (it was new, so most pages were blank), even so, each one demanded careful scrutiny. Examination over, a short sharp 'wap' with a stamp, and I was unceremoniously welcomed into Russia.

Now onto the baggage hall where I expected I would be racing between outsized baggage for my bike, and the carousel for my panniers. When I reached the top of the stairs that descended into the hall, I was delighted to see my bike box waiting for me at the bottom. A quick glance at the carousel and I saw my panniers travelling merrily around.

I loaded them onto a trolley, and headed for the green channel, fully expecting to be stopped with such a large and unusual box. Surprisingly, I walked straight through. I was beginning to warm to Russia already.

I made my way to the taxi kiosk to find an enthusiastic English speaking young lady who efficiently handled my special requirement, namely an over-sized box that would necessitate a big vehicle. She instructed me to go Lane 3 outside the terminal and look for a blue Renault Kangoo which would be along shortly. As I made my way to Lane 3, I thought to myself that a Kangoo is too small to fit this box into. As I was crossing Lane 2, there was a burly man standing outside of a blue van waving at me. He had a big infectious smile. After mentally sizing up the bike box, he opened the hatch, lowered the back seat, and (with my help) managed to cram it in.

On the map, the airport looks relatively close to the centre of St Petersburg, but the ride took longer than I expected. My jovial driver was entertaining considering he only had a few English words, which to be fair, was significantly more than my Russian words. We managed a conversation nonetheless. It started with him pointing to the music he had playing on his radio, then pointing to himself:

'Drummer.'

'Your music…?'

Alan Deakins

'Da.'

'Cool.'

'Taxi…money…I drummer.'

'Nice. Whatever it takes…'

Maybe he didn't understand me, but I have respect for those who support themselves in whatever way they can so that they can do what they love to do.

He pointed behind us with his thumb over his shoulder.

'Bicycle…?'

'Yeah.' I made a peddling motion with my hands. 'St Petersburg to London.'

It took a few seconds for it to sink in, then a look of surprise came over his broad face.

'London…?'

'London,' I nod.

He immediately thrust his big hand forward, and we shook hands. Mutual respect. The rest of the journey was mostly silent as I tried to get a feeling for St Petersburg by observing the sights passing by my window.

Every so often, he would look over to me, smile and shake his head.

'London…'

As we progressed into the city, the shopping malls and petrol stations gave way to a denser, more traditional eastern European city, the architecture was a bit tired; we passed through less affluent neighbourhoods mirrored by the drab dusty shop fronts. Soon we were approaching the centre, and the grandeur of the city began to be revealed. Majestic buildings, a beautiful palace, sweeping bridges that enhanced my view of everything as we crossed over them. It was stunning.

I pointed ahead and tapped my watch asking the driver how much longer. He held up his hand and flashed all five fingers twice, so I texted Arseniy to let him know I would arrive in 10 minutes.

When we pulled up in front of the building where I would be staying, two very nice young men (Arseniy and Dmitry) were waiting at the door. They seemed open and hospitable. The bike was out of the taxi in a flash and the lads cheerfully bundled it into the building. I offered the driver a tip, but he refused, shook my hand and said 'London' while shaking his head.

The flat that was to be my home for two nights was on the first floor. The entrance hall was exceptionally wide. There were already five bicycles parked in one corner. My box was in the centre. I was shown around and made to feel at home. My space was a snug room off of the sitting room, separated by a curtain. It had a double bed and a small lamp on a table. There was room enough for me to unpack and sort out my gear. I was happy with it.

I had brought two bottles of Pimms that I bought in Duty-Free. I thought 'something British' would be an apt gift. I explained that it needed to be mixed with lemonade, of the 7-up or Sprite variety and lots of ice.

I asked where could I unpack and assemble my bike. They all agreed that the sitting room would be OK. I didn't want to be in the way, but I was told it was no bother, they hardly use that room, and feel free to spread out. Dimitri helped unpack the bike and all of the paraphernalia I managed to cram into the box. As I was putting it together, I had all sorts of questions about Russia, shops, where I could buy things I needed. Everyone was helpful, searching the internet for shops or texting friends for information. I didn't feel out of place, nor did I feel any age gap, even though I was 40-50 years their senior.

As the afternoon progressed, everybody had to get on with their lives, and I was left to get on with mine. I finished building my bike. It looked splendid in the rather grand high ceilinged room, resting on its newly purchased Amazon kickstand. I had a sense of accomplishment. I also had a massive amount of packing, bubble wrap, cable ties and bits of padding strewn all over. I stuffed it all into the large box and put it out onto the landing outside the flat. I would ask when people returned where I could dispose of it. I hadn't eaten since Heathrow, where I had a quick sandwich. So I set off in search of food.

It was early evening, but pleasantly warm and the sun was still high in the sky, reminding me of how far north St Petersburg is. I wandered around the neighbourhood, which was mostly residential, made up of tall elegant early 1900's apartment buildings. It didn't take long to find commercial activity. I spied a small café which had an empty table outside. I deemed it the perfect spot for me. My preferred way to 'see' a city is to find a place to sit, ideally with a glass of wine and watch its inhabitants pass by. The friendly efficient waiter from Belarus sold me on a homemade wine that his father made. It was unusual but pleasantly drinkable. He suggested a spicy lamb stew and fresh bread which seemed very reasonably priced. Out it came with a generous sprinkling of fresh coriander. I had a lovely relaxing hour enjoying my Belarus dinner and a couple glasses of rustic wine, while St Petersburg paraded itself in front of me.

When I returned to the flat, I noticed that my bike box had disappeared from the landing. No one was about. I could tell that someone was watching television on one of the bedrooms, other than that, quiet. I was tired from the day's travel, anxiety and wine. I had a quick shower, retired to my little snug and fell into a deep sleep.

DAY 2
ST PETERSBURG

'You can see a lot just by observing.'
-Yogi Berra

Morning comes early to St Petersburg in Summer. Just as well, I had a busy day ahead of me. My first task was to find breakfast. There was a tiny bakery with a couple of tables where I enjoyed a warm eggy dumpling sort of affair and a good strong coffee, as I watched the comings and goings of people on their way to work. Once fed, I could turn my attention to my impending trip and the few things I needed to buy before my departure tomorrow.

My first stop was Sport Master, an outdoor shop fairly near (more than walking distance) that apparently stocked camping gas for my stove. This outing would give me a feel for St Petersburg as well as the experience of negotiating roads amongst Russian drivers. It would also give me the opportunity to try Google and Apple maps as navigational tools. I knew I would have to rely on one or the other when I needed to go somewhere outside of the route that I configured with RideWithGPS.

It was good to be back on my bike again, and I found it thrilling to be riding it in St Petersburg.

'This is it, Deak,' I said to myself out loud. 'You're here. You're ACTUALLY here.'

I find that I talk out loud rather frequently while I cycle. Perhaps it's because I ride alone, and I'm the only company

I've got. But I'm not the only one I talk to...there is my bike, drivers, the weather...I'm always commenting about something.

I don't know why I took to calling me Deak. First, it was my father's nickname when he was in university over ninety years ago. I too was dubbed Deak in high school, and it pretty much stuck with me up to my hippie days. For some reason, I found it appropriate on this trip when conversing with myself.

I thought I might have problems riding on the right, but I quickly adapted. As I headed from the residential streets towards the river, I would have my first test in proper traffic.

I crossed two bridges over the River Neva, then along Admiralty Embankment. I was enthralled with the grandeur and beauty of this fine city. I had to keep my eyes on the road and be aware of the very fast drivers around me, so I would stop every so often to take it all in. This was a city to take at a slow pace in order to savour its splendour. It seemed to me that the only ones in a hurry were the drivers. Fortunately, I had read that it was acceptable to ride on the pavements with the pedestrians, which in many instances saved me from dangerous encounters with exuberant motorists on narrow roads.

I turned and rode through Aleksandrovskiy Garden, a leafy park shaded by massive mature trees. The paths were wide and easily negotiable amongst the tourists and locals enjoying the warm sunny day. It was nice to see a mixture of Westerners, Chinese and Japanese. It was World Cup week, so obviously there would be more tourists than usual, but I could see that it wouldn't take a special attraction to entice people from around the world to visit.

I stopped at a kiosk, bought an ice tea and found a bench to sit on and watch. A young American family walked by with two toddlers. Were they tourists, or did they live here? I imagined what it would be like to permanently reside in St Petersburg.

Even though it was western in many ways, there would still be enormous cultural differences to reckon with…let alone wrapping my head around the complexity of the Russian alphabet. Still, the idea had its appeal. I've been an American abroad for forty years, and even though Marnie and I became British citizens, and have made Europe our home, every so often, I still feel that I am a traveller. That pleases me.

Google maps guided me easily across the Moyka River, into the Admiralteysky District and onto the very grand Moskovsky Avenue. I was directed right up to the entrance of the shop. Great. I could rely on Google maps.

Finding the camping section was easy for me, it was next to the bicycle department. Unfortunately, the camping gas on display did not have the screw-on fitting that my stove required. The English speaking assistant assured me that this was all they carried. Disappointed, I headed back to the flat. It was not an entirely wasted trip. I managed to see more of St Petersburg, get a feeling of riding on the right with Russian motorists and I thoroughly enjoyed myself.

Back at the flat, I searched online for screw-on camping gas canisters, and the only source that I could ascertain was Sport Master. I found that another branch in the Vasileostrovsky District had two large 450g canisters in stock. It meant a longer ride in another direction. It was a lovely day, and I had another opportunity to see more of the city.

I decided to use Apple maps for this journey, and it too was accurate, directing me to a moderate shopping centre. I locked my bike to a railing outside a café where several people were dining on the outdoor veranda. I figured it would be safe under the scrutiny of so many eyes. Sport Direct was on the second floor, and the gas canister was easily located and purchased. At 300 rubbles, (about £3.20) it was more than half of what it would have cost in the UK. Such a small event, really, but I had a huge sense of accomplishment.

As I mounted the escalator to return to my bike, I suddenly felt quite dizzy and weak. Alarm bells started ringing loudly in my head. I began to panic. Was this another stroke? But before I could think it through, strong pains gripped my stomach and I realised I was hungry. In fact, I was ravenous. I was so intent of exploring the city and securing the camping gas that I totally forgot to eat. I had underestimated the number of calories I had expended on my two rides. In an instant, I was overwhelmingly consumed with the thought of food. St Petersburg, camping gas, my impending trip across Europe were nothing compared to the desire to shove something, anything, into my mouth.

I made it to the café as quickly as I could. Fortunately, most of the food was already prepared and on display, so all I had to do was to point at something that looked appetising and it was instantaneously plated for me. I chose a schnitzel looking piece of meat with chips and a salad. I found a table on the edge of the veranda and bolted the first few bites down without noticing the taste or texture of what I was consuming. As quickly as my hunger attack hit me, my panic eased as those first bites arrived in my stomach. Very quick communication from my gut to my brain, I thought. I relaxed, sat back in the chair, and surveyed my surroundings. First off, I had chosen a good meal. It wasn't a culinary tour de force, but it was flavoursome and agreeable. I looked over to see that my bike was still chained to the rails exactly as I had left it. Now I could relax.

The next thing I noticed were three young people (I guessed late teens) walking together. Two boys and one girl. Nothing unusual in that, but they were in identical navy blue uniforms. If they were walking through an airport, I might have mistaken them for flight crew. Another thought crossed my mind that perhaps they were ushers at a posh venue. As I considered that possibility five or six more young people passed by in uniforms. I then thought they could be from a local academy, or perhaps they were naval cadets. More came walking by, only this group were dishevelled. Their ties were undone, some wore dirty trainers with no socks, others had their shirt tails hanging out from under their jackets. They had to be students. I estimated that at least fifty or sixty passed by in various states of neatness, most of them on their mobiles, or sharing something on their screens with one another. I thought no matter how you dress a youngster, that person is still a youngster. They were no different than a throng of UK teens leaving school, except for the uniforms. It was an entertaining spectacle that added to the enjoyment of my lunch.

On the way back, I rode alongside a wooded park behind a wall. When I came to a gate, I decided to ride through the park since it ran parallel to the street. Within a few meters, I realised I was in a cemetery. It was quite unusual to my Western eye. I dismounted, removed my helmet and walked with my bike. Most of the graves had the Russian Orthodox three bar crucifix. Some of the more recent grave stones had photographic likenesses of the deceased etched into the granite. Some were of militarymen posing rigidly in their tunics adorned with medals.

One stone stood out, the etched picture on it was of a smiling young couple in their bathing costumes sitting on a beach.

So many lives lived in so many different ways. Most of the

graves had colourful bouquets of flowers placed on them. Upon closer inspection, they were invariably artificial. Most of the graves had seats, some with small tables at the foot where I observed a few people sitting in silence. Some of them had their lunch unpacked on the small tables and they sat and ate alone with their loved ones. I was quietly touched.

I lugged my bike up the wide stairs to the flat, along with my prized camping gas canister. It was early evening, and I expected to see my hosts, but all was quiet. So I thought it a good time to get my food shopping done for my departure in the morning. I headed in the same direction as last night, I wasn't in the mood for further exploring so a familiar route suited me. I found a market across from the Belarus café, where I bought packets of instant soup, cheese, coffee, tinned beans, nuts and a few bananas. I hadn't made any plans on the food for my trip, so I was just guessing what I would need, and what I could cook on my little stove. I was also wary of carrying too much weight.

Alan Deakins

I decided to visit the café once again for a glass of Dad's home-made wine. The waiter smiled as I entered.

'Nice to see you again.'

'And you. I'll have a glass of your father's brilliant wine, please.'

He laughed and promptly had a chilled glass in front of me. Life on the street was different than the relaxed weekend atmosphere of last night. The end of Monday, produced a scene of people in a hurry, disembarking from busses, scurrying along the pavement, anxious to get home. In the midst of it all was a small man (or perhaps a woman) dressed in a character costume, which was a cross between Super Mario and the Swedish Chef from the Muppets handing out leaflets to the disinterested passers-by. Under his comic oversized costume shoes, I could see his very worn trainers. At one point, he sat on a low wall where he kept his frayed bag full of leaflets. His character face was constantly smiling, but underneath I imagined it was hell on this hot evening.

I didn't stay long because I wanted to see my hosts before I set off in the morning. I was disappointed to find the flat quiet on my return. I packed my food and began sorting my clothes. I guess I was exhausted from the day because I promptly fell asleep. I woke with a start an hour later. I passed the kitchen on my way to the loo, and Lena was sitting at the table with a bottle of the Pimms.

'Hi there.' I was pleased to see her.

'Hi. I have Russian lemonade.'

'Cool. Do you have ice...?'

We set about mixing up Pimms, Russian style. Lena had bought a lemonade that was bright green, not clear like 7-up, and it had the same consistency as a thick orange juice.

When mixed with the Pimms, it resulted in a brownish sludge that was, for lack of a better description, 'different'. Nonetheless, we persisted and clinked glasses with 'Prost' and chatted. Elena was an engaging young woman, a psychologist who related to my efforts for the Samaritans. Her approach to psychology is unique, which involves music, art and nature, as far as I could understand. I thoroughly enjoyed talking to her.

Before long, Dmitry and Arseniy joined us, and we mixed more 'Russian Pimms'. Both lads politely described the concoction as 'interesting'. Dmitry is interested in architecture and is involved with building an eco-friendly house for a friend, and Arseniy is a software designer. I loved that we were talking without a perceived age gap between us.

I told them that I considered myself fortunate for being able to stay with them, given the response I had received

from the St Petersburg Cycle Club. They told me that they were going to raise their rate for the World Cup week, but when they got my request, they thought having me as a guest would be interesting, so they invited me at the usual rate. I was flattered, but what could be so interesting about an old man?

They wanted to know what it was like to be a hippie. A period of my life that was a million years ago, which I abandoned to find a normal drug-free life. Still, to them, it was colourful and glamorous. I told them about San Francisco in the late '60s, the scene, the music, the people, and the drugs. The good times, the weird time and the bad times. I tried to explain how it was so long ago and was only a fraction of what defines me as a person today. I don't know if I succeeded in that, the 'brown sludge' was having its effect on me.

One thing that stood out to me about our evening together was there was no mention of politics. No Trump. No Putin. No Brexit. If there was a political elephant in the room, it was very small and very quiet.

It was a thoroughly enjoyable evening, but sadly, I had to take my leave. I had promised myself that I would be off by 5.00 tomorrow morning to avoid the rush hour traffic. We said our good-bye's and that was the last I saw of these gracious hospitable young people.

I lay awake while all sorts of thoughts, doubts, anxieties and wonder raced through my head. Here I was, a kid born and raised in 1950's Erie Pennsylvania, in the country of our arch enemy (so the American indoctrination impressed upon us). Not only here, but getting along. I liked that. But then, doubts crept back, and my inner voice began working overtime.

'Are you mad?'

'What have you let yourself in for?'

'You're old. You're weak. You've had a stroke.'

'How far will you get before you pack it in?'

'You promised so many people, and you won't make it.'

DAY 3
ST PETERSBURG – GLUKHOVO

*'Jump, and you will find out
how to unfold your wings as you fall.'
-Ray Bradbury*

It felt like I was awake all night. All of a sudden, I sat up with start at 5.00. Damn, I overslept. I quickly gathered my things together, had a quick cup of coffee, and quietly trundled my gear and my bike down to the pavement outside and posted the keys into their letterbox. As I closed the front door, I felt a twinge knowing there was no going back.

It was just me and my bike.

Old Hippie on a Bike

I wanted to film my departure from St Petersburg, so I pulled my two GoPro's out and spent the next half hour fitting them to the bike. I was now anxious about taking so much time to set them up. I set off with both cameras running. I got about 200 metres when one of the cameras tilted which needed adjusting and tightening. Another 10 minutes were taken up.

I also had to stop again because I forgot to start my 'RideWithGPS' maps app on my phone, which was to be my guide for the entire journey.

Finally, I was truly away. The early morning riverside was brilliant in the clear warm early light, and the streets were relatively empty of traffic, which I appreciated. Across two bridges, along Admiralty Embankment, which ironically turned into English Embankment. Sharp left, across the Moyka River. Stop again to adjust the camera. Carry on. A bit further along, I started hearing an ominous a musical sound: DA-dum, DA-dum, DA-dum. I couldn't figure it out until I looked down at my map. It was telling me that I veered off course. The annoying thing was, it didn't offer an alternative route to get me back on course. I didn't know what do do, or where I was, so I turned around until the sound went: 'BLIIII-ING'. I thought if this is what I have to do every time I go astray, I'm in for big problems.

Before I crossed the Fontanka River, I decided that I had enough with the cameras. They were getting in the way of my paying attention to where I was going. Also, the traffic was getting heavier and faster. I stopped at a small park, disassembled the camera gear and packed it away. I figured that the effort to get some footage has taken up at least an hour of my time. I was not amused. I continued heading south paying particular attention to the map, and the mounting traffic. The cars were hellishly fast, so my full attention was needed. I began looking less at the sights and more in my rear-view mirror to see what was bearing down on me.

I crossed a canal and passed hundreds of people entering a factory to start their workday. I wondered what the sight of an old man with a white beard on a loaded bike meant to them. One of the workers in the crowd gave me the thumbs-up sign. I shouted out 'HELLO!' Although at this point, my mood was anything but cheery. I had been on the road for two hours, and I was still in St Petersburg, and I was worried about my ability to navigate with the maps on my phone. I was tired and needed a rest. I had to keep going because there wasn't anywhere to sit down.

I was hoping for a shop or café to appear, but there was nothing but kilometres of huge bland blocks of flats. I was forced to ride on the edge of the road with the traffic because the shoulder was dirt. I rode until I came upon a commercial district with shops and bus stops. I couldn't find a café, but I stopped at a kiosk and bought a bottle of ice tea. I rode on for another kilometre or two when I spied a park on the opposite side. Even though the road had narrowed to two lanes at this point, it still was difficult to cross because of the sheer speed of the traffic.

I found a place to sit under a monument to WW2. It was an actual vintage Russian tank on a plinth. I walked around it out of curiosity. It was small (by today's standards) and considerably rudimentary. It looked as if it had been slapped together. The armour plates were roughly welded and riveted. It was ugly and crude. I was reminded of a documentary that I saw recounting how these little basic tanks defeated the superior meticulously engineered German tanks just by outnumbering them. Stalin had said that the quality of the Russian tanks was their quantity. I could only imagine the horror of those times.

A couple of kilometres further, I saw a small homemade kiosk outside a factory gate. An elderly woman had a few small fried items on display. Were they sweet or savoury? I had no way of knowing. She carefully wrapped the one I pointed to in paper and picked out a few roubles from the coins in my outstretched hand. It was savoury, a bit of cheese and cured meat. Not hugely flavourful, but welcomed nonetheless.

I had been travelling for hours and I was still cycling past more blocks of flats so dense, they were like a giant cliff wall. I hadn't realised how slow I was travelling, fighting the traffic, taking every footpath, pavement or parallel road I could manage to keep as far from the speeding traffic as I could. And to be fair, a good part of my journey thus far was on these relatively safe alternatives. But unfortunately, the vast majority of them were rough, badly maintained and strewn with holes and high curbs to slow me down.

The road rose sharply to pass over a railway, which was not only steep but had no room for a bike. My maps had no other route indicated, so I headed under it in the same direction as the road. I found myself passing through the station amongst the passengers to cross the tracks.

Further on, the road turned into a six-lane motorway with a spaghetti junction I had to navigate. This was particularly difficult because I had to straddle the white line separating the slip roads from the main carriageway while cars and lorries zoomed past on either side of me. It was harrowing. I would have had my doubts that a cyclist should be on this hazardous interchange if it wasn't for a young local cyclist passing me heading in the same direction. I pedalled as fast as my tired legs allowed, but my speed felt ponderous and inadequate in the face of this traffic.

When I finally got through, I was utterly exhausted, in need of a rest. I saw a welcoming site of what looked like the roofline of a shopping centre. I pulled off the main road and entered a huge empty car park. I was deeply disappointed. As I turned to get back onto the road, I noticed a new looking coffee kiosk with lights on and a car parked next to it.

The young proprietor looked up from his mobile phone as I entered. A large menu in Russian and English was on the wall. Nice. I ordered a large Americano. There wasn't any food on the menu, so I picked out a packet of biscuits and instead of sitting inside, I elected to stand at the tall tables outside. My bum also needed a rest. The coffee was rich, but the biscuit was extremely dry. I turned to select something else, but the young man was locking up, and without a word, he hopped into his car and sped off. I washed the biscuit down with the coffee and departed.

I was beginning to wonder if St Petersburg would ever end. After a while, the conurbation began to thin out, blocks of flats gave way to simple single dwellings. I was hoping I could relax, but the cars were still rocketing past my left side at astounding speeds.

No sooner had I thought I was free of the metropolis, more, newer, larger blocks of flats appeared, and my spirits fell. I wanted to find a secluded lane for a place to stop, break out my camp stove and eat. I pressed on unenthusiastically.

Then I came upon a huge roundabout with a monument in the centre. It looked newly built, as did the road that surrounded it. There were youngsters riding around in the middle on their bicycles. They stopped and stared as I rode by. I carried on past more enormous blocks of flats.

'C'mon, MATE. There's gotta be an end."

Another couple of kilometres, once again, the flats disappeared, and small wooden single houses were the only dwellings on either side. The road too had changed. The shoulder was more narrow, the paths along the side were just dirt, so riding on the edge of the road became necessary. The drivers

Old Hippie on a Bike

didn't slow down; they were still screaming past me. All I could do was keep going with my eyes to the road...placing my fate in their hands.

I carried on looking for a side road where I could be secluded for a while. The countryside was open flat fields with little in the way of hiding. I expected something to turn up...and it did, but not what I wanted. I came across road construction. It was obvious that the road was being widened. Traffic was being funnelled into two extremely narrow lanes. Too narrow, I quickly realised, for me to be included.

I noticed that the new road surface, which was still being laid by the work crew, was accessible to me simply by riding between the cones that cordoned this section off. I was so relieved to be riding on a perfectly smooth road completely devoid of any vehicle but mine. I was heading towards the working crew, and I fully expected they would kick me off, but at least I had two kilometres to myself. As I approached, one of them waved me past the heavy equipment. A lorry driver stopped to let me pass in front of him. Fantastic!! I carried on for a few kilometres until I re-joined the main road with the rest of the traffic.

A few hundred metres along, I happened upon a small road leading to what I perceived to be a small village nestled under mature trees. Perhaps there would be a café. It turned out to be a tiny hamlet of a few houses. Two young boys stood in the dirt road open-mouthed as I rode by. I decided to ride a bit further into the countryside to at the very least, find a tree to pee behind. I followed the dirt track until I saw a small clearing that I could reach by walking my bike through tall grass. I could hear machinery and I realised that the track had led me in an arc back towards the road construction. It was about a hundred metres away separated by trees, so I felt secluded enough.

I tended to the urgent need first, then unpacked my folding

Alan Deakins

chair, the stove and cooking gear. I dined on a tin of beans. Not gourmet, but hot. It was, I reminded myself, what to expect for the rest of the journey. I leaned back in my chair to contemplate my next move.

My mind said, 'You haven't gone very far, the sun is still high in the sky. '

My body said, 'I've had enough. I'm staying.'

I pitched my tent.

DAY 4
GLUKHOVO – GURLOVO

*'It is a common saying, and in everybody's mouth,
that life is but a sojourn'*
-Plato

My first night "under canvas" was by and large OK. I lay there for some time listening to the sounds around me. I wasn't worried about creatures, but I harboured a thought that people knew where I was. Morning came quickly. Upon emerging from my tent, I was accosted by mosquitos. I hadn't expected that. I quickly sprayed myself with Deet-free insect repellent. It kept them at bay, but the smell was to me, repellent.

It took over an hour to brew a coffee and pack things up, which I vowed to better in the future. Because I was so close to the E-20, rather than double back the way I came, I took another track that led me to the road quickly. I was hungry.

After twenty minutes, I spied a kiosk on the other side of the road. I stopped to investigate. I peered through the window. Inside was a man tending a large stone oven, he was stacking what looked like bread onto shelves for display. I pointed to them. He took one, wrapped it and handed it to me. It felt so very warm in my hand.

"Coffee...?"

He had a pot brewing near the oven, and he poured it into a paper cup. I held out a handful of coins for him to choose from, which he carefully did. I placed my breakfast on my saddle and unwrapped it. It was large. Bigger than my saddle. I tore off a piece and ate. It was a bit like a filo pastry filled with a ricotta type cheese, all warm and gooey. I stood there on the side of the road next to my bike gobbling it down in a matter of a few minutes. I was surprised by how hungry I was.

The road was straight...very straight. I didn't like it for two reasons. First, I could see for kilometres, so I knew what was coming up. No surprises. Second, drivers also had the same view. If the road was clear, they stepped on it. If there was traffic approaching, they stepped on it. I saw cars thundering past doing more than 130 kilometres per hour less than two metres apart. Crazy. Reckless. Stupid.

No matter what car was being driven. It had to be driven at full speed. At one point, an old brown Lada four-wheel drive screamed past. Its engine sounded like someone shaking a tin can full of nails.

'You're not gonna last long in that, MATE,' I said aloud.

I stopped at a small market for something to cook for dinner, two bananas and a carton of drinkable yoghurt which I had while sitting on a bench in the sun. When I returned to the road, I could see blue flashing lights on the horizon, about three or four kilometres away. I could see a fire engine and police car on my side of the road. As I got closer, I was shocked to see the brown Lada down an embankment wrapped around a tree. The driver was still in the car, his head bent back. The emergency crew were standing around, there was no sense of urgency to get him out. I felt terrible.

I carried on. Cars slowed down at the scene of the accident, but they were back up to full speed within a few hundred metres. I had enough for the day. I began looking in earnest for a side road that led into a wood.

Several kilometres later, I saw a track that looked passable, but not well used, which meant the chances of someone driving up it tonight were remote. I found a suitable hidden spot on a rise with a view over a small valley. I made camp, cooked my dinner and sat in the late afternoon sun. That unfortunate Lada driver was heavy on my mind.

I thought of how we have such a tenuous hold on life…and yet we tenaciously cling to it with everything we've got.

DAY 5
GURLOVO – NARVA, ESTONIA

*'Almost all of your life is lived
by the seat of your pants.'
-Ron Perlman*

My itching forehead woke me. I tried to open my eyes, but only my right complied. I rubbed my left. It felt puffy, and my eyelid was also itching. Something was wrong. I put on my glasses and surveyed my surroundings. On the inside of my ten, were ten or so snails clinging to the flysheet above me. SHIT!

I scrambled out into the morning light. Another dozen snails were stuck to the outside of my tent. I quickly detached the flysheet and shook it as hard as I could, dislodging most of them, but I had to prise a few stubborn ones off. During this frenzy, I hadn't given notice to the early morning mosquitos until I felt a few bites on my legs. Out came the bug spray.

My left eye was swollen shut and my face was itching. Obviously, I didn't secure the netting on my tent well enough, and the little bastards spent the night feasting on the only part of me that was exposed outside of my sleeping bag. I was anxious to get out of there. I fired up the stove for coffee and began packing as fast as I could. It still took close to an hour before I was ready to travel.

Back on the road, I was having a difficult time with the sight of one eye to stay on the narrow shoulder. I was also having a hard time covering any distance because I was ravenous. Vulnerable and hungry...not a good combination.

'You're not going to last this whole trip, Deak.'

My entry on Google maps told me that a café was two kilometres ahead. I doubted it would be opened at 6.00. When I got there, my left eye was halfway open and I could see that there were a few lorries parked outside. I was relieved. Before entering the restaurant, I took a selfie of my swollen face. I was not a pretty sight.

Once breakfasted, I felt closer to normal. Even my left eye responded to food by opening once again. But I felt grubby, and whiffy from the bug spray. I needed a secluded spot to wash and change, and the basic café toilet wasn't it. Another kilometre down the road, I found a track where I could turn off, wash with the adult size moist wipes I brought from the UK, and change my clothes. I felt much fresher and ready to get on with the day.

I decided to mount the cameras on the bike before setting off, to film the precariousness of my riding with Russian drivers. It took over thirty minutes to fit them. Once on the road, the lorry drivers seemed to oblige me by driving very fast and very close and buffeting me about. I was suffering for my art.

I pulled off the road in front of what looked like a small café to readjust the cameras and hopefully get a coffee. It was closed, so I drank some water and started to adjust the camera mounts. Suddenly, my bike fell over. On picking it up, I discovered that my new Amazon kickstand was irreparably broken. An elderly woman came rushing out of the café and held my bike upright as I assessed the damage. There was nothing to do but remove it.

'Coffee...?'

She nodded and retreated back inside. The bike fell over again as I was removing the kickstand. Fortunately, the woman didn't speak English, so my expletives fell on deaf ears as she returned with a styrofoam cup of instant coffee. I began adjusting the camera mounts, but stopped when I thought: "Am I on a film shoot, or am I on a bike tour?' I answered myself by packing all of the camera gear away.

Kingisepp was ten kilometres away. I had not planned to stop there. My intention was to make it to Narva, Estonia by the end of the day. I had no choice, I couldn't very well continue on a bike loaded with 18 kilos of gear without a kickstand.

By the time, I reached Kingisepp, there was a light drizzle in the air. On a junction near the centre, I saw a McDonalds. Perfect for a number of reasons: a dry place to sit, electricity to charge my phone, free internet to search for a bicycle shop, decent coffee and cherry pie. Even though I'd never had the latter before, it appealed to me. I was acquiring a voracious appetite. I found one cycle shop on Google It was a long way, but I decided to head there after I devoured the super sweet pie.

As I headed for the bike shop, I came across an outdoor market of numerous vendors. I thought it worth a quick look, perhaps there would be someone selling bike parts. A quick walk through with my bike revealed nothing but stall after stall of cheap clothes. I emerged from the labyrinth and looked for somewhere to lean my bike against to take a picture. I was awkwardly trying to lean it against a rickety fence when a woman approached.

'Do you need help?'

'You speak English...!'

'Yes. Where are you coming from?'

'St Petersburg.'

'St Petersburg?! You are crazy! How is your ass?'

'My ass is fine. Thanks for asking.'

Of course, she was curious to see an English cyclist in Kingisepp. When I explained my predicament, she had the perfect solution.

'My good friend repairs bikes.'

'Really...?'

'I will take you there.'

'My name is Alan, by the way.'

'I have the most common name in Russia. Natasha.'

Alan Deakins

During the ten-minute walk, I learned that she had graduated an engineer, but ended up teaching English in a local school. She was friendly, full of questions and such a pleasant person to be with.

We ended up in an alley behind an old commercial building. She knocked on a door, and a man appeared. I was introduced, and she explained about the kickstand. He surveyed the damage, disappeared behind the door and emerged with two kickstands. I chose a very substantial affair, which although not pretty, would definitely see me through the journey.

He then proceeded to check the entire bike over without being asked. He oiled my chain, adjusted my brakes and tightened a couple of spokes. Finally, he presented me with a small bottle of oil, and a paper towel in a plastic envelope. Final charge: about £10. Bargain.

Before we left, he stroked my saddle in admiration.

'Broooooks.'

'He says this is the best saddle in the world. Very expensive.'

I had a feeling this would be the closest he would ever get to one.

As we left, Natasha turned to me.

'You have been camping for two nights. Would you like to come to my flat for a shower?'

That was an offer I couldn't refuse. Although I had a wet-wipe bath on the side of the road, a chance to properly wash off all the bug spray was most welcome. She lived in a block of flats that looked like it was built in the '60s. It was a typical Russian, no frills, utilitarian type of building. Her flat was on the fourth floor. I asked where I could lock my bike, she said it needed to go up to her flat, otherwise, it would be gone in a matter of minutes. I took my tent and panniers off, and she completely surprised me by grabbing the bike and starting up the stairs.

'You don't have to do that...I'll carry it.'

'It is fine. I carry mine and the children's' bikes every day. I'm used to it.'

The stairwell was drab and colourless, but Natasha's flat was warm, comfortable and colourful, filled with the paraphernalia that goes with raising kids. I liked it. The bath was behind a sliding door in the corridor. On the wall between the sink and bathtub, was a large hot water geyser with a long tap at the bottom that could be swung between them. I haven't seen this type of set-up since we first moved to Britain in the late '70s. It instantly brought back memories and the knowledge of how to operate one. The water was hot and soothing. Shampooing my greasy hair was a luxury. Washed, dried and dressed, I found Natasha in the kitchen. She had prepared a simple lunch. We sat at the small table and spent well over an hour chatting.

I told her about the unfortunate Lada driver and how fast Russian Drivers were. She told me that many Russians don't take a driving examination, they simply buy their drivers licence. Corruption, it seems, is still alive in Russia.

We talked about the Samaritans, families and travel. Although she didn't say it, I felt that she was a bit envious of my trip. She had wanted to travel when she was younger, but visas were expensive and difficult to obtain.

'I am happy now. My family is my world.'

I said that I would email her every time I crossed a border into a new country, but she couldn't see the point of people staying in touch when they wouldn't be seeing each other again. I asked how far were we from Estonia. When she told me it was 20 kilometres, I thought I could make it before the end of the day. Getting back to the E-20 was a bit complicated, so rather than trying to explain, she would ride with me. At her insistence, she carried both bikes down the stairs.

On our way to the main road, she said, 'I am happy and proud to be riding alongside you.'

I too felt the same. The very same.

We reached the point where I was to continue on my own. We shook hands, I thanked her for her kindness, she turned and rode towards her life without looking back. With renewed energy and higher spirits, I headed to Estonia.

It began raining again, so I stopped under an overpass to don my waterproof jacket. The traffic was thundering past. I considered pulling out my GoPro's to film it, but the thought of unpacking was too much, so I relied on my iPhone.

About five kilometres from the border, I approached an army

checkpoint. There was a queue of cars and trucks waiting to be checked. I had read somewhere that when presented with a queue at borders, ride your bike to the front, no one will argue. What could I lose? It was getting late in the afternoon, and I needed to cross the border before nightfall. I rode past scores of cars and trucks for about a kilometre to the head of the queue. A Russian soldier stepped forward.

'Passport.'

I handed over my British passport. He looked at the cover for several seconds.

'UK...?!'

'Yes.' I pointed behind me. 'St Petersburg...' I then pointed West. 'London.'

'London...???'

I made a circular gesture around my temple with my index finger.

'I'm crazy.'

He laughed, handed my passport back and waved me through. Now I know how to handle queues on a bike.

Closer to the border, I approached another queue, and like the first, I kept riding. It too was at least a kilometre long. When I got to the front, I could see that the traffic was being guided into four or five lanes and heading towards drive up windows for passport control and car searches. I began riding into a lane when a petite young female soldier stepped forward and held up her hand.

'Niet.' She pointed to an unpaved path down a steep embankment where I could see people on foot.

'No.' I pointed towards the windows. 'I belong there.'

She stood in my way and pointed again. I had no choice. It would have been a struggle getting down that dirt path without anything to carry, but with a bike loaded with eighteen kilos, it was positively dangerous. Towards the bottom, I stumbled, but luckily a young man saw me and rushed forward and guided me and the bike down safely.

I followed the crowd walking my bike beside me. I knew I was misguided by the young soldier when I came to the building that housed passport control. There were steps, or a small wheelchair ramp, nothing to really accommodate a bike. I couldn't very well turn back. For one thing, I wouldn't physically have the strength to push my bike up the embankment. With difficulty, I hoisted the bike up the stairs and entered.

The queue for passport control was the usual 'switch back' affair that was invented by Walt Disney and familiar to every traveller around the world. I've stood in hundreds of them, but I never had to negotiate a bike through one. It was difficult getting it around each turn. Everyone was dressed in mostly grey, black, brown or navy blue. Everyone had either hand luggage or rolling cases. I, on the other hand, was dressed in a bright yellow hi-viz jacket and a red, white and blue helmet. I must have been a spectacle. One man began talking to me. He seemed to be reprimanding me for being there.

'Sorry mate, I was told to come here.' He kept on talking slapping the palm of one hand with his index finger to make his points, whatever they were. 'I know, mate. Tell it to the soldiers.' He kept on. I shrugged and ignored him until it came to my turn to approach the window.

Again, each page of my virtually empty passport demanded meticulous scrutiny before being stamped and handed back to me.

Entering Estonia was easier than leaving Russia. The queue

was shorter and the passport inspection was briefer. My last trial was to guide my bike through a very narrow door. The handlebars were wider than the opening, so I had to get the front wheel and the left side of the handlebar through, then turn the opposite way while pushing to clear the right side. At the same time, I had to squeeze myself through alongside while keeping the heavily sprung door open to clear the panniers. By now, I was exhausted. It had been a full-on day. But at least I was in Estonia. Or so I thought.

Outside was a caged walkway that ran parallel to the motor traffic coming from customs. I partly rode and partly walked, weaving my way around slower pedestrians, the last two or three hundred metres before exiting through a gate into Estonia. By now it was early evening, and I didn't have a clue where to go.

This would not be the first time I visited Estonia. I was sent

Alan Deakins

here in 2010 to film a pig farm for a livestock feed company. We flew to Tallinn, drove two hours to a remote farm, to film pigs enjoying the scrumptious feed that my client was producing. A few things about that trip remain in my memory.

I remember Tallinn being a nice provincial city, judging from the two nights we stayed there. The people were friendly and the restaurants, on the whole, were agreeable. Not much of an assessment or recommendation, I suppose, but unfortunately, that is the nature of filmmaking on a budget. You aren't sent there to explore; you are there to do your job in the shortest period of time possible. Fly in, eat, sleep, wake up early, travel to the location, film, travel back to the hotel, eat, sleep, wake up and fly home. The glamorous life of a corporate filmmaker.

It could be hard work, but it did have its moments. There was a particular incident on this Estonian shoot that still makes me chuckle. When we arrived at the location, the farmer showed us into the barn where we would be filming. Colin, my cameraman, set his camera on a bench so that he could walk around to assess where he would put his lights, much to the farmer's amusement.

'You don't want to put your camera there.'

'Why not...?'

'That is where we service the bulls,' making a masturbating gesture with his right hand.

In the twenty years I've worked with Colin, I've never seen him move so fast. It was the only laugh that day. To see how mother pigs were constrained in the farrowing crates with their babies was depressing.

On this excursion, I was about to redress my limited experience of Estonia.

Old Hippie on a Bike

The rain had stopped. The nearly empty main square of Narva was glistening in the evening light. I took out my iPhone to take a picture of my bike against this backdrop to post on Instagram and Facebook. Three days into my journey, I had a minor sense of achievement.

Suddenly, I heard a voice behind me. I turned to see the man who lectured me in the immigration queue. I presumed he was still banging on about my being in the queue.

'I agree! I had no choice.'

He kept rattling on.

I held up my hands, uttered, 'Police,' and shook my head with a smile.

He laughed, shook my hand, slapped my shoulder and departed.

I now had to face the fact that I did not know where I would spend the night. I thought it too late to carry on out of town to find a wild spot. Nor did I fancy the idea of setting up in a wet forest after the long day I had. I decided to ride around looking for B&B signs. I got halfway across the square when I saw a tourist information centre. It was still open. Although the advisor was enthusiastically helpful, she had no B&B's on her list, but she did know of a reasonably priced hotel about a five-minute ride away. I was too tired to think of my meagre budget, so I reluctantly accepted her directions and headed for the Vesta King Hotel.

It looked pleasant from the street. There was an inviting beer garden with tables nestled under mature trees. It would have been the perfect place to enjoy a drink if it wasn't so wet. The staff were accommodating. A secure storeroom was made available for my bike, and my room looked comfortable. I dumped my panniers and headed straight for the bar. A day in the saddle is thirsty work. A half litre of A. LeCoq was drawn and placed before me on the bar. I immediately took a picture if it.

I called it my 'Ice Cold in Alex' moment in my blog. This, of course, was an utterly over-stated appraisal of my modest accomplishment. In the movie, John Mills, Sylvia Syms, Harry Andrews and Anthony Quayle spent weeks crossing the Sahara Desert fighting off Nazi's, spies, hunger, thirst and death to be rewarded with ice-cold Carlsberg's when they reached Alexandria. I camped two nights, was bitten by a few mosquitos and picked a couple dozen snails off my tent. Hardly a comparison, but I was pleased to be in Estonia, and the beer tasted good.

Back in the room, I texted Marnie and emailed Natasha.

> *Hi Natasha...*
> *I made it to Estonia in good time. The first thing I did was have a very large cold beer. Thanks again for your kindness.*

A shower before dinner was in order. I took my clothes in with me and washed them also. I then put camera batteries on charge and returned to the restaurant which was empty except for one other table occupied by a couple with a young delightfully precocious daughter, who danced around the empty tables while humming to herself. It was quite entertaining. I ordered goulash soup for a starter, and pork loin for mains. My appetite knew no bounds since St Petersburg. Until the soup arrived.

A bowl the size of a tureen was placed in front of me, along with a brick-sized chunk of bread. This was my first properly cooked dish in three days. I dived in and thoroughly enjoyed it even though I knew another course was to follow. The pork loin was astoundingly huge but equally delicious. Try as I might, I had met my match, and regrettably left a good deal of it on my plate.

I had packed in such a chaotic hurry to escape the mosquitos in Russia, I was faced with the task of unpacking and re-organising everything. While I was sorting out the camera gear and recharging the batteries, my original question came back to me. 'Am I on a film shoot, or am I on a bike journey?' I hadn't enjoyed using the cameras; I didn't have a definitive film in mind to think of sequences to shoot; the energy to set them up far outweighed the footage I was getting. It was obvious. I took the cameras, batteries, cables, mounting kit and iPad Mini and placed it all into a plastic bag. I was sending the lot home. I also chucked in my waterproof trousers and socks. I had ridden in the rain with my Gortex PacLite jacket and quick-dry shorts comfortably enough. It would be good to rid myself of the weight.

I checked my emails.

> *Hi Alan Deakins!*
> *So you are closer to home now.*
> *hope your trip will have many adventures.*
> *Natasha from Russia*

I slept well. Free from mosquitos. Free from snails. Free from the worry of being discovered. Free to fall into a deep, deep sleep...and dream.

DAY 6
NARVA – JOVHI

*'You don't need a weatherman
to know which way the wind blows.'
-Bob Dylan*

The morning was bright as I set off. I stopped at a market to stock up on food for the day, then to a post office to send the cameras and clothes home. The package weighed more than 2.5 kilograms. That would reduce the load on my bike to fifteen and a half kilos. I couldn't say it felt lighter to ride, but I felt lighter. I had less gear to look after.

The route I had mapped out was to take me on the main road (E-20) for about fifty kilometres towards Tallinn to Jovi, from there I would head south for another fifty kilometres to the north shore of Lake Peipus. This distance was not achievable in one day to my mind, but I should be very close to the lake before I stopped for the night.

On reaching the outskirts of Narva, I was delighted to see a new wide cycle path about ten metres from the road stretching as far as I could see. I felt that this would be a good day. This feeling was short-lived, however. It wasn't long before I was riding against a strong westerly headwind. I hoped it would die down or change direction; I didn't fancy fifty kilometres of it. I pressed on. The wind got stronger. It was becoming hard work. It took a couple of hours to go twenty kilometres; I was tired and my legs felt weak. I stopped frequently for breaks. The wind was now gusting which was even more frustrating. Just when I thought I could make progress, a huge blast would set me back.

A bit further on, the path ended, and I was back on the road. Riding was precarious because the gusts of wind made me unstable, and I tended to weave without warning.

I rode on for another hour. I was exhausted. I found a place in the sun outside a school to rest. It must have been lunchtime. Several students stared at me as they passed by. I tried eating a sandwich, but a gust of wind blew half of it off the wall I had placed it on. Now I was angry. I shouted at the sky.

'C'mon, MATE. Throw more at me!'

'Mate' was my generic name for whatever I thought was working against me, be it a deity, the weather or individual vehicles. It didn't matter. I tended to put a bit of an Essex accent on it…which sounded halfway between 'mate' and 'mite'. I supposed it humoured me, even though by this time I had lost my sense of humour. At least talking out loud kept me company.

Further on, I headed into roadworks. I was dicing with traffic, but this time I was at a total disadvantage. Not only was I at the mercy of the thundering lorries and speeding cars, but it also began to rain. Short sharp showers slapped me with the gusts. The wind got stronger. My legs were no match for it. I was forced to dismount and walk my bike several times.

'I can't DO this! I can't fucking DO this!!!!'

It was more a cry of frustration rather than capitulation. Even if I wanted to give up, I would still have to get myself to somewhere. I trudged on.

Alan Deakins

About a kilometre later, I saw a log cabin with a tin roof on the other side of the road. It had a picture of a frosty glass of A. LeCoq on the side and a hand-painted sign reading: 24h. I immediately looked for a break in the traffic to cross. I entered a room about four metres square. The log walls were as dark as the outside. There was a service window about a metre wide at chest height. Behind the sliding glass, I could see a young woman sitting in the kitchen staring into her mobile phone. Next to her was a small griddle and a glass fronted fridge. I could see my old friend A. LeCoq sitting on the top shelf, and at one euro for a half litre tin, I considered it a bargain. I flopped down on one of the three shabby mohair brown sofas arranged in a U facing a disused fireplace. After a sip, and staring at absolutely nothing, I caught my breath and my bearings. I ached. My left ear was ringing from the traffic roaring past me for hours. A couple more sips were quenching and I began to feel a bit better. I pulled out my iPhone to consult the maps, but I had no signal whatsoever. Damn. Nothing left to do but sit and savour the beer.

I would have stayed longer, but I needed to get a signal to see where I was. It quickly returned outside, and I reckoned I was 5 kilometres from Johvi, where I would be turning south and out of the wind. By the time I got there, the sun had come out, and the wind had subsided. I had planned to have a proper meal here, but it had taken me so long to get this far, I decided to rely on the delicacies of the petrol station that straddled the junction so I could press on to find a spot to camp before nightfall. I made do with a hot dog sort of affair that was inserted into a soft roll that had been hollowed out. A brief respite in the sun on a grassy patch outside was curtailed as I felt the wind pick up, and saw ominous clouds rushing across the sky.

I didn't get far before the heavens suddenly opened up, and the wind gusted with a vengeance. It was quick and fierce. I couldn't stay on my bike and was even struggling to stay upright while pushing it.

'C'mon MATE. Throw it all at me!!! You bastard!!!'

One prolonged gust stopped me dead in my tracks. I literally couldn't take a step forward.

'I can't fucking DO this!!'

My frailty was all too apparent. Maybe I was too old or too weak from my stroke. Maybe this whole trip was folly, a pipe dream. I clearly wasn't a match for this kind of weather, and there was nowhere to take shelter. I felt vulnerable. Not only was I at the mercy of the traffic but also the elements. Either one could do me in within an instant, and there was nothing that I could do about it. One lone fragile being with feeble defences. This thought played heavily on me.

As quickly as the weather overwhelmed me, it abated. The wind dropped considerably to a breeze and the clouds parted to allow the warm evening sun through. I set about looking for a track into the pine forest on either side of the road to camp. I came upon one that looked promising. Fifty metres in and I could see that this particular track was used for fly-tipping. There was garbage strewn everywhere. I turned around, and as I approached the road to resume my search, I suddenly felt cold and weak. I needed fifteen minutes off the bike and something warm inside me. I fired up my stove and made a cup of the instant soup that I bought in St Petersburg. It would have to sustain me until I settled for the night.

It had taken me nine hours to travel less than sixty kilometres.

The further I rode, the thinner the forest became. I began to worry when I came to the edge that I wouldn't find a secluded place to pitch my tent. I finally found a track across a field that led to a small copse. It ended in a nice flat clearing, which cheered me until I heard a familiar crunching under my feet. Snails. I looked down to see hundreds of them. I've never seen so many gathered in one place. I had stepped into the Woodstock of snail events. I settled for a small snail-free patch on the side of the track quite close to the road. I might be seen by passers-by, which made me feel vulnerable, but I had no choice; it was late and I was completely drained.

As I was about to fall asleep I heard dogs barking and men's voices nearby. I didn't sleep well all night.

DAY 7
JOHVI – MUSTVEE

*'Who comes to the lake for water
and sees a reflection.'*
-Rumi

I was travelling on the main route to Tartu. Although not as busy as the E-20, it had its moments of crazy fast drivers. As I got closer to Lake Peipus, I started seeing roadside kiosks brightly painted with fish on their sides and bold letters: 'Suitsukala.' I thought it must be local fisherman selling their catch. I turned off onto a rural road that skirted the north shore. This was the first quiet road since I started this trip. It was still, warm and sunny; I was thoroughly enjoying the quiet relaxed pace that I settled into. No hurry. I passed quaint wooden houses, small churches and local people walking and cycling the road. It was an idyllic day.

I noticed that the forest on my left had become less dense, the soil was sandy and there were footpaths running between the pine trees. It was instantly familiar to me. Memories of my childhood living next to Lake Erie came flooding back. I stopped and walked my bike with a bit of difficulty in the sand. I came out onto a prominent edge. Stretched out in front of me was the expansive lake and below was a pristine beach. I hid the bike in a thicket and clambered down the steep embankment. I was the only living being on the beach as far as I could see in either direction. I was elated. Bright cumulus clouds hung over the lake stretching out to the horizon. A gentle fresh onshore breeze wafted over me. I had it all to myself. I laid on the sand and fell into a peaceful sleep for an hour.

Back on the road, I came across a brightly painted small 'Suitsukala' caravan with a table and chairs outside. I decided to have a look. I soon learned that suitsukala was smoked fish. The cheerful young lady had an array of perch, small pike, bream and other unrecognisable fish on display. She also had fresh bread and a small fridge with soft drinks. For two euros I had a small perch, a fresh crusty slab of buttered bread and an iced tea. The smoke flavour was delicate and delicious.

This was quite obviously more of a holiday destination, even though there were no hotels to be seen, only private houses, and the occasional store. I would guess that the majority of the houses were either holiday lets or second homes. There was a mixture of old and new. I was attracted to the old single-story wooden cottages with doorways so low, I would have to stoop to enter. Most of them were in disrepair. It seemed that people preferred to build something new.

It reminded me of a time in the early '80s when I was filming in the Wicklow Mountains outside of Dublin. At that time, people were abandoning their quaint stone cottages and building new houses next to them. I was told the cottages were symbols of poverty which people wanted to forget. Perhaps it is the same here as Estonia crawls out from under a shadow in the post-soviet era.

I stopped at a small church nestled in the pines. It had a rather large graveyard scattered amongst the trees. A few metres away, at the top of the brow, was a splendid view of the lake. 'If you have to be dead, it's a nice spot to be buried,' I thought. I supposed it was nicer for the living who visited than for the deceased. Most of the graves had elaborate artificial bouquets of flowers, much like the St Petersburg cemetery. There was one unusual plot that caught my attention. It consisted of three graves market by one cross and two modest stones. In front of each was a small real red flowering plant growing out of the sand, and the sand was carefully raked in a pattern, much like a Japanese garden. It was simple and poignant.

It was early afternoon, and I had no idea where I would be spending the night. It was pressing on my mind because I was constantly seeing 'Camping Forbidden" signs all along the road. I searched Google Maps for campsites and found a few in the vicinity. The first one looked bleak from the road. The second had several tables with umbrellas set back from the road, and the grounds were nicely shaded under a pine canopy. At five euros for the night, including shower and WI-FI, I was pleased.

A cold A. LeCoq and I were soon seated at one of the tables where I could look at my map and text Marnie. A couple of touring cyclists arrived and sat at a nearby table. They said a few words to each other in German, then pulled out their mobile phones. They were the first travelling cyclists I had seen.

'Hi there.'

'Hi.' She looked up from her phone. He didn't.

'Have you travelled far...?'

'Not far.' This time she didn't look up.

And that was the extent of our conversation. And at that moment, I suddenly felt very lonely.

When you ride a solo bike journey, you have to be prepared to be alone. You will spend hours on the road and pass long nights in a small tent with just you for company. Your days will be filled with being an observer rather than a participant. It is the nature of the beast. So when you do have a chance for interaction, a conversation, a laugh, it feels like a gift. There is a difference between alone and lonely. You can live with the former if you like your own company. But it takes someone else to assuage the latter.

DAY 8
MUSTVEE – JOGEVA

'Rainy days and Mondays always get me down...'
-Karen Carpenter

The morning was decidedly grey. It didn't look promising. My weather app agreed. Light infrequent showers were forecast. Light and infrequent I could deal with. It was a short ride along the edge of the lake to Mustvee where I would turn west on Route 36 and travel across Estonia to Parnu on the west coast, a three-day ride.

Aside for the first ten kilometres of muddy roadworks, the road to Jogeva was fairly new with a metre-wide shoulder for me to ride on. Unfortunately, once I was clear of the works, it began raining. So much for infrequent showers. The noise of the lorries zooming past was even louder due to the hissing of their tires on the wet road surface. It was tiring. I stopped several times at various bus shelters to catch my breath out of the rain.

Closer to Jogeva, the ruins of an ancient castle on a hill next to the road caught my interest. I didn't have the inclination to explore it in the rain, but a covered seating area adjacent to the car park was the perfect spot out of the rain to brew a coffee.

Eight kilometres from Jogeva, I saw a bicycle route sign and decided to follow it. I rode through Laiuse, a tiny hamlet. On the other side of the village, was an enormous ancient white church set back amongst mature deciduous trees. It was so colossal; it took my breath away. The imposing spire shot up above the trees and beyond. I had never seen anything quite like it. The rain had subsided, so I stopped to take a picture of my bike next to it. It was impossible to get the entirety of the spire in the same picture. The door was locked. Disappointing. I would have loved to see inside.

Alan Deakins

I carried on this lovely peaceful road for approximately ten kilometres where a sign pointed me to Jogeva, which was another eleven kilometres. So this enjoyable detour was thirteen kilometres longer than if I had stuck to the main road. When I arrived in Jogeva, just about everything was closed. I found a café and had a forgettable chicken burger and fries.

I set off to look for a place to set up camp for the night. As I headed into the countryside the sky suddenly got black, I knew what was in store. By the time I turned my bike around, the rain was already pelting me. I found refuge in a bus shelter. Camping would be impossible so I searched for accommodation on Google Maps. I didn't understand why my phone's battery was so critically low. I discovered that the cable to the solar panel had somehow been disconnected. I pulled out my battery bank, it still had a small charge left. I thought it best to save that. Google offered up a few expensive hotels, and one reasonable bed and breakfast on the other side of town. I decided to head there. Maps was draining the juice quickly and before I got to the destination, my phone died.

'SHIT!'

I relied on my memory of the map and found myself outside a house on a small dirt lane next to a factory. There wasn't a B&B sign and no lights on inside. Did I get it wrong? I needed to find shelter, the rain was getting heavier. I headed towards the main road and saw a restaurant next to the road. When I approached, I could see that it was closed. I was deflated. There were tables and chairs on the covered patio, so I brought the bike in, and sat. I connected the phone to the battery bank, but it did not respond. It was totally drained; it would take mains power to charge it. What was I to do? I resigned myself to spending the night there by pulling a few chairs together and wrapping myself in my quilt. God. How depressing. After twenty minutes, I knew this wasn't going to work. I decided to go back to the house.

There still was no sign of life as I opened the gate and walked my bike around to the back. I came to a glass veranda, and I could see a woman standing in a dimly lit room. I tapped lightly on the glass, hoping not to startle her. She immediately came to the door.

'Hi...uhm...room...zimmer...chambre?'

'Of course. Come in. It is not good out there.'

I wanted to give her a big hug! The house was split in two, with her quarters on one side. I was the only guest, so I had the entire other side to myself, consisting of a kitchen on the ground floor, and three bedrooms, a shower and a large warm sitting room furnished with two overstuffed leather sofas on the first floor. It was heaven. I had very little cash. No problem, she took cards. It couldn't have been better.

I immediately set my phone and battery bank to charging and jumped into the shower. With coffee in the kitchen and enough food in my panniers to tide me over until morning, I settled in. I texted Marnie, caught up on the news, blogged on my Instagram and Facebook pages and planned my route for tomorrow on the very fast WI-FI which was also included. I slept soundly in the superb king size bed.

DAY 9
JOGEVA – SUURE-JAANI

'The journey is the reward.'
-Steve Jobs

It was still grey the next morning, but the clouds were moving swiftly, and momentary shafts of sunlight shot through. It was going to be a good day. I left a thank you note in the guest book, quietly let myself out and packed my bike in the garden. I looked up at the house. It had been a godsend. It was fortuitous Google Maps had found this haven because it was near to the junction of Route 37. The road I was to travel on today.

I remembered passing a petrol station in the rain last night less than half a kilometre away. I breakfasted there on coffee, yoghurt and an egg sandwich. I was in the lap of luxury.

The road to Poltsamaa was badly in need of repair and resurfacing. Once again, I was riding on the very edge of a road without a shoulder to speak of. The tarmac was cracked and potholes were dotted all along the 30 kilometres. It there was any sights to be seen, I most probably would have missed them because I had to keep my eyes on the narrow strip I was riding on. Even though the day was pleasant, and the traffic was light, the cars passed blindingly fast. I was not enjoying it.

Poltsamaa was a sizable town. It seemed quite pleasant as I rode into the centre. I stopped at a supermarket to shop for lunch. My plan was to find a shady park to eat and rest.

Alan Deakins

On the way, a small squat little building caught my eye. In fact, it leapt out and assaulted my eye. It was painted a bright shocking fluorescent pink. I was convinced it would glow at night. It was a little café called Kaie Juures, and I was utterly attracted to it. The food in my pannier was to become my dinner because now I was destined to lunch here.

It was a simple establishment. The dining area was furnished with picnic tables. There was a serving hatch to place my order, and a large menu hung on the wall that I didn't understand. A lady behind the hatch asked me a question, just as a waitress walked by carrying a plate of what looked like Chinese dumplings.

'Do you speak English…? No…? Ahhh…' I pointed to the passing plate of dumplings.

She asked another question. I shrugged.

'Sorry.'

'She wants to know if you want pork or chicken.'

I turned to see a smiling lady who cheerfully helped me place an order of chicken dumplings with fries and an ice tea. She told me this little cafe was a favourite of hers and her family's. She then returned to them to finish her lunch. How very kind.

Before long, a plate of fried dumplings was placed in front of me along with a generous pot of sour cream. They were 'Deep Fried Bliss'. I thought to myself, 'This is what I want…moments like this.' I left heavier but happier.

Despite the added weight of the dumplings, the thirty-three kilometres to Vohma was relatively straightforward. The road surface improved, I had a bit of a shoulder to ride on, and it felt good covering a fair distance in a trouble-free day. The landscape was familiar to me, much like Suffolk and Norfolk at home: flat, rural and farmed.

On reaching Vohma, I stopped at a supermarket for a cold drink. I couldn't resist a buying bottle of wine also. About five kilometres from Suure-Jaani, I found an ideal spot next to an abandoned barn. I made my way into long grass next to a small copse, tramped down a clearing, set up my tent and opened the bottle of wine. Since the grass was tall enough to hide me from the road, I could relax for the rest of the night. I enjoyed the remainder of the warm evening sun along with my heated tin of beans and a couple glasses of an agreeable red.

Alan Deakins

DAY 10
SUURE-JAANI – PARNU

*'When you're being stalked
by a mob armed with raspberries,
the first thing to do is release a tiger.'
-John Cleese*

Suure-Jaani is a pretty village nestled in a valley. It looked inviting in the clear morning light as I approached in search of breakfast. I had a good feeling about today. It was to be a warm sunny, calm day and I would soon be on a beach in Parnu where I would spend two days resting. On the map, I had approximately fifty to sixty kilometres to ride. It looked fairly direct through a national forest. I also coordinated the route with Google Maps, just to keep me on course. I was going to enjoy it.

After a quick ride around the village, I found nothing open except for a small petrol station. I bought a sandwich and bananas and sat outside observing the local farmers filling their tractors and chatting to each other. Watching the slow good-natured pace put me in a relaxed mood.

Before setting off, I stopped in a layby to straighten my handlebars which had become annoyingly off centre. I took my helmet off and put on a baseball cap to shade my eyes from the sun. Straddling the front wheel to straighten the bars required the removal of my front bag. It was taking longer than I expected and I was getting impatient to get on the road.

Five kilometres out of Suure-Jaani, I realised I was riding with my baseball cap on. 'SHIT!' It was only then I looked down to see that my bag was not on my front pannier rack as it should be. Damn, my camera, Kindle and American passport were in it! I immediately turned around and pedalled as fast as I could with my heart in my mouth. When I approached the layby, I saw they were not where I had left them. I panicked. I jumped off my bike, frantically looking around. And there, on a bench, my bag and helmet were sitting side by side. Some kind stranger had picked them up off the ground and placed them there. There was nothing missing.

I sat there hoping the good Samaritan would come forward so that I could offer my heartfelt thanks. After about twenty minutes, I mentally offered my gratitude and left.

I turned off the main road onto my scenic route through the forest. After three kilometres, the road abruptly turned into an unpaved dirt track. Did I take a wrong turn? I checked with Google Maps, and a cheerful voice instructed me to proceed for nine kilometres. Riding wasn't easy in the loose dirt, but rather than turn back I figured I could last for that distance. When I approached that point, the voice directed me on to a newly paved road for twenty-one kilometres. Great.

It was a smooth, calm, comfortable ride as I entered the forest. About four or five kilometres along, once again the tarmac ended and I was dodging loose rocks on a dirt washboard. At this point, my thought of turning back wasn't feasible, I would have to stick it out. I would just have to slow down and take it easy.

'You can stand on your head for sixteen kilometres, Deak.'

The going was difficult, my front tyre would skid when it hit a loose stone, sending a shock through my whole body as I compensated to stay upright. I finally found that the only way to safely move forward was to ride in a track that a previous car or lorry had imprinted in the dirt. By now, the temperature had climbed and I was sweating profusely.

Then, the black flies found me. Huge monsters, the size of wasps descended upon me. Biting and menacing. Diving and buzzing around my face. They found their way behind my sunglasses and in my ears. I pedalled as fast as I could to outrun them. Still, they attacked. I rode as hard as I could in the narrow tyre tracks, dodging rocks and potholes. It was a frantic run to escape. Faster. Faster!! Surely they can't fly this fast.

Little did I know that insects can smell a human from hundreds of metres away. So, in fact, I wasn't out-running them; I was attracting more as I passed through the forest. I was a moving lunch. The neighbourhood ice-cream van with children's music blaring, come, eat, enjoy.

Google Maps called out a new message to me, 'In two hundred metres, turn right.'

OK! Not far! I made it! When I got to the junction, I saw that the same tortuous dirt hell lay in front of me. Google cheerily instructed me to proceed for a further twenty kilometres. I was stunned. I had given it everything I had in me. I was spent. I cried.

If a man screams in the middle of a forest, and there's no one around to hear. Does he make a noise? I can categorically say, YES! I screamed, I heard it. There was no one around. Not a living soul. I was totally on my own.

The onslaught increased. Mosquitoes joined the party. They began feasting on my legs. I slapped. I swore.

'I can't fucking DO this! I fucking CAN'T!

The only weapon I could think of was insect repellent. I rummaged in my pannier. When I found it, I took my glasses off, closed my eyes and sprayed everywhere. Then I sprayed some more. I reeked of the acrid citronella pong. The oily spray stuck to my sweaty skin. It felt terrible. It didn't seem to make a difference. The flies were still dive bombing me. The mosquitoes were still buzzing in my ears. I quickly downed a litre of water and got back on for a further run. I had no choice.

I attacked the tyre tracks as best and as fast as my aching legs

Old Hippie on a Bike

would allow. My bike was taking a terrible beating. I could feel the weight of my gear on the back pounding unforgivingly with each bump. I feared it would break. If it did, I would break. I would not have the strength to walk a broken bike out of there.

Suddenly, I hit a hidden rock. The handlebars jerked out of my hands. I was down. I felt a sharp pain in my leg, but I didn't care. I jumped up. I was gasping for breath, I needed more water. I gulped another half litre. I then noticed all was still. There were no flies or mosquitoes swarming me; the repellent was working. Finally, I was free of insects, but I was not (as the saying goes) out of the woods yet.

At least I could slow down to rest my legs and ease the trauma on my bike. The forest finally started thinning out, as I travelled and I could see open fields. I came to tarmac once again. 'Finally,' I thought. Three hundred metres on, I crossed a bridge over a small river. Another three hundred metres and I was back on a dirt track again. I was being tormented.

'C'mon on MATE!'

Another cyclist, fully loaded with baggage appeared from around a bend. We stopped to greet each other. He was Italian, he had been on the road for two months. He was carrying twice the bags I was. I told him about the flies, the mosquitoes, the road, the distance and the heat.

He shrugged nonchalantly. 'I will be OK.'

I watched him for a few minutes as he disappeared into that forest.

'I wonder. I wonder if you will be OK. I wasn't.'

I was soon back on a properly paved road, and within a kilometre, I happened upon a café. I was famished. God knows how many calories I had burned in the last few hours. Everyone looked up from their meals as I entered. I felt a bit self-conscious. A visit to the toilet explained it to me. My hair, matted and stiff from the insect repellent, was sticking straight out in all directions. My face was dirty, except for around my eyes. Much like a vintage race car driver, when he lifted his goggles after a race.

After a quick wash, I sat down to a cheese omelette, fries and a very cold beer. I recovered quickly and was ready to tackle the remaining kilometres to Parnu.

I had planned to reach Parnu by midday, but my deep forest encounter set me back several hours. The run into Parnu seemed fine for the first few kilometres until I starting hearing an irregular grinding noise coming from somewhere on my bike. I got off, rolled the bike along listening, but couldn't find the cause. I got back on and rode for another few kilometres. But then, the back end felt unstable. I stopped and checked. The back wheel was loose at the hub. I tightened the hub nut and rode on for another kilometre. The wheel was still wobbly and looking closer, I saw it wasn't the nut that was loose, it was the hub itself. I wasn't surprised, it had taken a pounding in my flight in the forest. I would need to find a bike repair shop in Parnu.

Luckily the remaining distance was on smooth cycle paths, so I was able to ride into Parnu without a complete breakdown. I had Googled campsites and found Konse Camping close by on the Parnu River. On the way there, I saw another, called Green Camping. It looked fairly empty. A young man climbed out of a squat tin shed that looked like a bunker as I entered.

'I would like to camp tonight.'

'Fifteen euros.'

A bit steep, I thought.

'Do you have showers?'

He pointed to an old dirty drab building that looked like an abandoned factory with a large iron door.

'WI-FI...internet...?'

'No.'

Do you take cards...?'

'No.'

Did I want to stay?

No.

I carried on to Konse. It was clean, bright, and modern with friendly staff, unlimited showers, a café on the river, WI-FI, electricity and a nice shaded green area to pitch my tent...all for nine euros. Fantastic.

Set up the tent. Shower. Beer in the café as I search for a bike repair shop. Relax. Dinner. Finish the half bottle of wine I still have. Sleep. It was an ambitious agenda, but I managed to complete it.

Alan Deakins

DAY 11
PARNU – REST

'Anything can happen. And it usually does.'
-Murray Walker

I awoke to a beautiful warm morning. I could feel another great day coming. The first thing to do after coffee was to get my bike repaired. The shop, Parnu Ratas OU, was less than a kilometre's ride. It was easy to find. Two amiable English speaking chaps inspected the hub, and their verdict was the wheel was most likely irreparable. New wheel prices started at fifty euros. I explained that I was riding for charity, and my budget was minuscule.

'Come back in four hours.'

'OK, how far is the beach?'

'I will loan you a bike.'

I left there on a basic one-speed shopping bike. It had a hand brake for the front wheel. To apply the brake to the back wheel, I had to pedal backwards, much like the Schwinn bikes I grew up with in America. It was rudimentary, but I was grateful to have a way of getting about.

It was a short enjoyable ride to the beach, meandering through lovely narrow streets lined with beautifully ornate wooden houses and buildings that have been standing there since the turn of the last century. Parnu, in a word, is stunning. It is rediscovering and restoring itself. I can only assume that the Nazi and subsequent Soviet occupations didn't decimate the town. Sprinkled amongst these colourful gems was the occasional art deco or ultra modern house. It all worked. Simply charming.

White sand, blue sky and a gentle offshore breeze was a promising welcome as I stepped onto the beach. Little wonder it was so crowded. I walked along towards the outlet of the Parnu river to find a more secluded spot. It soon became apparent that I had entered the clothing optional section. This option suited me better because I didn't have a bathing suit. I lay on my towel, and the combination of the warm sun and cool breeze felt wonderful on my body.

One of the concerns I had in planning this trip was my body. Could it stand the challenges? Would it let me down? Would it last the course? Of course, I anticipated aches and pains along the way, I was seventy-two, an old man. It goes with the territory, doesn't it? I had fully expected to be crippled this morning after my 'Black Bomber Fly' ordeal, but apart from a large black bruise on my leg, I was delighted to wake up feeling surprisingly fine for a septuagenarian. Admittedly, I had to crawl out of my tent on all fours, then stagger around for a couple of minutes as my body unknotted itself, but that is what I have been doing every morning on this trip. I had demanded more from this body than I thought it was capable of, and so far, it had responded without aches or the need for the painkillers that I packed in my first aid kit.

The sun had warmed me to the point that I needed cooling off in the sea. I walked into the water up to my knees and thought it was warm enough for a dip. WOW! It was, to put it mildly, refreshing. Exhilarating was a better description. I would have stayed in the water if it wasn't for a seagull ransacking my clothes.

'HEY! HEY!' I ran out of the water waving my arms wildly. At the same time, a young man who was closer to the thief ran towards it clapping loudly. The bird dropped my wallet and flew off.

Paul and Elsa were a young Swedish couple sitting close by. If it wasn't for Paul, I would have lost my cards and driver's license. They were on a trip around the Baltics in their camper van.

'Vintage split screen VW?'

'No. We drive an old Mercedes Vito.'

I wanted to take a picture of us for my blog but thought it more prudent not to since we were all naked. Instead, I asked if they would take a picture of me; they courteously obliged.

I was growing rather fond of my simple loan bike as I rode it back to the bike shop. It did what it was supposed to do: go forward and stop. It had heart, but I missed my bike. My fondness for it was growing stronger by the day. It had convinced me to do this trip, and thus far, carried me so many miles without complaint. The brutal pounding it received yesterday was not its fault. I was anxious to get it back. I braced myself for the news.

'Your hub was rusted inside, and full of dirt. The bearings were no good...'

'I'm not surprised. So...?'

'I cleaned it out, and I had the bearings...so it is OK now.'

'Really...?! How much?'

'Twelve euros.'

For the second time on this trip, I wanted to hug someone. He had gone out of his way. It would have been less effort (and more profitable) for him to replace the wheel. Instead, he listened to my plea. On top of that, he replaced my mirror which he accidentally broke. No charge.

I had been advised by countless people in the UK to watch out. Be careful. Take every precaution. All I've encountered on this journey thus far is open honest people who go out of their way to help. The only thief that nearly robbed me was a seagull. I felt safe. But I still locked my bike when it was out of my sight. I may be trusting, but I'm not reckless.

It was a lazy afternoon. I napped, sunned and sat under an

umbrella at the café reading my Kindle. I chatted with a very pleasant couple from the UK who were touring the Baltics in their motorhome. She had been a Samaritan and kindly made a donation.

I thoroughly enjoyed my rest, but my thoughts were increasingly turning back to the road.

DAY 12
PARNU – SALACGRIVA, LATVIA

*'I trust down the road
our chance meeting will make perfect sense.'*
-Nikki Rowe

I had hoped for an early start, but, as usual, it took me more than an hour to prepare myself and pack everything. It was a warm, pleasant morning, perfect for cycling. The route south started on a wide cycle path well away from the road and carried on for about five kilometres. It was nice being out of the traffic to find my rhythm again. Once back on the road, I had a decently wide shoulder to ride on.

Even though this was the main road to Riga, the traffic seemed lighter than I was used to. For the next twenty kilometres I could appreciate the forests, tidy farms and gentle countryside without constantly feeling threatened, although when the lorries did roar past, I was reminded not to become too complacent. And my left ear took a bashing once again.

As I passed through Voiste, a small hamlet, I noticed a curious little green shop. It had a most unusual crescent-shaped roof that sat on it at a noticeably jaunty angle. There was a familiar red round Coca-Cola sign fixed at a right angle to catch the attention of passing motorists, and outside was a bright red table and chairs. I had to stop.

Old Hippie on a Bike

Inside was a surprise. It was tiny, but very well stocked. Every shelf and display was crammed full of interesting foodstuffs and souvenirs. There were cheeses and prepared snacks in a refrigerated glass cabinet. The cheerful shop keeper was busy tidying the shelves as I entered. It was obvious she was proud of her little establishment. And rightly so, it was charming.

As I browsed, I told her about my ride to the UK. And my ringing left ear.

'So you will be taking the old Riga road?'

'I don't know about it.'

'Ah. You will want to go on that road. It is good for cycles. Very quiet.'

'Where is it?'

'Another 3 kilometres, turn right when you see a sign to Vana Riia Monument.'

Alan Deakins

I sat outside at the bright red table on a bright red chair with a freshly brewed coffee and an indulgent sweet pastry before thanking her and heading for the quiet road.

The old road was narrow, primitively paved and thankfully tranquil. I was enjoying a nice effortless, albeit slow pace. I was in no hurry to get anywhere. Today was a day to savour.

Two touring cyclists approached from the other side of the road heading to Parnu. Their cheery 'HELLO' instantly compelled me to stop.

Waldek and Tanja were German serial cyclists. They've been wandering on and off for years. Europe, Australia, America and Asia. I immediately liked them. They were warm, attentive and affable. They listened with genuine interested as I talked about my trip and the Samaritans.

Waldek's enthusiasm was infectious.

'How wonderful! Riding for the good of somebody else!'

'It's quite special to me.'

'I am glad. I am also glad for you England won in the World Cup last night.'

'Sorry about Germany.'

'Don't be!! I am so happy we lost! We don't have to ride fast to find a television every night. I can now enjoy cycling again.'

'That's one way of looking at it.'

'No more television, no internet…no electronics…' He looked at my iPhone attached to my handlebars.

'Now Waldek…don't start…'

'No electronic maps…paper maps are better…'

I pulled out my map. 'Like this one…?'

With a shout of glee, he rushed forward and gave me a big hug. It was a spontaneous gesture that said to me, 'You are a kindred spirit.'

We talked further of life, cycling and Brooks saddles. Waldek pointed out how mine was laced incorrectly. It felt like we could have happily passed the rest of the day chatting, but we all knew that we had to carry on with our respective journeys. Before we parted, I suggested a selfie.

They came close, putting their arms around my waist, Waldek rested his chin on my shoulder. I hoped the picture would capture the mutual familiarity and fondness that happened between strangers in such a short space of time on a remote road in Estonia.

I rode off thinking of exuberant Waldek and gracious Tanja travelling the world enchanting everyone they came in contact with. I was a fortunate recipient. I had been truly enchanted.

I was in high spirits all that day. The weather was perfect, the road quiet and the scenery was lovely. I passed through lush forests and tidy villages with wooden churches. My unstructured day was pleasantly unfolding as if it had been meticulously planned to satisfy my wishes.

I stopped to take a picture of a Eurovelo sign. A man staggered out of a little shop with a vodka bottle.

'English...?'

'Yes.'

'Where are you going...?'

'London.'

'A long way. You like Estonia?'

'Very much. It is beautiful.'

'It is quiet. Very quiet. Too quiet.' He pointed to a modest well-maintained house across the road. 'That is my house.'

'Very nice.'

'Good luck.'

With that, he quietly crossed the quiet road to his quiet house for a quiet drink.

And I quietly thought, 'Why not?'

The Old Riga road sadly came to an end and re-joined the busy Route 4. Once again, I was in the thick of it, enduring fast drivers, and the deafening thunder in my left ear. Up until now, I hadn't given much thought of camping for the night. Salacgriva was twelve kilometres ahead, I would sort it out there, and in the meantime, I would look for camping signs along the way.

On the large tourist map in Salacgriva, I saw there was a tourist information office. After I figured out the directions, I realised the office was ten metres behind me. The advisor pointed me to a camping site two kilometres out of town on the road to Riga.

'Go past the church, and look for a sign saying ROKI'

I found the sign easily enough, which was reassuring, but it pointed me up a dirt track. Visions of my 'black fly' experience almost stopped me from turning. 'I'll give it five minutes...no more.' Fortunately, after two hundred metres, I came to a pleasant house with a wide gate leading into a welcoming courtyard.

I was greeted by Janis ('Spelled like the rock star, but the J is pronounced like Y', he told me). He had a lovely little traditional cottage for €20, or I could pitch my tent in his attractive garden for €8, mindful of my budget, I opted for my tent. He pointed out the shower at the end of the garden, which was gravity fed from a large tank above it.

'It may be a bit fresh, I filled it this morning but maybe the sun has warmed it by now.'

Indeed, it was fresh…breathtakingly fresh…shockingly fresh. But I must admit I felt rejuvenated and enjoyed sitting in the warm late afternoon sun to dry my hair.

Janis had built a rustic veranda with a hammock, table and chairs, stereo system and microwave. I was there charging my phone, and organising my gear when he approached with two beers. We sat and chatted. He had led an interesting life, having worked most of his adult years abroad. Recently, he had a desire to return to Latvia, so he came here, his family home, to rebuild it into a holiday site.

Two beers led to two more beers. I warmed to Janis. He was a gentle practical man, returning to where he was born, doing everything he could to make a success of his burgeoning business so that he could stay here. I felt it has been difficult for him.

After he left, I continued organising my gear and microwaved a modest dinner. I loved this space. I felt comfortable and welcomed. I reflected on my day filled with wonderful people. For the first time on this journey, I didn't feel alone.

Janis returned with two more beers.

'I thought you might like some company.'

He thought right. His company was most welcomed.

DAY 13
SALACGRIVA – LAKE DZIRNEZERS

*'Who told you you're allowed
to rain on my parade?'*
-Bob Merrill

It had rained during the night. I brewed coffee while packing everything under cover of Janis's lovely veranda. He came out to say goodbye before he departed for Riga. I asked how much I owed him.

'Eight euros.'

I couldn't agree to that; he hadn't included the beers. We came to an arrangement. He was a wonderful, generous host. His kindness was large in my mind as I too headed south on the road to Riga.

The sky was threatening to the point that I had considered staying another night with Janis; I really didn't want another experience as I had in Jovega. The clouds were moving swiftly, though, and before long; the sun began peeking through. The E67, although busy, was bearable because it was relatively wide, and I had the luxury of a metre-wide shoulder to ride on. I felt safer, but my left ear didn't agree. The lorries were loud as ever. Even so, I had an uneventful forty-kilometre ride through dense forests and broad fields, broken up by the odd stop for a stretch.

Fortunately, I was able to turn onto a quiet road that would offer respite for twenty kilometres. I assumed it was the old Riga road. I happened upon a little outdoor farmers' market in

Saulkratsi, a small, attractive, well-manicured town where I bought a rather nice pork pastry for lunch.

I was hoping for an unhurried day, but the sky was getting darker, telling me to press on. It was a pleasure to travel this road through Saulkratsi and its neighbouring town Saulkratsu; the majority of the ride was on smooth bicycle paths. It was nice to see that Latvia also was accommodating cyclists. Just before I joined the main road, I stopped at a petrol station for a cold drink. I was pumping air into my tyres when I heard shouting.

'HEY!! HELLO!!! HIYA!! YO!!'

I looked up to see a cyclist on a light road bike with a small pack on the back waving enthusiastically. I waved back. He rode on quickly with bright white and red lights flashing on the back.

'There's a man in a hurry,' I thought.

Further along the road, it began raining. I wondered if I would miss not having waterproof trousers, but I felt comfortable in just my waterproof jacket and quick dry shorts. I guessed I was burning enough calories to stay warm. It wasn't long before I saw the young man who waved at me standing under a tree. I stopped.

'Everything OK…?'

'Yeah. Just getting my waterproofs out.'

We talked for a few minutes. His name was Manny, a Lithuanian travelling around the Baltics visiting family. I told him briefly about my journey. It was a nice chat, but I thought I better get going.

'I'll be off. You will be passing me soon enough, I reckon.'

About thirty kilometres from Riga, I happened upon a campground. The gate wasn't locked, but it didn't look like anyone was there. By this time, Manny had caught up with me.

'It doesn't look promising.'

'Is the gate locked?'

'No.'

'Let's go in.'

We rode further into the camp. It looked derelict. The cabins were in various states of disrepair, the paths were overgrown, various dilapidated cars were parked under the trees covered with ragged tarpaulins. The whole place was tired and wet in the rain.

'Looks a bit grim.'

Then an old man came out of one of the cabins and ambled over to us. He and Manny conversed in Russian.

'He has rooms, twenty-five euros for the two.'

'That's a bit steep. My last campground was eight euros.'

Many spoke to the old man.

'Ten euros each. For another ten euros, he'll cook dinner. I'm staying.'

'OK. Does he take cards?'

'No.'

'In that case, I'm off, I only have five euros on me.'

'The weather is not good. Stay. I will pay as a donation to your charity.'

'Does he have beer?'

'Yes.'

"I'll pay for the beer.'

The old man led us down a rough track to the lake, and there standing on the shore was the strangest cabin I've ever seen. It was about three metres square, and two stories tall. A rotting staircase on one side led to a door on the top floor. There was a porch attached covered in sheet plastic flapping in the on-shore wind. Some of the floorboards were rotten, so we had to be careful where we stepped.

Manny wanted to work on his bike in the room, so I took the top floor. As I climbed the stairs, one of the treads snapped under my weight. This place has seen better days. The theme continued in the room. For a start it smelled mouldy, not surprising, there were damp patches on the 1960's flowered wallpaper. The mattress on the small double bed was thin and lumpy. It too had a damp smell. I decided that the best option was to roll out my sleeping bag, rather than rely on the thin blankets. A single bare low wattage bulb hung from the ceiling casting a dim depressing glow over the whole scene.

Never mind. At least it is out of the cold rain. Besides, there is a hot meal to look forward to.

The old man summoned us to dinner. We were ushered into a room that was actually a lean-to tacked onto his cabin. It had a corrugated plastic roof and clear plastic sheeting for windows. He brought the beers and a plate of sliced white bread, followed by a tureen of a thin chicken and rice soup. It was under seasoned, but comforting.

I was enjoying Manny's company. He and his wife had immigrated to Florida, where they raised their family. He founded a business that he runs with his wife and son. 'I make boxes.' Well done him for carving out a happy life. He talked about his trip. He has relatives all over the Baltics, and to visit them, he was doing upwards of 160 kilometres a day. He had an extremely light road bike, and he packed light also, opting for hotels rather than camping.

The old man shuffled in with the main course, along with two more beers. We dined on small pork cutlets, pickled vegetables, and a potato/cabbage dish. It was modest but surprisingly good.

Manny supposed that this campsite had its heyday during the communist era. It is obvious that the old man has been struggling with dwindling funds and strength to keep it up.

We finished dinner with sponge cake and coffee. At the end of it all, I thought the old man did well. I was filled, warm and in good spirits.

The rain had stopped. I walked along the shore of the lake in the fading evening light. I saw several pedal boats lined up pointing towards the water. Their paint had turned to powder, from years of waiting, their pedal gears had rusted. I saw affluent communist officials and their families enjoying hot summers on the lake in them, with the old man, young and prosperous looking on.

DAY 14
LAKE DZIRNEZERS – LAKE KLIGU EZERS

'I think life is pretty strange.
It is wooo, wooo, wooo"
-Annie Leibovitz

A squeaking door woke me up. I looked out to see Manny packing his bike. It was not quite 05.00.

'I could brew you a coffee if you're not in a hurry.'

'I can't say no to a coffee.'

I set my stove up on a little table sheltered from the onshore wind behind the plastic sheeting. I soon had two mugs of coffee ready, and Manny shared a couple of energy bars he had in his pack. A quick breakfast before we shook hands and he departed.

I felt sadness. Was it because I was alone once again? Was it the dull grey chilly morning? Was it the crumbling decaying campsite? I didn't dwell on it. I packed as soon as I could and left. The old man was nowhere to be seen as I closed the gate behind me.

I was on the road by 06.00. The one question on my mind was: 'What do I do with Riga?' I would be there by 09.00, too early to check into any sort of accommodation. I didn't fancy roaming around five hours with my bike. And if I was perfectly honest, I don't particularly enjoy exploring cities alone. I'm not an ardent sightseer.

By the time I reached the outskirts, I had decided to pass

through, and find a campsite west beyond the airport. I accessed my 'RideWithGPS' app to get me through. The route to the centre looked straightforward. All I had to do was follow the A2 to the Daugava River.

I expected to fight rush hour traffic, but I had very little trouble. What traffic I did encounter, or held up as I rode through roadworks, was patient. I didn't feel threatened or pressured. It was a good ride and rewarded with a rest in a lush park next to a canal before I crossed the river. The Akmens Tilts (Stone) Bridge had a wide cycle/pedestrian lane. It was nice to see scores of cyclists travelling into Riga for work. I stopped for a few minutes to watch the river traffic, and to take a picture of my bike against the skyline of Riga.

Once I crossed the river, I relied on the map app to lead me on a somewhat complicated route to get around the airport and on to the A9 taking me to Liepaja on the west coast. I rode through expansive tree-lined parks, affluent, middle class and poor neighbourhoods.

Every so often I would hear the irritating 'DA-dum, DA-dum, DA-dum from my phone telling me I am off course. I would

Alan Deakins

have to turn around to get the 'BLIIIING' to say I'm back on course. Annoying as it was, I was making good progress and enjoying riding through ordinary neighbourhoods observing ordinary people.

At one point, I stopped at a Y junction to have a sip of water. A young man came walking along. He stopped, looked in his bag, pulled out a slip of paper and walked over to me.

'Take this. You will get a free coffee there.'

He pointed to a café with inviting outdoor tables under wide umbrellas, before walking off.

My first thought: 'Scam.' My second thought: 'Doesn't hurt to check it out.'

I entered a dark velvet lined room with glitter balls and fairy lights. At the foot of a wide staircase, sat a scantily clad young woman in what appeared to be a ticket booth.

'Definitely a scam,' I thought.

'Hello,' she smiled.

I sheepishly held up my coupon, and she pointed to the bar area. A young man smartly dressed in a crisp white shirt and black waistcoat was busy arranging pastries on the bar.

'Hello, Sir.'

'Hi. I've been given this…'

'Very good. What would you like? cappuccino? Americano? Latte?'

'Cappuccino.'

He pointed to the assortment of pastries. 'Would you like one of these?'

'Here we go,' I thought. 'The scam. Free coffee…ten-euro pastry.'

'How much?'

'Fifty cents.'

Amazing. It turned out that this was a casino/bar promoting itself with the free offer.

I sat outside in the sun, and before long, the young man cheerfully served the coffee and a sweet cherry pastry with a skilled flourish. I sat there enjoying my treat musing that I would have missed this lovely experience if I had given in to my scepticism rather than my curiosity.

It took another hour through suburbs and narrow country lanes to finally reach the A9. The road surface was excellent, and I wondered if this was a new road. There seemed to be very little in the way of services or restaurants that I had become accustomed to in the past twelve days, just fields and forests.

It was early afternoon before I finally found Laci, a restaurant and food store. The car park was full of Mercedes, BMW's, Range Rovers and Audi's. Well-dressed diners were seated on the patio in the afternoon sun. It was apparent to me this was not the place for a sweaty cyclist. I opted for the shop instead. Even there, I was out of place among the chic people buying exclusive wines, exotic cheeses, organic produce, and trendy loaves of bread from stylish wicker baskets. I found a slice of pizza for four euros. I sat on a bench on the edge of the car park eating my very expensive small lunch.

It was getting late, and I had already travelled eighty kilometres. I began to worry about accommodation. A Google map search proved unsuccessful. Nothing to do but press on. Ten kilometres later, I saw a restaurant/hotel set in a lovely copse. The shaded patio was very attractive and all the tables were immaculately set with tall wine glasses, polished cutlery and linen tablecloths, another establishment catering for the high end of the market. Oddly, there were no customers to be seen. I was still hungry. The woman behind the bar looked startled as I walked in.

'Hi there, can I get a bite to eat?'

'Moment.'

She scurried out of the room and returned a few seconds later.

'No.'

"No food...?'

'No food.'

How about a room? Zimmer...? Chambre...? For the night...?'

'No. Full.'

As I rode out of the empty car park, I mused to myself, 'Was it something I said...?'

The next twenty kilometres of open fields offered no hiding spot for wild camping. Google maps were still drawing a blank, and I was getting tired. One hundred kilometres is the furthest I've ever travelled in a day. I came across a café on a junction seventy-two kilometres from Riga. My intention was to buy a coffee, but the fridge full of beer quickly changed my mind. It was a bonus that the friendly waitress spoke English.

'I don't suppose you know of any camping around here.'

'Oh yes. There is a very nice place on the lake five kilometres from here.'

'Really...? Where?'

She pointed to the opposite side of the A9. 'Go on that road for three kilometres, then turn left. It is at the end of that road. You will see it.'

I set off down the road. 'Five kilometres. I can do five kilometres.' After five hundred metres, I was dismayed, but not surprised to see the smooth road turn into a rough, dusty, gravel track. I cursed. I swore. I had no choice.

I dodged stones and ruts for a further two and a half kilometres, where a camping sign directed me left as the young lady had described. I thought it odd that there wasn't a similar sign on the A9. This road was a rock hard bone-shaking, bike rattling washboard. I had to go slowly, for fear of breaking my wheel again. I could see the campsite in the distance, but I could also hear loud motor sounds. It sounded like there was a race going on with highly tuned high RPM cars. It reminded me of the sound of the Grand Prix races the boys and I attended.

I rode through the gates and headed straight for the noise. I was surprised to see radio controlled boats screaming around buoys in the lake. Scores of people were on a pier watching. The boats were about a metre and a half long. They were tremendously fast and loud. The sound filled the whole campsite. There were numerous tents dotted all around, filled with men working with rapt attention on their boats. This wasn't a just good-natured pastime...this was serious, and no doubt seriously expensive. Win at all cost.

I searched unsuccessfully for an office, or reception in the main building that housed rooms, showers and toilets. I walked around only to find tents and cabins. Finally, I approached the tent of the organisers. I was informed that the owner of the campsite was on the lake in the rescue boat, and he'd be there until the end of the races in two hours' time.

I decided to pitch my tent in the meantime, one more among the dozens there wouldn't make much of a difference. A light rain started to fall, which didn't deter the racers in the slightest. The screaming engines were as loud as ever. I sat in a picnic shelter and ate the soup and sandwich I still had in my panniers. That was the extent of my supplies. All I had left was coffee for the morning.

I fell asleep in my tent to the buzzing of the boats. Sometime later I was awakened by a band playing thumping bubble gum dance music accompanied by the whoops and shouts of the revellers. Latvian model boat racers really know how to party. There was no way I would find the owner in that cacophony. So I tried as best I could to sleep.

DAY 15
LAKE KLIGU EZERS – SKRUNDA

*'If you celebrate the small victories,
you will eventually win the war.'*
-Ian K. Smith

The stillness woke me at 05.00. It had rained in the night, and although it had stopped, the morning was grey and the air was wet. I brewed coffee, packed up and rode towards the gate. I was surprised to find it locked with a chain and padlock. The perimeter fence was three metres high. It seemed there was no way out. I had to take matters in hand by unpacking the bike, climbing the shoulder high five bar gate, and passing my panniers and bags over one at a time, then with much effort, lifting my bike over. I then suffered the five-kilometre washboard to the main road.

Coffee is not a breakfast, and by the time I found a small shop I was famished. Fresh coffee and warm sausage roll was all I needed to press on into the wet day.

I stopped at a petrol station/café in Saldus after two hours of rain-soaked riding. I was standing in the queue for the coffee machine when a young man behind me struck up a conversation.

'Did you come far?'

'St Petersburg.'

'St Petersburg...??!!'

'And I'm going to London.'

'Woah Dude, you're crazy!'

'That's what my wife said.'

'Wow. Respect, Dude.'

'Thanks.'

I selected a sandwich and sat in the window next to an electric socket to charge my phone. Outside, the young man was smoking a cigarette and looking at my bike. He looked up at me, gave me the thumbs up, then got in his car and drove off.

I was weary of the rain, but I had to get to Skrunda. Forty kilometres to Skrunda. I would celebrate in Skrunda. I will have travelled five hundred miles when I get there.

The clouds were lifting as I approached Skrunda. I promised myself that I would stop at the first café I encountered. Luckily it was a lovely little place with a young waitress and chef. It just felt comfortable and right. I noticed straight away that they had chilled wine in a glass fridge, I ordered a glass and was rewarded with a rather nice dry white. My celebratory meal was a spicy chicken kebab, salad, and a huge gut busting pile of chunky chips. I couldn't eat them all, but with my increasing appetite, I gave it a good try. I asked the waitress if there was a place to stay, and she pointed to an unassuming tavern directly across the street. Cool, I would attend to that shortly, but first, I had another glass of chilled white.

My fifteen-euro room was above the bar. The landing at the top of the stairs was big enough for my bike. I immediately unpacked, showered and washed my clothes at the same time and hung out everything to dry all over the room, before falling asleep.

I woke up early evening. I decided to go down to the bar for dinner, but it was closed. I looked across to the café, it was also closed. A quick calculation and I realised it was Sunday. I found an open supermarket, which meant either a cold dinner or soup on my camp stove. I chose the latter. I also stocked up on provisions for my run to Liepaja.

DAY 16
SKRUNDA - LIEPAJA

'It's like deja vu all over again.'
-Yogi Berra

Another dull, grey, wet morning. It was difficult to work up the enthusiasm to face a rain-soaked highway. Spending another day in my little room in Skrunda didn't fill me with joy either. If the traffic was light as it had been the past two days, it would be tolerable. I was cold at first, but I soon built up heat and was making good time.

The traffic was heavier than I'd hoped for, but I realised that it was Monday morning. It was odd to lose track of the days. In my life at home, I was always functioning by the clock. Wake time, breakfast time, work time, lunch time, store hours' time, Samaritan shift time, dinner time, television time, bedtime. I wonder how often I glanced at my watch during a normal day.

Since the start of this journey, I'd been functioning on two different but connected calibrations: distance and hunger. The more distance I covered, the more food I shoved into my face at every given opportunity. I once read that cycle touring is a physical activity where you don't lose weight. I could understand why; I was replacing the calories I was burning at a phenomenal rate to keep my machine going.

Some unexpected steep hills, the increased rain and the constant spray of the lorries were slowing me down considerably. It was also having a negative impact on my mood. This was hard work; I was not enjoying it at all. At one point, on a particularly steep hill, I saw a snail crawling towards the road's edge. It struck me that we had a lot in common: we were both slow, carrying everything on our backs and wishing to be off this road. I stopped and filmed it sliding along as the lorries thundered past for my blog.

The only relief was a simple little café just off the road where I enjoyed a rich espresso for sixty cents while sitting outside under a clearing sky.

A nice wide tree-lined cycle path carried me into Liepaja. I immediately liked the ageing neighbourhoods I passed through. Even though the buildings could certainly benefit from maintenance, it definitely was 'Old Europe' unashamedly facing the present while retaining its venerable aged face.

I loved the scale, the old weathered wooden houses and the cobblestones that either edged the streets or actually were the streets. I easily could imagine what life would have looked like between the wars. It was exciting me.

I stopped several times to photo the textures and aesthetically appealing details of the ornate houses. There had to have been an optimism when they were built, and it still shone through in my mind, after decades of war, occupation and repression.

I crossed a channel over a low bridge leading to the centre and found a modest café on its edge for lunch. I searched for accommodation and was pleased to find a moderately priced hotel right next to where I was sitting.

The exterior of the Royal Hotel was not as grand as its name would suggest. It was industrial, perhaps a former warehouse, given its proximity to the waterfront. I wasn't prepared for its totally berserk interior. The reception was very large, with a desk on one side, and a bar on the other. At one end of the room, a huge three by four-metre television screen was showing World Cup highlights. The elephants in the room, however, were several large gilded Rococo sofas and chairs arranged in groups, filling the room with theatrical golden kitsch. Visually, it was mad, nutty and wonderful. I instantly wanted to grab a glass of wine, and sink into the fabulously faux splendour of one of the chairs.

The pragmatic part of me decided to secure my bike, a room, a shower and a change of clothes first. The cordial receptionist was most welcoming. And soon I had my bike firmly chained to the staircase railing, my gear unpacked on the single bed in my narrow but agreeable room and myself washed in the spotlessly clean communal toilet/shower room, all for twenty euros. After my mad night with Latvian boat racers, and my wet noisy seventy-five-kilometre ride, I conveniently forgot about my minuscule budget.

If a film production company needed a period set, Liepaja is perfect. Prewar, postwar, between the wars, there are streets that could undoubtedly be appropriate backdrops. It was so easy to imagine life here forty, fifty, sixty, seventy, a hundred years ago. As I explored the cobbled lanes near the hotel, I could picture dark figures darting in and out of the shadows in an effort to escape Nazis patrols.

Life still goes on in these streets. New life. Young people are renovating the lovely old wooden buildings for cafés, coffee houses, bars and real ale pubs. What I admired most was their efforts to keep the weathered character of the neighbourhood without introducing twee modernism to cater to the tourists. And to their credit, there wasn't a souvenir shop in sight.

As I was walking around, I happened across a bicycle shop called Gandr. I had been considering a red flashing light for safety on the dull wet roads.

Alan Deakins

Eventijs, a personable young shop assistant, was patient in helping me choose a bright rechargeable light that I could mount on my helmet. He took the time to talk about the coast road heading south, the weather, and routes in Poland. A simple sale became a thirty-minute conversation. He then rung up my purchase on his staff discount. A small kindness that meant a great deal.

Back at the hotel, I managed to sink into the ersatz rococo grandeur with a rather pleasing white wine, and I took the advantage of the WI-FI to update the operating system on my iPhone that Apple had been relentlessly reminding me to do.

Old Hippie on a Bike

DAY 17
LIEPAJA – KLAIPEDA, LITHUANIA

*'Reality is an illusion
due to the lack of alcohol.'
-W.C. Fields*

My plan to have a leisurely ride down the Latvian coast lounging periodically on the sandy beaches were crushed when I came down to breakfast. It was raining. It was grey. It was depressing. Sitting in a hotel for another day was not an option, I headed off.

The ride to the Lithuanian border was uneventful, except for the wet weather, and numerous road resurfacing works. There were several single lane stretches about three kilometres each, with the same distance between them. I rode to the front of the queue of traffic waiting at the lights, and entered the works against the red light, and rode on the side that was cordoned off. By the time I reached the end, the traffic I had passed caught up to me. Three kilometres later, I passed them again waiting in a queue for the next section, this little game was the only excitement in an otherwise dull ride.

About ten kilometres from the border, I came across a small gazebo near the side of the road. Access to it was a small footbridge that spanned over a ditch that ran alongside the road. It was a tiny structure, eight-sided and about two metres in diameter.

Inside was a seat, a small round table in the centre with a candle on it. Outside, stood a crucifix with a small bunch of fresh flowers at its base. I imagined that someone lovingly built this modest structure as a shrine to the loved one who died on this spot. And that he or she comes every evening to place the flowers, light the candle…and wait.

Seven kilometres inside Lithuania, I stopped at a restaurant. I was desperate for a break. The proprietor met me on the steps to tell me that the kitchen was closed, and the only thing he could offer was coffee. Perfect, that's all I wanted. He served me a deep dark delicious espresso made from an old polished Gaggia machine, along with a pretty little sweet cake.

There was another couple there, and I overheard the proprietor talking to them about his wife who was a famous singer. We gathered around his computer screen as he proudly showed us a couple of YouTube clips of her performances. She is Birute Patrikyte, a well-known star in the Baltics. Interestingly, the name of the restaurant is: 'Birute's Uoste' which translates to Birute's Port of Call. Apparently, she loves to return to the restaurant after every tour. Lovely.

For some reason, I started having trouble with my iPhone. Every time I accessed my maps, a window annoyingly popped up over them saying: 'This accessory may not be supported'. I had no idea why this was happening, but it was making navigation difficult.

The rain continued, convincing me that I had to make it to Klaipeda. Even if I could find a campsite, pitching a tent in the cold rain did not fill me with joy. Having said that, I didn't relish the thought of paying for another room.

Entering Klaipeda was a mixture of dual carriageways and cycle paths. It seemed a long way to the centre, perhaps my sense of distance was clouded by my cold wet mind. I didn't get a sense of the town, as my only focus was to find accommodation. My battery was low again as I searched Google maps.

I found a hostel which was reasonable but turned it down because my bike would have to stay outside exposed to every passer-by in a dubious neighbourhood. I was sure it would not be there by morning.

The only other option I could find before I got the 'This accessory may not be supported' warning and my phone dying from a drained battery pointed me towards a nice tree lined street. When I arrived at the address, all I could see was a small office. I asked the young lady behind the desk if she knew of a B&B on this street.

'It is here.'

'Fantastic…do you have a room for the night…?'

Her rate was much more than I expected. I explained that I was riding for charity, and my budget was extremely tight. She kindly offered a discount and said I could keep my bike in the office overnight as well.

Alan Deakins

'Do you want breakfast?'

'Is it extra...?'

'Yes.'

'How much...?'

'OK, OK,' she laughed. 'I will give it to you.'

By the time I settled in the room, it was getting late. I needed to get something to eat. I found a supermarket close by and chose something that I could microwave in the communal kitchen. I also chose a bottle of wine to ease my cold aching legs. When I got to the cashier, I was informed that I couldn't purchase the wine because it was 3 minutes past 20.00. Lithuania had recently changed its alcohol laws. How frustrating. Should I be grateful that the Lithuanian government was protecting me from myself?

My night consisted of: a nice room is a period house, a dry

bed, a nondescript microwaved meal, a hot shower and...NO WINE. I was comfortable, but not amused.

DAY 18
KLAIPEDA – NIDA

*'Why don't you go and live
in a hostel to save cash?'*
-Prince Philip

A pretty little basket was waiting outside my door. In it were two rolls, butter, cheese, jam, yoghurt, a cereal bar and a banana. I ate a roll and packed the rest in a pannier for later.

When I collected my bike, I was disappointed to see that the young lady was not there, I would have liked to thank her, and get a selfie with her. I was rested, and eager to set off in the clear warm sunshine to Nida.

Nida is the southernmost Lithuanian community on the Curonian Spit, a long thin peninsula shared with Kaliningrad. The Russian part of this peninsula is known as the Kaliningrad Oblast. The whole spit is a UNESCO World Heritage Site. The entire length of it is lined with beautiful sandy beaches. I was determined to spend some time on at least one of them to make up for the wet ride from Liepaja.

The fifteen-minute ferry ride across the channel to the Spit was the first travelling on this journey that wasn't under my own power since the taxi ride from St Petersburg airport. In a small way, it excited me.

I've always had a fondness for big boats. It started when I worked a season in the Merchant Marines on the Great Lakes as a deckhand to help pay for university. Since then, I've been on various ferries around the world, filmed on aircraft carriers, battleships, submarines and large tankers and freighters. Every time I climb on board a ship, I'm thrilled.

And this little ferry was no different. I loved walking my bike on board, and basking in the morning sun as we slowly steamed across the channel. I loved the feel of the steel ship vibrating under my feet. I watched the crew as we docked on the other side. It fascinated me.

This was the start of a perfect day; I could feel it.

The fifty-kilometre cycle path to Nida started well enough through a peaceful pine forest. It was wonderful to ride, and the only sound I could hear was my own breath. It beckoned me to slow down, relax and enjoy. I could just ride, stop when I wanted for as long as I wanted.

Alan Deakins

A few kilometres later, the path skirted very high dunes. I stopped and climbed a staircase to the top of the dune. The beach below was smooth, wide and totally empty. I hid my bike in a clump of trees and descended onto the beach to enjoy an hour of solitude in the sun.

Back on the path, I found a little kiosk with tables and chairs. I sat in the shade with an ice tea watching the world go by. At midday, I found an open air café on a beach for a large burger lunch.

The path led me through fields covered in wildflowers, then into forests, and out onto beaches. The Curonian Spit was wonderful, and I could understand why it is so fiercely protected, and seemingly respected by everybody. I didn't see any litter on the entire ride to Nida.

My iPhone was still acting up. Every time I accessed Google maps, the 'This accessory may not be supported' window popped up over the app, making it extremely frustrating searching for accommodation. I decided to just go there and look for signs. By this point in my journey, I was less worried about where I would end up for the night. Something would turn up. It had so far.

It was a steep uphill climb approaching Nida, and equally steep descent into the town itself. I entered a pleasant compact neat town on the lagoon side of the Spit. It was obviously a tourist town with numerous outdoor restaurants, bicycle rental shops and various kiosks selling everything from sun hats to ice creams to corn on the cob snacks. Business was brisk, but I didn't sense that the town was overrun with tourists.

It was close to midday when I found the Zuna Hostel situated on a lovely waterfront promenade. The ten-bed dormitory had extremely large windows on three sides with no curtains. To say it was bright would be an understatement. Most of the beds were already taken; I chose one next to the washing machine, which I considered might be a mistake if someone wanted to wash their clothes in the night, but it did offer shade from the huge windows. On the other side of the bed was a hand basin. No doubt that could be a distraction, but it did offer a bit of space between my bed and the next.

Alan Deakins

Alone in the room, I set about making my bed and organising my panniers. It wasn't long before a young Canadian backpacker entered. He was a cheery, open lad who travels Europe every summer. He thought this hostel was brilliant. I had to admit so far, the only brilliance I detected was the sunlight streaming through the windows.

He dumped his shopping on his bed, and as he was leaving, a young lady, in her early 20's quietly entered. I said hello, she nodded without a word, walked over to her bed, sat on the edge and stared out of the window. I felt perhaps she wanted to be alone.

I decided to explore Nida, and find lunch. I walked along the terraces of the open air restaurants filled with holidaymakers, hungry as I was, I didn't fancy sitting at a table alone in a crowd, so I opted for a kiosk, bought a sizeable sandwich, made my way to the promenade, sat on a bench under a tree and enjoyed looking out over the lagoon.

There was a bike rental shop opposite the hostel. I stopped in and asked if they could de-grease and oil my chain which was starting to squeak. They quoted fifteen euros, more than I paid to have my back hub rebuilt in Parnu. I decided to do the job myself.

When I entered the dormitory to retrieve the oil I was given in Russia, the young lady was still there on the edge of her bed staring out of the window. She must be travelling alone.

I found a bottle of degreaser and a roll of paper towels for three euros at the local supermarket and managed to service my chain in a boatyard without making a mess.

As I was returning to the hostel, I noticed the young lady sitting on a bench on the promenade staring across the lagoon. I wondered if she had broken up with her lover, and was now travelling alone, waiting for his (or her) return.

I bought a cold beer and sat on the veranda of the hostel in the afternoon sun catching up on my blogging. I was joined by a Lithuanian who struck up a conversation about England since his daughter worked for a large bank in London. He declared that he visited her and that all food in England was expensive shit. Obviously, he thought highly of his educated observation from three days in London. I showed him pictures of Zack's food which abruptly ended the conversation. Fine with me, I find opinionated people like him extremely irksome. Even though I welcomed just about any kind of company, I preferred my own to his.

The dormitory was filling up. A young Spanish couple were making their beds in the far corner. A young man was sitting on his bed polishing his clarinet. In the other corner, a young woman in a bathrobe was texting on her phone. A middle-aged woman and her young teenage daughter arrived. The daughter found a bed on the opposite side, and the mother claimed the one next to mine.

I wondered what the night had in store.

I wanted to get an early start, and the dormitory was relatively empty as darkness fell, except for the young Spanish couple who were in the corner facing each other and shining their mobiles in each other's face while whispering, and the young man with the clarinet, who was just about to leave. I felt I could possibly turn in and be asleep before the others returned.

I was just about to doze off when I heard a clarinet playing classical music just under the front window. The young man is obviously accomplished, I thought. I personally had heard enough after fifteen minutes. After a half hour, I felt that he had practised enough. Finally, after another twenty minutes, he finished, followed by applause and shouts of 'BRAVO'. And I finally had given up on a proper sleep.

Alan Deakins

I dozed on and off, being woken by peoples' movements. At one point, I got up for a pee. As far as I could tell in the dark, the young couple in the corner was still whispering. The lone young lady was sitting on the edge of her bed, Mum and her daughter were tucked in. As I got to the door, I noticed a bowl of wrapped sweets on a table. I took a packet, unwrapped it to discover fluorescent green foam earplugs. Fantastic.

DAY 19
NIDA – PRIBREZHNYY, KALININGRAD

*'Back in the USSR.
You don't know how lucky you are, boy.'
-Paul McCartney*

I woke just before five, the dormitory was still, except for the young teenager who was talking in her sleep. The Canadian lad had a lady in bed with him. Was she his travelling partner, or did he meet her last night? I silently left, loaded my bike on the promenade watching the sun rise over the still lagoon, and set off in the early light.

Alan Deakins

It was only two kilometres to the border. I assumed I was the first to cross that day since I was the only traveller there, which led me to assume that this would be quite swift. I hadn't counted on the Russian Immigration Officer. Maybe because she didn't have any other travellers to deal with, she would hone her skills on me with a thorough inspection.

She held up my picture page in front of her, then her eyes darted back and forth between my picture and me. She did this at least a dozen times as if she couldn't believe the last time she looked. I began to feel a bit uncomfortable. She then proceeded to check each page, first by reading all four entries, then by holding each page up to a strong light. She then re-read the entries, before holding the picture page up and scanning back and forth between it and my face a dozen more times. Finally, she stamped it, and before handing it back to me, she held up the picture page for a dozen final scans to make doubly sure that I was still the same person who had stepped up to the window five minutes ago. Who knows, I could have slipped into a disguise, or substituted a refugee in my place while she was stamping my passport. Can't be too careful.

On the other hand, the soldier tasked with searching for contraband was exactly the opposite. He stepped forward and pointed to one of my panniers.

'Open.'

I undid the buckle and was about to open it.

'OK.'

He waved me through. As I passed through the gate into Kaliningrad, a young cyclist approached passport control. I knew he was in for a long wait with the immigration officer, and I also knew he would catch me up soon enough.

The road surface in Kaliningrad was crude in comparison to

Lithuania, but still adequate to cycle on. It was completely empty so I could enjoy the surroundings more.

About three kilometres inside the border, I came to a barrier guarded by a soldier. I dismounted, and he pointed to a hut with a window. I dutifully walked up to the window. No one was on the other side. I looked back at the soldier and shrugged, and he motioned to knock, which I did. Suddenly, a bleary-eyed dishevelled young soldier appeared from the shadows. His shirt was undone, and so was his trousers. I really did not need to see his bright blue boxer shorts so early in the morning. I held up my passport, and he waved me off and disappeared back into the darkness. My presence obviously disturbed his activity, whatever it was. When I returned to my bike, the other soldier was chuckling to himself.

Before I set off, I could see the other cyclist in the distance. I figured it wouldn't be too long before he caught up with me. It would be sooner than I anticipated because, after another kilometre, I suddenly stopped.

In the middle of the road thirty metres ahead, stood an adult wild boar staring straight at me. I sat there warily looking at him, my left foot on the ground and my right foot on the pedal. This is the first time in my life that I've been confronted by a dangerous animal. My mind raced. I remember hearing that they are easily provoked, and extremely fast. I knew I couldn't ride past him, nor could I turn around and outrun him should he attack. I decided it was best to be still and wait.

I could see in my rear view mirror, that the other cyclist was fast approaching. It wouldn't be too long before he was alongside me. Perhaps the boar sensed it wasn't worth confronting two people; he sniffed loudly, turned and headed into the underbrush. He didn't disappear completely; I could see his head popping out a few times.

The young cyclist pulled up, and I explained the situation.

We waited a few minutes, then decided to proceed with quiet caution. He must have wandered off. The road was clear and we rode side by side chatting for the next fifteen kilometres. He was a Danish lad returning home after a tour of the Baltic coast. We talked about our trips, bike routes and tents.

He was good company, but I was aware that I was holding him back. I suggested he could head off, but he said he was in no hurry and was enjoying our conversation. We came upon a petrol station, I offered to buy him a coffee, but he said he would get going. I figured as much, he was so much quicker than me. Still, I appreciated his riding with me.

I walked up to the service window. The woman on the other side of the glass was staring into her mobile phone.

'Coffee?'

Without looking up, she replied, 'Niet.'

The Kaliningrad Oblast was much different than the Curonian Spit. Apart from the rudimentary road surface and lack of cycle paths, the forests were wilder. Many more fallen trees and thick underbrush. There were also fewer paths to the beaches. In fact, most of the Oblast seemed to be off-limits and protected. I assumed that the forests were left to their natural devices, rather than being managed like the Lithuanian side. Maybe that's why I had the meeting with the wild boar.

I was running short of supplies and was pleased to see a small supermarket in the village I was passing through. Outside were two fully loaded touring bikes. One of the cyclists was sitting on the steps, her face lifted to the warm sun.

'Hi...'

'Hello.'

'Have you come far?'

'Berlin.'

'Are you heading home?'

'No, we're going to tour the Baltics.'

Her partner emerged from the shop, and we talked about each other's journeys so far. I found this quite useful. They thought that the city of Kaliningrad was ugly and depressing. Since I'm not a keen city explorer, that's all I needed to hear. I had pretty much decided to not stop there, but rather pass through.

I was able to offer them insight about the Baltics. They seemed seasoned cyclists; they probably researched their planned journey more than I had. I was naïve to think I could hop on my bike in Russia and have a trouble-free unplanned journey with rudimentary maps, a dodgy phone and wild camping across northern Europe. I was making it so far, but for how long? I wondered.

Once off the Oblast and on to the mainland, the roads changed to more urban wider roads to handle the denser traffic. There were even the occasional welcomed cycle paths. I was making very good time; it was just turning lunchtime. I found a small café in Zelenogradsk. The mother and daughter had a variety of appetising handmade savoury pastries on display. We all knew that our mutual language barrier would be a problem in distinguishing what was inside them.

I pointed to one and did my best chicken impersonation with flapping arms and 'clucking' sound effects, which they found hysterical, and they pointed to the chicken pastries. I then made a cow sound, and they pointed to the beef ones. We were getting along famously. There was one row left. I oinked like a pig, they shook their heads, so I reckoned vegetable.

I chose a chicken and a mystery one. I was right, it was a nicely seasoned potato and spinach affair. They were so filling; I could only manage half of each. Mum kindly wrapped them up for me, and I packed them away in my pannier.

Even with the cloudless sky giving my solar panel unlimited access to the sunlight, my iPhone still refused to charge. And every few minutes or so, the annoying 'this device may not be supported' window popped up over my maps, making navigating extremely difficult. If I left my maps on permanently, my battery drained at an alarming rate. If I turned them off, I couldn't navigate at all. So very frustrating.

Kaliningrad isn't that big, and there aren't that many roads that I would get lost. All I had to do was follow the road signs to the city. What could be easier? I turned my phone off. All went according to plan as the road was wide enough to accommodate me alongside the traffic. It was particularly hot, but I was making good progress.

About ten kilometres outside Kaliningrad city, the road became a newly built six-lane motorway, I didn't see any signs forbidding bikes, and I felt safe enough on the two-metre-wide shoulder, I continued on.

The road was higher than the surrounding landscape, providing me with a good view of farms and fields. One incongruous sight that stood out was a gleaming polished emerald green Rolls Royce parked on a dirt track next to a field with all four doors open. A rich farmer? There was no one about. That kept my imagination occupied for a while until a car pulled over in front of me. The driver got out, lit a cigarette and nonchalantly puffed away, watching the traffic slowing down to get around him.

I knew from experience that Russian drivers were unpredictable, and I thought I had seen it all until a couple of kilometres later when I passed a car parked on the shoulder of an elevated section. I had to ride into the traffic lane to get around, and as I passed, I caught a glimpse of a couple in the front passenger seat having sex. It was mind-boggling bizarre. The idea of a 'quickie' took on a whole new meaning for me at that particular moment on the edge of a motorway leading into the city of Kaliningrad.

I got off the motorway to pass through the city and connect with the road to the Polish border, which meant I had to turn on maps and drain my battery. Kaliningrad was surprisingly congested with traffic. However, the streets were wide, as well as the pavements, so I managed to get to the western edge without too much drama.

I stopped at a McDonalds for a cold drink and a quick charge for my phone. There was a group of young friendly and curious Russian cyclists sitting outside. We talked briefly about accommodation or camping on the road to Poland. Unfortunately, they didn't have any suggestions, nor did I manage to find a plug for my phone.

The road skirting the edge of the Vistula Lagoon was lined with several restaurants and karaoke bars, but I didn't see any signs for accommodation. At one point, I stopped at a restaurant and spoke to the chef, who advised me to go back to Kaliningrad for a room. To me, that wasn't an option.

I pressed on hoping I would find a spot where I could wild camp, but my energy was waning. I had been riding for twelve hours, covering one hundred and twenty kilometres; I had enough.

Finding somewhere to spend the night seemed a distant possibility. My only options were to either keep on going in anticipation or use the remaining battery life on my phone in hopes of finding some sort of shelter. Google maps revealed one B&B on the Lagoon five kilometres behind me. I thought of calling, but with the language barrier and my dwindling battery, I might not have had enough energy to navigate my way, so I turned around and peddled as fast as I could.

I was led up a rural flat road towards the coast. I passed a large factory. Scores of people were rushing out of the gates in a hurry to get home. I turned as directed, and found myself riding down a crudely paved road lined with several large blocks of flats, ten stories high. The rendering on most of them was either extremely weathered, of crumbling off. The various cars parked in the dirt parking areas told a story of people of very few means.

Maps directed me to turn onto a narrow dirt road lined with small modest bungalows on either side. Some of them were barely shacks.

I began to worry. I couldn't imagine that the upmarket B&B I found on maps would be here. I thought I was being led on the wrong path. At the end of the road, I came upon a large crude half-opened rusted industrial gate. I entered what looked like a boat yard. A few men were working on various small boats in disrepair. I was about to approach one of them for directions, but my battery had run out, so I had nothing to show them on my phone, and I seriously doubted they spoke English.

In looking about, I noticed that I had entered a small narrow inlet, and beyond the boatyard, there were houses lining either side. Most of them looked homemade, mostly out of breeze block, or wood and most built within a strict budget. They were far from elegant, but the community had a certain rudimentary charm. For no reason, I headed towards the end of the inlet to find a place to sit and consider my plight.

At the very end of the inlet, stood the B&B I was looking for. I was utterly amazed but relieved. As I approached, I could see that all the windows were shuttered up. The gate was opened, so I entered. There was no response to my repeated knocks on the door, it was obvious that there was no one about. There was a chair at the edge of the jetty; I sat and weighed up my dwindling options. I could wait here to see if the owners returned. It was late, so I doubted that would happen. I could make my way back to the main road, and continue riding. I was exhausted, so that wasn't an option. All I could do, really, was wait.

I wandered around, and at the very end of the property, on the edge of the lagoon was a small garden about seven metres square with a grassed area that had recently been cut. I thought it would be the perfect spot to pitch my tent.

I would be in full view of the cottages on the other side of the inlet, and the B&B owners may discover me on their return. I concluded that the worse they could do was kick me out.

So I set up camp and no one seemed to notice. A calm breeze and the gentle lapping of the water on the edge of the jetty soon lulled me to sleep. It definitely was the most peaceful wild camping I had done on the trip thus far.

Old Hippie on a Bike

DAY 20
PRIBREZHNYY – ELBLAG, POLAND

*'Some people maybe still live in the Cold War.
But this is their problem. Not mine.'*
-Thomas Piketty

In the morning, I brewed a quick cup of coffee while I struck the tent and packed my bike. I was surprised but pleased to see that my battery pack had fully charged my phone during the night. The B&B was still boarded up when I opened the gate to leave. I left the little garden as I had found it so my stay would not be a problem for them.

It was thirty-five kilometres to the Polish border. I pressed on as fast as I could, but I was hampered by hills, a stiff headwind, and hunger. A cup of black coffee is hardly a breakfast for a cyclist. I needed sustenance, and I found it in Ladushkin, a small village with a large church.

Just opposite the church, I saw a queue outside a small store. Sensing food, I stopped and joined it. I was rewarded with a lovely warm hand made, fresh out of the oven sausage wrapped in a doughy soft bread which had soaked up the juices of the meat. I sat on a bench next to a tiny old woman who was waiting for a bus. The first bite was melt-in-my-mouth deliciousness. I had underestimated my hunger. Had my face been big enough, I would have devoured it in one bite.

I sat there savouring my breakfast with my diminutive companion when all of a sudden we were hit with the loudest blast of music from the church across the road. Granny nearly fell off of the bench. It was the typical thump-thump-thump eastern European rock music, which quite frankly, I detest. Three women came running out of the church shouting into microphones and dancing. They were obviously inviting everyone within earshot (a hundred-kilometre radius in my estimation) to their event. It was time for me to leave.

The road to Poland was pleasant enough, except for the headwind which was seriously hampering me. I was stopping at just about every petrol station I came across for a cold drink and a break. The traffic was thinner the closer I got to the border. Most of the vehicles seemed to be coming from the EU.

In Pyatodorozhnoe, a village about 7 kilometres from the border crossing, I was stopped by soldiers standing in the road. They were, of course, fascinated with my passport. I managed to tell them I had come from St Petersburg and was heading for the UK. I did the spinning my finger around my ear 'crazy' gesture, which greatly amused them. They all shook my hand, and one of them slapped me on the back.

I had been raised in 1950's America. The good ol' red, white and blue, Mom and apple pie, Howdy Doody and Buffalo Bob. In the post-war world I grew up in, communism was feared, and socialism was considered the work of the devil. Anxiety and mistrust were drilled into us. We hid under our desks at school during practice air-raids, knowing at that young age that a wooden desk was wholly inadequate protection against an atom bomb. We were shown black and white films about evil Russian plans to defeat America. We stood every morning with our hands on our hearts to pledge allegiance to the flag (which I still can recite sixty-five years later). We were being benevolently indoctrinated to mould us into good God-fearing, Russian hating Americans because we were a nation 'under God', which meant all other nations of the world were not...especially Russia.

Alan Deakins

And yet, a Russian soldier slaps me on the back, gives me the thumbs-up, and says to me, 'Good.'

I wished my father was alive so I could tell him.

The queue of cars and lorries at the border was longer than I expected. People were sitting outside their vehicles picnicking, chatting to their fellow travellers and sunning themselves. No one was in a hurry, except me. I kept on riding past car after car, lorry after lorry. No one said anything. No one seemed to mind.

I rode straight up to the passport window to watch the Officer go through her motions of a thorough check once again. I got the dozen or so glances back and forth from my passport photo to my face. Passport to face. Passport to face. What was she looking for? What was going on in her brain box?

Eyes. Eyes...Check.
Nose. Nose...Check.
Mouth. Mouth...Check.
Ears...On wait, his ears are hidden by his hair.
Start over.
Eyes. Eyes...Check...
Or are they his eyes?
Eyes. Eyes. Check...

The soldier on the forecourt wasn't the least bit interested in my panniers; he nonchalantly waved me on.

'Great,' I thought. 'I'm through.'

But two hundred metres on, I was confronted with hundreds of cars and lorries split into six lanes waiting to get into Poland. I weaved my way around them and rode straight up to one of the Polish passport windows. A young uniformed lady came rushing out waving her finger at me and yelling at me in Polish.

'Uhm...? English...?

'Can't you read the sign? You must wait behind the white line!'

'Sorry. I'm an old man.'

Her eyes lit up, and she laughed.

'Give me your passport, I will get you through.'

She went back into her booth. When I was called to her window, she pointed to another window further along.

'You must speak to my colleague.'

I went along to the other window where another young officer was waiting for me. She looked at me sternly.

'Anything to declare?'

I thought of the fabled Oscar Wilde quote: 'I have nothing to declare but my genius" but instead opted a more pragmatic line with a smile.

'Nooo...!'

She smiled. 'No? Of course not! Welcome to Poland.'

She handed my passport to me, and I was off. What takes hours for motorized travellers, took me less than twenty minutes, thanks to my bike, and the kindness of strangers.

Crossing the border into Poland called for a celebration. I stopped at a little roadside bar. I bought a not so very cold beer from an ancient lady and sat on the small porch watching the cars and lorries that I jumped in the queue trundle by.

After a few minutes, a battered Mercedes and a white van pulled up in the dirt car park. A rotund man jumped out of the car, opened the back doors of the van and pulled out two very large bottles of vodka. He quickly headed straight into the bar.

It wasn't long until he emerged folding his thick wallet and casting a smile to me. He jumped into the Mercedes and sped off in a cloud of dust followed by the van. I mused to myself, 'Here I am, a lowly boy from Erie, Pennsylvania witnessing an international smuggling ring, and living to tell the tale.'

I didn't finish the warm beer.

My initial ride inside Poland was on a relatively smooth tree-lined road. I didn't have much of a shoulder to ride on, but the traffic was light, and everyone was giving me space as they passed. Or if there were oncoming vehicles, they patiently waited until it was safe to pass.

It was an increasingly hot day, possibly the hottest of the trip, thus far. The trees were welcome for a bit of shade. But sadly, a few of them told stories. Once in a while, I would see a bunch of flowers, or a small hand made shrine attached to a tree, a sad reminder of a lost life, and a mute testament to the fact that trees planted on the very edge of the road are beautiful, but deadly.

My hot sweaty ride ended in Elblag, situated, curiously enough, on the Elblag River. I found a campsite on the edge of the river near the centre. The area reserved for tents was small but nicely shaded. It was furnished with tables and chairs, and there was easy access to the river's edge. I felt quite comfortable.

The only other tent there was occupied by a friendly French couple, who I immediately struck up a conversation with. They had travelled across the northern Polish coast, south through Gdansk to Elblag following a Eurovelo route, which they found very hard going. They also described their experience north of Gdansk as a horrible ride through an industrial wasteland. I was planning on touring this route, but their description made me want to have a major rethink.

That evening, I cooked a ravioli dinner on the riverbank, and over a couple of glasses of wine, I contemplated where to go next.

DAY 21
ELBLAG – STAROGARD

*'It's no wonder truth is stranger than fiction.
Fiction has to make sense.'*
-Mark Twain

I was up early, packed and was ready to go by 7.00. It was a beautiful morning; in all likelihood, it would be another hot ride.

I had decided to take the straightest possible route across Poland, following Route 22 to Walcz then Route 10 to Szczecin, about ten kilometres from the German border. It would shorten my trip considerably, but I had weighed up a few factors in making my decision.

The first was my budget. I was haemorrhaging money. I hadn't counted on paying for my accommodation every night on this trip, nor had I any idea on how much I would eat and drink. I couldn't do without either, so I figured fewer days would obviously work out cheaper.

Secondly, this would be an easier route to travel, avoiding the hard going of the Eurovelo the French couple described to me. Admittedly, I was fitter and more confident that I had anticipated I'd ever be, I was still mindful that I was seventy-two. I had hit the sweet spot of chugging along at a steady pace, a pace that suited me.

Last but not least, annoyingly, my iPhone was a complete pain in the ass. It had taken on a mind of its own since I upgraded the Operation System. It sporadically charged with the solar panel or the battery pack but constantly blocked my maps with that irksome window telling me it didn't like the solar panel every time a direction appeared. I reckoned that following one route would be easier since all I had to do is follow road signs.

It was already hot as I rode out of Elblag. I had no plans on how far I would travel before the heat would grind me to a halt. Although Route 22 was relatively busy, it was not a main road, sparing me a constant barrage. Villages dotted the route every six to ten kilometres, which added interest and allowed me to frequently stop for cold drinks.

On the other hand, the road surface was badly cracked and full of potholes along the edge which impeded my progress. I found myself constantly weaving into the road to avoid breaking a wheel.

At one point, the road became a twenty-metre-wide cobbled surface, which was arduous to ride on. I assumed by the vast width of cobble, it would be a short distance. After five kilometres, I began to comprehend the immense scale of it for what it was. This must have been a huge undertaking to build; it would have taken thousands of people on their hands and knees labouring for years to lay each brick one by one to traverse this modest distance. The cost must have been enormous. It didn't make sense. The one question that stuck in my mind was: 'Why?'

I was riding through flat open farmland. Because there were few trees along the side of the road, the ruthless sun was beginning to take its toll. I was wet from sweat. Even my bum cheeks were wet. I found a clump of trees for a pee break, and to remove my lycra shorts, which I had been wearing under my normal shorts. I dried off and continued on commando. The difference was remarkable. I instantly felt cooler in the nether region, making me more comfortable in the saddle.

It was past midday when I saw a sign for a restaurant off the main road in Swarozyn I was sorely in need of a break. I was wondering how much more stamina I could muster in this heat. The Woda na Mlyn was no ordinary roadside café. It was a rather grand establishment, with a vast shaded veranda overlooking the surrounding countryside. Even though I was a dishevelled cyclist, I was graciously welcomed. The heat had suppressed my appetite, so I chose a cold summer soup and bread. I was pleasantly surprised with an elegant delicious dish of a high culinary level. It was rich, refreshing and zingy. I was sure Zack would have been impressed. Although this wasn't a large meal that my 'eating machine' usually required, I left completely satisfied thanks to the intense flavours and beautiful presentation. This was indeed another place that I added to my "Little Gems" list.

Feeling replete, I felt I had the strength to last the fifteen kilometres to Starogard where I would find accommodation. The road seemed to comply by offering up a wider shoulder to ride on. I was comfortable in many ways.

By the time I reached Starogard, I was totally spent, in need of a shower, and a cold beer. For some unfathomable reason, my iPhone decided to allow Google maps to appear without that pesky warning window. The Hotel Ren seemed the most reasonable of the few choices that came up, so I headed there.

I peeled myself off my saddle and walked into an empty reception. The first thing to assault my senses was the thump-thump-thump of the dreaded bubble-gum Eastern European rock music. Luckily for me, it was in the background. I approached the smiling receptionist.

'Hello. Uhm, room? Zimmer...?'

'Oh, I'm so sorry, we are fully booked. We have a wedding reception happening.'

'I can hear. Can you recommend anywhere else? A camp Site would be nice.'

I briefly explained my trip, riding for charity and the desire to find cheap accommodation.

'I would have to make phone calls.'

I pointed to the large glass fronted refrigerator filled with bottles of beer next to the desk.

'Could I please buy one of those...?'

'Of course, we brew our own beer. We are quite famous around here for it. Please sit over there, enjoy your beer, and I will see what I can do for you.'

I sat on a soft sofa, took a sip of the ice cold lager, and began to cool off when suddenly all hell broke loose. The doors next to the reception area burst open, and people in their best finery began spilling out. The music was deafening. Women in revealing satin dresses sat on the remaining sofas excitedly chatting. Other people milled around singing, shouting, hugging and kissing one another. They were a good-natured raucous bunch intent on having a good time. In my own little way, I joined in by drinking my beer with a smile for everyone. What they made of an old bearded sweaty cyclist sitting in their midst was anybody's guess.

At one point, a huge bull of a man with a belly that looked like he had a watermelon under his shirt, took a beer out of the fridge. The half-litre bottle looked tiny in his bear-like hand. He opened it, lifted it to his massive face, tipped it upside down, and drained the entire contents within three seconds. I had never seen anything like it. I thought, 'What's the point?' He didn't have time to taste or savour it. If his aim was to add to his enormous girth, I supposed he was doing an admirable job.

In the spirit of the festivities, I helped myself to another beer and watched the merry mayhem until the receptionist came over to me.

'I hope you have been comfortable.'

'Yes, thanks, and entertained.'

'I have managed to find you a room at the Hotel Bachus.'

'Great.'

'Unfortunately, they are having a wedding reception also.'

'Oh.'

'But she said she will find you a quiet room.'

'You've been most kind.'

I thanked her for going out of her way for me in the midst of this pandemonium. As I got up to leave, the bull was lifting

Old Hippie on a Bike

another beer to his face. It would be down his neck before I reached the door.

At the Hotel Bachus, all was quiet as I entered. A cheerful young lady, Pauline, was there to greet me. She knew all about my journey.

'I have a quiet room for you.'

'Will I be able to eat here tonight?'

'Of course, the wedding reception will be in another room. You are welcome in the dining room.'

She directed me to a carport behind the hotel where I could secure my bike, and to my room at the very top of the building as far away from the wedding festivities as physically possible with large windows that gave me a commanding view of the surrounding countryside. I could hear a pin drop. Perfect.

I had a long hot shower, and poured myself a glass of wine I had left over from Elblag, and sat looking at the scenery. It had been a relatively short day (only forty-five kilometres), but considering the heat, I was satisfied with my progress.

Before dinner, I returned to my bike to retrieve my Leatherman from the tool bag. I was surprised to find it neatly covered with a tarpaulin. An elderly man came running up to me.

'Telephone! Telephone!'

He had thought that the case on my handlebars still had my phone in it, so he covered the bike to hide it. He was relieved to see that I had my phone in my pocket. It was another act of kindness that greatly impressed me.

The dining room was totally empty. It seemed that I was to be the only one dining tonight.

My waitress was none other than Pauline, which pleased me; I enjoyed her sunny demeanour. As a complimentary offering, she had prepared a stupendous plate of various cheeses, accompanied by special little berries that are grown in the hotel garden. I was touched.

Even though I was the only one dining, I didn't feel alone. Pauline approached often to chat and ask about my trip. She was gracious and convivial. She was the perfect end to a short, difficult, hot day. I knew I had made the right decision to take this route across Poland.

Old Hippie on a Bike

DAY 22
STAROGARD – CZLUCHOW

*'To be a little further on the road,
a little nearer somewhere.'*
-Arthur Symons

I woke up with a start. I felt sick. I lay there hoping it would pass.

'What's going on? Was it something I ate…? Did I have too much to drink last night…?'

Before I could consider answers, I had to jump up and run for the loo to vomit. The convulsions were coming on strong and fast. In desperation, I flung the bathroom window open, and the fresh morning air that rushed in instantly revived me. I felt fine.

'What was that all about…?'

I was anxious to get on the road. I quickly packed, ate a hearty breakfast, said good-bye to Pauline and thanked her for her hospitality before setting off.

Today was to be a special day.

I wanted to make it to Czluchow, a relatively short eighty-six kilometres away. The road was nicely paved with a wide shoulder to ride on minimising my efforts in the heat.

When I'm on difficult, broken surfaces, my eyes are constantly on the road no more than five metres ahead, not exactly sight-seeing mode. When I'm on a smooth stable surface, I have the opportunity to look about me. Even though it was hot, I was enjoying my steady pace through farmland and young forests.

It was obvious to me, travelling along, that the Poles wear their religion on their sleeves. I was constantly reminded of this as I rode past numerous crosses, icons, and shrines erected on the side of the road. Some were to mark road accidents, but most were there just to be there. Some were modest homemade affairs; others were grand structures emphatically proclaiming their faith. It was a phenomenon I only observed in Poland.

Alan Deakins

On the western edge of Czersk, I happened upon a small Soviet military cemetery dated 1945. Compared to all the other cemeteries I've seen thus far, this was haunting and bleak. There were no benches for family members to sit on. No flowers. Just twenty-five plain identical headstones arranged in precise rows. I wondered if these individuals were now gone from peoples' memories and no longer cherished. I suddenly felt very alone.

My spirits were down even though I was riding through lovely pine forests. I stopped at a roadside picnic area for a snack and drink under the still trees. I rested and did the best I could to shake off the melancholy that descended upon me.

I continued on through the forest when it came crashing to an abrupt end. A combination of roadworks and deforestation thrust me into a bleak featureless landscape devoid of colour or life, except for a few scraggly twig-like trees that still clung onto life, probably because they weren't worth the effort to cut down. Surely there was a grand plan for a new highway and beautifully landscaped surroundings, but at that moment, in my low state of mind, it was horrid.

The roadworks transformed into a new motorway that bypassed the large town of Chojnice. Had I known it was a bypass, I would have exited and ridden through the town, rather than suffer the perils of a motorway with a shockingly thin shoulder. I felt vulnerable to the thundering traffic and the mind-bending speeds that people feel compelled to do when they are on this type of road. If the shoulder were wider, I would have felt secure. I didn't like it and was glad when the road narrowed back to two lanes. Oddly enough, this section of road had a much wider shoulder.

The approach to Czluchow, like most towns and villages on this trip, offered a nice wide pavement/cycle path well away from the road. It seemed a luxury to me. Before I reached the centre, I saw a sign for a campsite. I immediately followed the arrow into a wood next to a lake. I found a spot on the shore, pitched my tent and texted Marnie. She responded straight away, and I felt better.

It was an interesting campsite. Most of the motorhomes were quite old and some showed signs of being patched together. Likewise, most of the tents were mended or held together with homemade patches. It was a holiday destination for people of lesser means…much like me, I thought. But it wasn't holding them back from enjoying themselves.

There was a small promenade lined with food stalls selling the usual budget fare of pizzas, burgers, hot dogs, popcorn, and beer. I bought a burger, chips and beer, sat on a bench and watched all the variations of people on holiday. Children are children. Teenagers are teenagers. Lovers are lovers. Old people are old people no matter what their income. I enjoyed it.

I bought a second beer to celebrate my special day. I had completed fourteen hundred kilometres. I was halfway through my journey.

DAY 23
CZLUCHOW – WALCZ

*'Go not to the elves for counsel,
for they will say both no and yes.
-J.R.R. Tolkien*

Another early morning departure to start the second half of my journey. On the way out of Czluchow, I found a Tesco supermarket to buy breakfast. In many ways, it was much the same as a UK Tesco. As I entered it, I thought, 'I am halfway home.'

If I thought the second fourteen hundred kilometres would be all downhill, I had another thing coming. For a start, the road out of Czluchow was older; the deteriorated surface was difficult to ride on, and there was no shoulder to speak of, so most of my day would be spent in the actual traffic lane. Thankfully, even though Polish drivers are fast, they are patient.

Route 22 has quite a few villages, all of which have wide cycle paths at either end and a generous pavement in the centres, giving a bit of relief now and again from the poor road surface.

The road meandered through forests and over flat farmland, the only difference being that it was a bit cooler, and the intensity of the sun was filtered by high thin clouds.

The Polish passion to express their faith was on grand display today. I was impressed with their creativity exhibited in big and small ways. In Borkowo, a huge modern grey church with Russian influences dwarfed the village. I came across an old church in Cierznie. A wooden cross at least ten metres high had been erected and decorated with hundreds of flowers. A shrine made of stone to resemble a cave with an icon of the Virgin Mary inside stood outside a church in Szwecja. I also saw numerous small shrines or wooden crosses in small villages.

About five kilometres outside Walcz, I came across a wonderfully bizarre display that took great passion to make but had nothing to do with religion. In the middle of a forest, I found Bar U Majora. It was marked with a metre-tall hand carved smiling wood nymph standing at the edge of the road. Alongside her stood a sign which I managed to translate. It read: BAR. I could see a log cabin and umbrellas nestled amongst the trees. Its quirkiness instantly captured me. I had to stop.

Even though I expected something out of the ordinary, the spectacle of the characters and creatures who greeted me took me by surprise. First, there was the six-piece musical combo of elves sitting on toadstools in front of their woodland village all crudely but enchantingly carved from local logs. There was an accordion player, drummer, trumpeter, saxophonist, violinist, and a one-armed, one-legged banjo player (I suspect the weather was responsible for his loss of limbs.) They wore blue tunics, yellow tights and red caps.

I immediately ordered a beer and sat down on the bench in front of them. I was the only animate being there, but I was in good company sitting with this little witty silent band.

Old Hippie on a Bike

I couldn't tear myself away from this enchanted spot, so I ordered another beer, and walked down a path lined with large life-sized sculpted dogs sitting and smiling at me. They were fashioned out of (I can only guess) cement with the same unsophisticated charm as my musical friends. They were absolutely wonderful.

Gathered under low trees, was a trio of strange little hobbit-type gentlemen staring into large pots in front of them. I

186

think they were making a magic concoction to beguile me... and it worked, I was completely charmed. Inside the cabin, a large bronze bust of an austere Russian Army Officer stood next to the bar, keeping a stern eye over the proceedings. This little establishment was utterly bonkers, mad and whimsical. I loved it.

I had a smile pasted on my face all the way into Walcz.

I managed to squeeze a few hotels out of Google maps before, Apple stepped in with its ongoing argument with my solar panel. I settled on the closest, which turned out to be a modern characterless 1980's affair away from the centre of town.

A lone woman was sitting on an overstuffed, overdesigned beige leather sofa watching television in the empty dark reception. Her English was as fluent as my Polish, but we must have been on the same wavelength because we simultaneously pulled our phones out to find a translation app.

I preferred the sign language and animal impressions that I've relied on thus far, but somehow, I instinctively knew that flapping my arms with a clucking sound would not be terribly helpful in procuring a room.

We managed to negotiate a room. Then our digital conversation went something like this:

'Do you have beer?'

'How many?'

'One for now.'

'Order how many. Pay now. I will be leaving soon.'

'What about dinner?'

This surprised her. She looked at me and sighed.

"Schnitzel. 20 zlotys.'

I nodded.

'30 minutes.'

She then disappeared into the kitchen and suddenly I heard furious pounding. An unfortunate pork steak was being given an almighty thrashing. I retreated to my modest room, there was nothing I could do to defend it.

I had a quick shower and was descending the stairs thirty minutes later as she was marching up the stairs to summons me to dinner. I was marched into the dining room, where I would be dining alone.

The first course was an enormous tureen of thick vegetable soup. I managed a bowl. Next came an enormous platter with an enormous paper thin schnitzel hanging off the edges with an enormous pile of chips and another enormous pile of fried cabbage. I ate what I could, but nowhere near half, and had no room for the enormous slice of sponge cake she offered. I had to decline. I was enormously full.

As I made my way to the room, she was waiting at the foot of the stairs with another beer, which I figured was gratis because she didn't ask for payment. She was, in the end, a kind person who meant well, and was determined to give what she perceived value for money. I really couldn't ask for more.

I was in my room for not more than ten minutes when I observed her getting into her car and driving off. I spent a quiet night as the only guest.

DAY 24
WALCZ - STARGARD

*'From there to here, and here to there,
funny things are everywhere.'*
-Dr. Seuss

I woke up with a conundrum floating about in my head. How could I be hungry after such a huge meal? The only answer to it was to investigate the dining room.

I was cheerily greeted by my hostess who had laid out a massive buffet. I was astounded. Why would she go to all this fuss for one guest? It soon became apparent that I wasn't the only one being fed. Local people, mostly workmen, piled in and made short work of the pretty buffet. I was relieved but managed to hold my own against the cheery throng to get a decent breakfast.

I was to travel on a different road in my final leg to the German border. Route 10 would take me through Stargard and Szczecin before crossing the border. It meandered around many small lakes and through pine forests. It was a quite narrow road, affording me very little room to ride on the edge. Still, it was an enjoyable ride. Traffic was lighter than on Route 22. I had periods of my being the only one on the road.

I made the usual frequent stops at petrol stations. One particular one in Stacja Paliw, was unusual in that it had large planter boxes with full-grown trees between the pumps on the forecourt. The adjoining motel served a most welcomed rich espresso. These little stops were essential for a quick recharge to keep the momentum going.

I found a little café/bar at Slutowo for lunch. It looked inviting, neatly tucked away from the road, with a lovely covered outdoor seating area surrounded by lush greenery. The chef and his wife couldn't speak English, but we both had a rudimentary knowledge of German. We managed to settle on a very nice, substantial chicken and potato meal.

I elected to eat outside. There was an old gentleman seated at one of the tables with a beer, who nodded to me as I sat down.

'Englissshhh...?'

'I am, actually.'

'Ozzle glish slavvoovoooffssshh...'

This last attempt at communication indicated to me that there was the distinct possibility that the beer in front of him wasn't his first.

'Uhm...OK...if you say so...'

'Frajjjssh slophhhsss braphhzzz...'

I astutely observed that he was intoxicated. He unsteadily stood up, leaning against the table weaving to and fro, he fumbled around in his pockets until he fished out a set of car keys, which he triumphantly held aloft.

'Schloggghdddd....'

'I don't think that's a good idea, young man...'

The waitress came running out with my meal, followed by the chef who immediately rushed over to the old man snatching the keys out of his hand. The man was intent on getting into his Mercedes, the chef had other ideas of persuading him to sit in a small Renault. Finally, the chef won, and the old man relented. The chef jumped behind the wheel and sped off.

My lunch was exceptional. I had just finished when the Renault appeared. The chef got out, walked up to collect my plate as if he had just strolled out from behind the bar to serve me.

'Gut...?'

'Schon...danka. Well done, Mate.'

'Bitte Schon.'

My lunch had been delicious as well as entertaining. I love travelling.

I was enjoying the undulating road as it skirted close to some of the lakes offering glances of tranquillity. At one point, I was tempted to stop at a small lakeside motel, but it was only mid-afternoon, and I felt I should do more kilometres. I was also hoping to find a more budget-friendly campsite.

An hour later, ominous clouds appeared, and I thought perhaps I should have stopped. I pressed on and made it to Stargard in light rain.

My sporadic Google maps didn't offer up any campsites, but it did suggest a reasonable hotel converted from a Victorian mill. It was warm, dry and the young staff were gracious.

With my bike safely parked in the wide corridor outside my room, I showered and slept soundly. I had covered one hundred kilometres.

DAY 25
STARGARD – SZCZECIN

*'I'm not sure I can swagger anymore,
but I can limp with the best of them.'*
-Burt Reynolds

I had hoped this would be my last night in Poland, but the grey rainy morning outside my window told me that perhaps I wouldn't make it far today. I knew I would have to ride in the rain regardless, but I was in no hurry to get out there mixing with lorries on the wet road. I had a leisurely breakfast, packed my bike and waited close to check-out. I was determined to at least get to Szczecin.

There was still a slight drizzle when I departed, but breaks in the clouds were beginning to appear. Perhaps I would have a good day after all. Besides, it was only thirty-five kilometres to Szczecin, what have I got to lose?

The ride across Stargard to Route 10 was very pleasant through many parks and gardens. It is a lovely town. At one point, while I was taking a break in a park, I heard an emotional wail of a harmonica coming through the trees. Its mournful and haunting melody captured me, so I set out to find its source. I found a cemetery on the other side of the road. I entered the gate and walked about fifty metres towards the sound. And there, through the tombstones, I could see a gathering around a grave. A family had come to bury a loved one, and their farewell cry filled the air and all ears within hearing distance, proclaiming this person was truly loved.

The rain had stopped, so I took my Gortex jacket off and secured it to one of my panniers. On the western edge of Stargard, I stopped at a supermarket for supplies. When I returned to my bike, I noticed that my jacket was missing. Had it been stolen? Did it fall off? I had no way of knowing. I also had no way of retracing my route through Stargard, as some of it had been guesswork. I was very fond of that jacket. I reluctantly had to accept it was lost forever.

I continued in a rather glum mood keeping an eye on the sky because the threat of rain was starting to reappear. Route 10 for the most part of this leg was dual carriageway – four lanes. Thankfully there was a cycle track running alongside for most of the way. Occasionally, I had to ride with the traffic, but I had the luxury of a 2-metre-wide shoulder to ride on. So although the traffic was loud as it sped past me, I had my earplugs from Nada, and enough space between me and the vehicles I felt safe enough.

It was a relief to turn off the main road and head into Szczecin on a minor road. Unfortunately, it began to rain, light rain, but I knew that I had to find a jacket soon. I located a cycle shop in the centre of town with Google, and with the sky getting more and more threatening, it was a race against time to get there.

Approaching the centre of Szczecin from the east is not particularly a pretty ride for a cyclist. There are numerous overpasses that are just not practical for cyclists, so I was forced to take small rough roads under them that skirted the docks. I rode past piles of scrap, rusting metal and stinking rubbish. Not exactly a warm welcome.

The two bridges I had to cross had cycle lanes, so I was afforded nice views of the river and the city itself. The traffic was thick, almost to the point of gridlock. Tough for cars, no problem for a bike. Finding CoolBike was easy, and the young lady who attended to me was kind and helpful. The only jacket she had in stock was 800 zlotys (about £170) which was way out of my budget. It seemed that my getting my problem solved was more important to her than making a sale because she directed me to another shop about a five-minute walk. She kindly said I could leave my bike in the shop and she would keep an eye on it.

Halfway there, the heavens opened up with a vengeance.

Within a few minutes, I was completely soaked. Sloshing into the shop in a foul mood didn't deter the young assistant in finding me a passable cycle jacket for 150 zlotys (about £35). The rain was minimal when I emerged back onto the busy street, but when I reached the last intersection before crossing over to CoolBike, a deluge hit without warning. I ran up a couple of steps to take cover in a bank doorway until the pedestrian signal turned green.

When the light changed, I ran as fast as I could, totally forgetting that I was two steps higher than the pavement. As I flew through the air, I knew this was going to hurt. I managed to twist before I landed so that my hip, rather than my face, would hit the concrete first. I was totally dazed. I rolled over on my back and through my wet glasses, I could make out blurry images of people standing and looking at me. I managed to get onto my hands and knees, all the while mentally assessing my body for serious injuries. I struggled a couple of times to get up, to no avail. Then, I felt a strong arm lifting me. When I got to my feet, a young man's face came close.

'OK...?'

'Yes. I think so...'

'Your money...'

I looked down to see all of my coins had come out of my pocket and scattered across the pavement. The young man stooped down and began picking them up. I was too shaken to help. I stood there sheepishly as he collected every one of them.

'Where do you want to go...?'

I pointed across the street.

'OK...'

He took my arm and got me across the street safely. By the

time we reached the other side, I felt somewhat in control, except for a horrible feeling in the pit of my stomach. I thanked him for his kindness and he departed with a pat on my back.

My hip was throbbing, my head was beginning to ache and my gut was rumbling. I was wet exhausted, and, not surprisingly in need of sustenance. I hadn't eaten since breakfast. A small kebab shop on the corner was a few steps away. I could sit, eat and gather myself together.

A fully loaded chicken kebab and ice tea revived me. I had a desire to get my bike, find a room, close the curtains and hibernate. As I walked to CoolBike, I was unsteady on my feet, a not altogether unfamiliar feeling. My left foot was affected by my stroke. In the days after it happened, I noticed a difference in my gate, and I never fully recovered from it. On most days, I'm fine. But when I'm tired, I limp a bit as I did when I walked into A&E the day after my 70th birthday. In many ways, I'm more confident on my bike than I am on my feet.

The young assistant at CoolBike was pleased I found a jacket, and quite concerned about my fall. She was most helpful in ringing around for affordable accommodation close by and managed to find a single room with bath at the City Hostel, a short ride along old streets and lovely lush parks.

I wasn't expecting much from a hostel; my room was sparse but surprisingly comfortable. I decided to visit the local supermarket while I was still ambulatory for a bottle of wine. Upon returning, and pouring a glass, I was deeply disappointed to find that I had chosen a semi-sweet red. It was barely drinkable, but I was too tired to limp back for a decent bottle. I managed half a glass, and a hot shower before instantly falling into a deep sleep knowing I would be aching in the morning.

DAY 26
SZCZECIN – LÖCKNITZ, GERMANY

'Sometimes life hits you in the head with a brick.'
-Steve Jobs

I awoke at 7.00. The expected aches and pains were actually not too bad; I felt well enough to ride, but not in the rain that was pounding on my window. I rolled over and slept for another couple of hours. At 9.00, the rain was lighter, but still heavy enough to warrant a re-think. I had until 11.00, perhaps 12.00 at a push before I had to check out.

Because I had a decent internet connection, I had the time, and ability to do two things. Find a scenic bike route in Germany, and find out why my iPhone is practically useless when using maps or when it was charging.

It took a few minutes to sort out a straight forward route that would take me on less travelled roads, which pleased me. As for the iPhone situation, apparently in the interest of security, the upgrade I did in Klaipeda, prevented the phone from working with any device that Apple didn't approve of. It appears that the only way I can charge the phone with my power pack or solar panel is to turn it off first. Great, so I can't access directions while charging. Thanks, Apple, you are screwing my trip up. It's not as if I have the ability to find an Apple approved solar panel here in Poland. This angered me, it's my phone, I should be able to choose the level of security I want.

I packed and readied myself for a break in the weather. At 11.00, the sky was brighter, and only a light drizzle remained.

Old Hippie on a Bike

I was expecting to do a short run of about twenty-five kilometres, to cross the border, and reach another milestone: one thousand miles.

Szczecin is a lovely city to cycle in. With beautiful expansive parks, picturesque old streets, wide pavements, dedicated cycle paths, and patient drivers, getting to the western edge was a pleasure. Germany was just a few kilometres ahead, the sun was shining, my hip was coping well; I felt optimistic. It would be a good day.

I celebrated my good fortune with a sweet pastry and espresso at a tiny roadside café.

My remaining few kilometres in Poland were uneventful and sunny. A wide cycle path ran parallel to the road for the entire way. Shortly after crossing the border, I was directed by maps to turn onto a rural road, which I duly followed. The road was meandering, well paved and took me through little peaceful villages. It was, in short, an idyllic ride.

Nonetheless, it wasn't long before things began to go wrong. First, I was directed onto a narrow country lane. Totally ignoring the memory my Estonian experience, I carried on. After a kilometre, I was confronted with a cobbled surface, passable, but rough. After a further half kilometre, the cobbles were large, broken and totally unrideable. I began pushing, just a kilometre to go. A hundred metres on, the road was deep soft sand with the occasional cobble sticking out. Too late to turn around, impossible to navigate a different route with my poor phone signal, I had to press on. It took just about everything I had in me to push my bike with fifteen kilos of gear through the muck. I cursed Google maps, I cursed my iPhone. I cursed my stupidity of trusting either.

I finally came out onto a decent rural road, thinking the worse was over. I sat under a small tree to recover when suddenly, all hell broke loose with the weather. Within seconds, the sky turned black and it began bucketing. Not just a rain, but a torrential downpour. By the time I jumped up to get my jacket out of my pannier bag, I was soaked. The tree was hardly shelter, and being in the middle of farming land, there were too few trees to shelter under.

I began peddling in the direction that Google maps indicated. The rain was so heavy; I could hardly see. My wet, rain-soaked glasses didn't help either. I found a bus shelter and quickly brought my bike and me under cover. I sat there shivering for twenty minutes waiting for a lull that didn't materialise. It was a steady driving rain that was beginning to flood the road. I had to do something. On checking my maps, I discovered that not only was my battery low, but I had absolutely no phone signal.

I was in a bus shelter, on a road somewhere in the middle of nowhere, with no phone signal nor paper map which disappeared the day I lost my Gortex jacket. It wouldn't have helped anyway, the roads were so small and remote (especially the tiny four-kilometre sandpit I had just traversed). In short, I had no idea where I was, and I had no way of finding out. I felt totally helpless.

After another twenty minutes or so, the rain lightened enough for me to consider my options of escaping this hell. I decided to continue on in hopes I find a village or a road sign. The rain was indeed lighter, but it was still wet nevertheless. Every bit of me was soaked, and at the same time, I was sweating profusely from my exertion., which was a distinctly odd sensation. I was hot and shivering at the same time.

At one point, I saw a postal van heading towards me. I stopped and waved for him to stop. He cheerily waved back at me and carried on down the road.

'BASTARD!!!!!'

How was he to know? I was angry just the same. I had to blame somebody. So I directed my anger to the black sky.

'C'mon, MATE...!!! Throw it at me!! You're the bastard...!!'

With no shelter to speak of, I had no choice, I carried on. I finally came to a crossroads, giving me four options. I dismissed going back. Of the three remaining roads, I had to make a completely random uneducated guess.

For some reason, a friend of forty years ago in Los Angeles came to mind. Whenever she was lost, her solution was simple, 'Turn left.' No reason, no knowledge, no map, 'Turn left.'

I turned left. The sign read: LOCKNITZ 10KM.

A series of fairly steep inclines brought me out onto exposed flat farmland just as the heavens decided to have a second go at me. A fierce driving rain hit me hard with large painful drops. The surface water on the road slowed me down, making it difficult to peddle. The water found its way into my helmet then streamed down into my eyes.

I couldn't see, my eyes were burning, I had to stop. I stood there, every bit of me wet with rain and sweat, and screamed.

'Fuck it! That's it! I've had it! I'VE FUCKING HAD IT!!!!!'

For the first time on this trip, the thought quitting loomed large and real in my mind.

The first sign of civilisation was a drab and dreary campsite under scraggly wet pine trees on the edge of Löcknitz. It looked like a deserted military barracks no doubt left over from WW2 or the more recent Russian occupation. It was about as welcoming as Fort Dix in New Jersey where I went to boot camp as a twenty-year-old Army recruit in 1966.

The owner spoke very little English, but better than my German. I understood that the rate was seven euros for the night, and one euro for a three-minute shower token. He said something to the effect that I could turn the shower on and off during the three minutes, I guess to get wet, which I already was, soap up, then rinse. I was in a foul mood and this filled me with dread.

'Es ein Zimmer in…uhm…village…town…?

'Nein.'

I didn't know if he thought if I was asking for a room at his site. But maybe he was correct in saying there wasn't a room in Löcknitz. I held out my credit card.

'Cards…?'

'Nein. Supermarket. Fünf-huntret metres.' He pointed towards the centre of town.

'OK.'

I rode into the centre hoping I would see a sign for a hotel or B&B. I really wanted a room to dry out in, rather than set up a waterlogged tent on the wet ground. A ride to the edge of town produced nothing, so I reluctantly made my way to the supermarket for cash, food, and the deepest red wine I could find. I made sure that it was dry…very dry.

The majority of the campsite was made up of cabins, I assumed converted from the old barracks. Most seemed empty. The only other traveller was a gentleman in a huge motorhome. It was enormous, at least fifteen metres long, the largest I've seen in my travels.

My first priority was to set up my tent, which was, unsurprisingly, wet, but the inside of the groundsheet was dry enough to sleep on. My sleeping bag was also wet. A vision of a sodden night deepened my gloom.

'Shit! To hell with it.'

I decided to take my six-minute shower (I bought two tokens). Upon entering the shower cabin, I saw a washing machine that took euro coins and a dryer that didn't. It seemed that I had unlimited drying time for free. FANTASTIC. I immediately stripped off, threw everything (including my shoes) into the dryer, wrapped myself in my towel and ran out to the tent to collect my sleeping bag.

Once everything was stuffed in, I turned it on. The loud thumping of my shoes was disconcerting; I didn't want to break it, nor did I want to alert the others on the site that their dryer was being destroyed. I took them out. I would have to rely on my sandals until the shoes dried by themselves.

The shower was six minutes of hot bliss. Funny how hot wet is a comfort from rain wet.

Luckily, my spare set of clothes were in a separate dry bag, so I was able to dress, pour a glass of wine and explore the site in the moist air. I looked for an electrical outlet to charge my phone. It seemed that the only one available was in a station that the motorhome was plugged into. I approached the owner, a Russian, who graciously welcomed my meagre requirement.

As we walked around to access the powerpoint I saw that the back hatch of the motorhome was open revealing a massive cavern.

'You could get a Smart Car in there.'

'No. A Toyota IQ.'

'Really...?'

'Yes. My wife is driving here tonight.'

Alan Deakins

I thought, 'Why would someone pay £300,000 for a motorhome to stay in such a dank campsite?" I then shortened my thought, 'Why would someone pay £3000,000 for a motorhome?'

He seemed to enjoy it. To each his own. Who am I to judge?

I cooked soup in the fading light and finished the bottle of wine; I thought I damn well deserved it, even though it didn't lift my spirits. A text from Marnie was better.

I didn't sleep well; I couldn't get warm, I lost my enthusiasm and I didn't know how to get it back.

It rained all night.

Old Hippie on a Bike

DAY 27
LÖCKNITZ – NEUBRANDENBURG

*'I was far away from home,
haunted and tired with travel.'*
-Jack Kerouac

Even though the sky was clear, I woke in a dark mood. I needed to get out of this campsite as quickly as possible.

It was dry enough to unpack everything, repack the dry items, and do what I could to dry out any wet items. I was deeply dismayed to see that my lovely Panasonic GM1 camera was water damaged. It would turn on, but the display was blank and it would not take pictures. Painful as it was, I had to write it off. I had planned on selling it upon my return to help pay for the trip.

Some of my clothes were still damp, so I tossed them into the dryer as I struck camp. By the time I was ready to set off, the only things that were still wet were my shoes, which I tied to the back of my panniers. I would ride in my plastic Birkenstock sandals.

I found a café in Löcknitz for breakfast. They had WI-FI, so I blogged about my experience on Facebook and Instagram.

Maybe it wasn't the camp site's fault, but to me, it was wet hell, and I was glad to put it behind me. As the sun rose, the morning began to warm up as I exited Löcknitz on Route 104 towards Neubrandenburg. I was heading west, that was all I knew. Since my phone signal was practically nil, I figured I would find an internet connection that evening.

At least I had a nice paved cycle path running alongside the 104, making progress safe and relatively peaceful. I hadn't gone far when the path came to an end, forcing me onto the main road. Suddenly, a man came running out of his house frantically waving his arms.

'Nein! Nein! Nein!'

I immediately stopped.

He pointed to a side road. Spoke very quickly, from which I only caught, 'Du gehn...'

'I should go there...?'

'Wunderbar. Wunderbar.'

I took him at his word and turned off onto the side road. He was right, it was a wonderful peaceful smooth road to the next village, where I sat in a lovely square with an ice tea.

I settled into my usual cadence with an unfamiliar lack of zeal. The day was fine, the road was smooth and I was just about OK with it all. Just.

About three kilometres west of Strasberg, a car pulled up alongside me, the driver waved then pulled over in front of me. He jumped out pointing behind me.

'Schuhe! Schuhe!'

I looked at my bike, and my shoes were no longer tied to the back. Damn.

'How far..? Ein...zwei kilometres...?'

He held up one finger.

'Danka.'

I turned the bike around and was about to cross the road to ride back when another car pulled up. A young lady got out of the passenger side with a smile holding up my shoes.

Everybody laughed, wished me well, and went on their way.

I was thrilled. Grateful. Amazed. And happy. Very happy.

In a short space of time, three people went out of their way to help me, simply because it was in them to do something positive for another person on this planet. I was moved by their generosity of spirit and their good nature. I was touched that they were pleased that I was pleased.

If I were walking, there would have been a spring in my step as I set off. At it was, a renewed spirit pushed the peddles.

Germany seems so far ahead of the UK in renewable energy. In the UK, wind turbines are considered blots on the landscape. Here, I was riding through fields of these gentle, elegant giants slowly submitting to the breeze, allowing it to turn their wings in the bright sunlight. At some points, the cycle path ran very close, where I could look straight up to see the sun glinting off of their massive blades. I was in awe of their splendid presence. They were like colossal kinetic sculptures, I personally thought they added beauty to the landscape. It was in many ways a salute to the future. In the UK, they aren't embraced. They spoil peoples' view, which is why, I suppose, the UK is more of a museum, rather than a forward-looking country.

If it had been evening, rather than midday, I would have happily wild camped under them. The thought was enticing.

I found a roadside park, with a nice restaurant in the middle. I sat on the terrace among the trees enjoying my lunch and watching Germans enjoying their good fortune. I half expected to see a young blonde man stand up and begin singing "Tomorrow Belongs To Me". A song that has stayed with me for over forty years, from Bob Fosse's film "Cabaret", set in Germany between the wars. It is my most favourite film of all time.

Alan Deakins

My spirits lifted further as I inched towards Neubrandenburg, singing 'Tomorrow Belongs To Me" loudly to the mute silver titans standing over me.

By the time I reached Neubrandenburg, I was exceedingly tired. It had been a tough day, emotionally as well as physically. I had covered over ninety kilometres against a moderate headwind. I was well and truly in need of a place to lie down. I managed to get a 3G signal on my phone, but the battery was running low, no surprises there. Thanks, Apple.

I headed for the cheapest accommodation I could find on Google maps which was a hostel located on a large square with bars, a restaurant and some sort of venue on the opposite side. The square itself was filled with cars, every space was taken. There was an event taking place because the square was also filled with scores of young men wearing immaculately pressed white shirts and young women in formal gowns standing around. There were bouncers at the entrance to the venue. Was it an awards ceremony or film premiere? And why were all the young men dressed virtually the same? It was an incongruous site; I didn't get it.

There was no reception in the hostel, so I asked one of the white-shirted men who were running in and out of each others' rooms; he directed me to one of the bars next to the venue across the square. It was an odd feeling as a sweaty old hippie cyclist dressed in a T-shirt, shorts and plastic sandals walking through the throng of immaculately dressed young people. What was going on…?

A young man behind the bar explained that the hostel was full due to the event. I thought of asking about the event, but for some reason, I thought I shouldn't. I don't know why; it just didn't feel right.

He suggested another hotel, a few minutes away, which I

found. To my relief, they had accommodation, and a secure room for my bike. To my dismay, the rate was sixty euros. It was too late in the day, and I was too tired to consider an alternative. I accepted and headed straight for the bar for a cold one.

The room was well appointed as I fully expected for the price. I showered and made my way down to the restaurant. My plan was, early dinner, then sort out my maps while I had a decent Wi-Fi signal.

I managed to get the last table on the terrace. It was a warm evening and I didn't want to sit inside. I was enjoying an agreeable chilled white wine as I was waiting for my dinner when double doors opened at the opposite side of the terrace, and several white-shirted young men and young ladies in formal evening dressed emerged to have their drinks in the evening air. How bizarre, to see young people dressed the same as the other venue. I did truly wonder what was going on in Neubrandenburg, but I couldn't ask.

Back in the room, I logged into my Facebook and Instagram pages, to find several messages of encouragement and support from so many kind people. I was tremendously heartened by all of them. In my heart of hearts, I never doubted that I would complete this trip. I had promised I would. The notion that it would be done without much enthusiasm, was what disturbed me.

But I had a good day, where I experienced small acts of kindness, bizarre happenings and wonderful kind uplifting messages. I felt strong inside, and curious once again of what lay ahead. I was also aware that I was exhausted and I decided to heed the advice of most of my friends on Facebook and Instagram and take time to recharge.

I had checked my progress alongside the original route I made with RideWithGPS, and I discovered that I had been travelling in a north-westerly direction. I was well off course of my ideal route. I now needed to head in a south-westerly direction.

A quick search on Google showed several small lakes south of Neubrandenburg with numerous campsites dotted along their shores. I decided to spend a short day riding there for a couple days' rest. This plan suited me for two reasons. First, it was cheaper than a hotel. Secondly, and most importantly, I would be among people.

I looked forward to what I would find around the bend in the morning.

DAY 28
NEUBRANDENBURG - USERIN

'Go anywhere, as long as it's forward.'
-David Livingstone

Even though I was a guest in a three-star hotel, I felt uneasy. I was anxious to get on the road and sleep in my tent since that was my original intention when I decided to do this trip, and here I was in the lap of luxury, comparatively speaking, giving me a twinge of guilt. I spent six nights camping budget on this one night's stay. I wanted to put things right.

The usual German cycle paths accommodated my ride out of Neubrandenburg. To me, this was a luxury I deserved. There were a number of steep hills to start out with that I found quite taxing. I had to push my bike up a couple of them, but the ride down the other side was effortless, so things evened out.

About five kilometres out, the path ran through an enclave of houses. All of them fronted onto the path. I thought this was such a cool and forward-thinking community design. The main road that ran past the front gates of all the houses was quiet, simply because it was a bike/pedestrian path. I observed several people walking with their families and stopping for a chat with other residents. It was a pleasant environment.

Google maps directed me to turn onto a quiet country lane and I rode through rolling hills and lush farmland. All was peaceful and I felt good. I should have known better, however, because I was directed onto a dirt path. I fell for it again. Google must think that a barely useable path constitutes a cycle path. I was not about to embark on this path for five kilometres so I turned around, changed Google map settings from cycling to driving. It wasted an hour of my time, but at least I knew that I wouldn't be led up some impassable sand pit.

I turned off Route 104 onto the smaller and quieter Route 96 that ran into the forested lake district that would eventually lead me to Userin, a municipality surrounding Lake Bullowsee, where six campsites were situated. Because I would have a choice of camping and be in a good position to get back onto my originally planned route after my rest, I figured it was worth the few hours' effort to get there. Besides, it was an enjoyable ride on cycle paths that meandered through silent dappled forests. It was evolving into a ride without tension or angst. My relaxed pace and peaceful surroundings were already having a positive effect on me.

As I approached the vicinity of the lake, I found a supermarket where I stocked up on supplies for my rest. I went from there to the first campsite I came across. So much for choosing one out of the half dozen within a small radius. My needs were simple: a place to pitch my tent, sit in the sun and to do nothing for two days, and I was keen to start straight away.

My other priority was to be among people, rather than holed up alone in a room, and it appeared that I would get plenty of that with the campsite I landed in. For a start, I was welcomed by other campers as I was setting up my tent. Some were curious about my cycling journey, understandably; a white-bearded old man travelling on a bike is a bit of an oddity.

I was pleased to find a quiet spot on the shore of the lake to pitch my tent, and it wasn't long before I was basking in the warm afternoon sun with a cold beer. It didn't last long, however, when I was approached by two men who explained that they were from a charity that organised camping weekends for deprived urban children, and could they please ask me to relocate my tent so that they could set up their 'village' on the edge of the lake to give the children direct access to the water? They assured me that they would be well behaved and that directly after dinner, they would be singing around the campfire and retire early. I couldn't very well refuse. There go my peace and tranquillity.

It turned out that they were nice kids, early to mid-teens. They all pitched in to build their tent village, listened to instructions from their two leaders, enthusiastically joined in activities and generally were fun to watch as they got on with enjoying their time in the 'wilderness'. It was no hardship to move, and I was entertained by a bunch of cool young people.

Alan Deakins

The day ambled into the evening, and I found myself needing to turn in early. I had no trouble falling asleep to the sound of campfire songs from young voices accompanied by a lone guitar.

DAY 29
USERIN – REST DAY

*'If you're not in New York,
you're camping out.'
-Thomas Dewey*

I awoke to a hive of activity. The youngsters were busy preparing breakfast and packing some of the tents away. One of the leaders saw I was awake and came over to me.

'We will be leaving at midday. You can have your spot back. Thank you for understanding.'

'I'm fine here. They're a nice bunch of kids.'

'Yes. Two days in the country is not much of a holiday for them, but we do what we can.'

'They're having a great time thanks to you.'

I made my way to the little shop to forage some breakfast. I joined a queue who were receiving bread rolls from the shop keeper by giving their name. When it came to my turn, I confidently stated my name.

'Deakins.'

'He looked on his list.'

'Deakins…Deakins…Deakins…?'

'Yes…Ja…'

He shook his head. The chap behind me spoke up.

'Did you order yesterday…?'

'Uhm…no…'

'You have to order the day before, then they prepare for you the next day.'

'Oh…'

'You can have some of mine…I always order too much.'

'That's very kind…are you sure?'

'It is OK. Over there is tomorrow's list. Order what you want.'

I offered to pay him for his kindness, but he declined to accept any money. I could now add to my Kindness of Strangers list: The Generosity of Strangers.

I sat at a table near my tent with my two plump bread rolls brewing a coffee when a couple asked if they could join me. Of course! I welcomed the company. They had jam and butter, and I had coffee. Between us, we managed an adequate breakfast filled with conversation.

Stephan and Kathi were in a fairly new relationship. They had cycled up from Berlin. Stephan, a Project Manager for Siemens, was fairly new to cycling. Kathi had convinced him to do this trip. His reluctance reminded me of my early days on a bike, not fond of it, but doing it nonetheless. He, out of love. Me, out of a whim. And, like me, he wasn't too keen on camping either. We had much in common.

Kathi taught Syrian children who were fortunate enough to escape the terrible civil war there. Many of her children experienced the horrors of Aleppo. We talked about how mentally scarred they were, and the difficulties of working with them, not only because of their dreadful experiences but also their cultural upbringing that was incompatible with the West on many levels. She seemed very measured, patient and empathetic. I took an instant liking to these two. They were fun, interesting and energetic. Our lively conversation made a humble leisurely breakfast a joy for me.

They were going to spend the day cycling around exploring the area and invited me along. I declined, it seemed a bit of a busman's holiday to me. I would be back in the saddle soon enough. And, although I didn't say it, I didn't want to intrude on their time together either.

'Will we see you later on...?'

'Of course, I'm not going anywhere.'

'Good. They are setting up a big screen in the campsite to show the World Cup Final for everybody. There will be beer. Will you go with us?'

Alan Deakins

"I would like that.'

I spent the day lazing about in the sun, reading, a cold dip in the lake, napping and cooking a simple lunch. I simply had a simple day, and it suited me.

The venue for the World Cup Final was a three-sided marquee on the edge of the campsite with a large screen TV set up on the far inside wall. By the time Stephan, Kathi and I got there, the marquee was full, so we joined the crowd that spilt outside. This was preferable to me because it was more comfortable under the trees and we were close to the golf cart full of beer that the owner had prepared. The screen was bright, so we had a good view.

I'm not a great football fan, so the interest for me was crowd watching. I enjoyed peoples' reactions and interactions, which were good humoured and animated. It was hard to tell which team people were rooting for, perhaps the edge was for Croatia. But by and large, the crowd cheered with each goal and groaned with each near miss. And with everybody making plenty of trips to the golf cart, a good time was had by all.

I had made the decision to set off in the morning; the bend in the road was beckoning. I had to admit that my journey had truly become an adventure. Not an earth-shattering exploit, not a legendary achievement, it was more of a personal, compulsive desire to watch my constantly changing day-to-day life unfold in front of me as I rode unfamiliar roads.

DAY 30
USERIN – PERLEBERG

*'Most travel involves depending on
the kindness of strangers,
putting yourself into the hands of people
you don't know and trusting them with your life.'
-Paul Theroux*

I collected my bread rolls at reception and sat in the early morning light deciding my route for the day. I wasn't totally sure I was rested, but I was totally sure that I was totally bored of resting. Through Google maps, I decided on Perleberg as my destination, a rather ambitious ninety-five kilometres south-west. That would be halfway to getting back to my original route at Bad Bodenteich. I also decided that I would not programme Google maps for bike routes. I had had enough of horrible muddy or sandy or badly cobbled paths.

I had an unhurried breakfast. I didn't want to leave without saying good-bye to Stephan and Kathi, who were still asleep. I finished packing my bike and all was ready just as they were crawling out of their tent. We had a quick farewell; I would miss them, they were so familiar to me now, like friends should be.

As I rode out onto the road, I felt a little flutter of excitement. The morning was warm, calm and inviting. I rode on beautiful cycle paths that skirted the road through the forests. It was going to be a great day.

When the path ended, I wondered along quiet tree-lined

roads. An occasional car would pass, but it didn't really invade my tranquillity. Perhaps I was rested after all.

I was still having problems with my iPhone's reluctance to connect to my solar panel, which meant that I went for long stretches with the phone turned off so I could keep it charged for when I needed it. Every so often, I would turn it on, consult the map to see if my following road signs was keeping me on course. It was a convoluted way of navigating, but I had no choice.

Near Gershagen, I saw a sign for Pritzwalk, a town definitely on my chosen route twenty kilometres along Route 103. I checked Google maps, and a nice female voice cheerily instructed me to turn onto it. Access was via a slip road, which told me that I would be riding on a motorway. I carried on for three reasons. First, so far on similar roads in Russia, the Baltics and Poland there were no restrictions for cyclists. Second, on such roads, in most cases, I had a generous three-metre-wide hard shoulder to ride on, so I always felt safe enough away from the passing traffic. Third, there no signs forbidding my entry, like a bicycle with a diagonal line through it.

I had gone about a kilometre when some of the cars hooted at me as they passed. I moved as close to the edge as I could. Soon, lorries were hooting at me as they thundered past.

'Oh, oh. I shouldn't be on this road.'

I had at least eighteen kilometres to go, and I knew I couldn't turn back; riding against the traffic would be even worse. I had to continue on. I rode as fast as I could but knew that it would take at least an hour to cover the distance to the next exit. It was obvious my being here was untenable, but I really didn't have a solution for my predicament.

Suddenly, a sign for a rest area loomed up ahead. I rode as quickly as I possibly could for the remaining five hundred meters, perhaps there would be a trucker who could get me to the next exit. There were only two camper vans, and two or three cars there when I rode in. There was, however a family (Mum, Dad and teenage daughter and son), watching me. I felt foolish and stupid. Mum rushed forward talking excitedly in German.

'Sorry...Ich spreche...uhm... kliene Deutch...'

'You must not be on this road...it is very dangerous.'

She and the whole family looked genuinely concerned.

'I realise that now...but I can't turn back. I have to get to the next exit.'

'You must get off, maybe that gate is open. Moritz, go check.' Her son ran up to a gate in the perimeter fence about fifty metres away, and shook his head.'

'Perhaps one of these motorhomes will take you.'

Both motorhomes had empty bike racks on the back. I approached the Swedish one first. The couple spoke English but declined, citing insurance reasons. It would have been more honest to say 'We don't trust you and you're disturbing our holiday.'

She then approached the second motor home with me, since it had German plates. Inside, a rather rotund older couple was sitting at a table eating. As she asked them to assist, neither one of them looked up from their plates. The man just shook his head. She spoke more urgently, 'Bitte…' Still, he shook his head while staring at his sausage.

She turned to me, 'I must apologise for my fellow Germans and for their rudeness.'

'Don't worry. Thanks for trying. You've been most kind. I will wait for a truck to stop.'

She walked over to her family who were standing next to their fully loaded car, with two bikes on top and two on a rear rack. They huddled close together for about thirty seconds. They turned and walked over to me.

'We will take you.'

Alan Deakins

From then on, I was under the wing of Kathy, Rico, Leni and Moritz.

Rico removed my front wheel and mounted my bike to the roof alongside the two other bikes. He then secured the wheel to the bikes at the rear using cable ties. Kathy, Leni and Moritz would squeeze in the back seat with my panniers and tent on their laps and I would be in the front with my handlebar bag.

As Rico, Leni and Moritz were sorting out the logistics, Kathy queried my ride, and I told her about the Samaritans, which seemed to genuinely please her.

Before we set off, they readily agreed to a selfie with humour, enthusiasm and jollity. I took several shots. We were having fun. We laughed. I was so relaxed with this wonderful family.

We all piled in and were soon covering the eighteen kilometres at a speed that I haven't experienced in well over a month, in cool air-conditioned luxury. I couldn't believe my amazing good fortune.

'Alan, you are a radio star.'

Kathy explained that an announcement had just come on the local radio notifying all drivers on the autobahn to be aware of a cyclist heading south. We then saw a police car with lights flashing speeding north, no doubt to the next exit to turn south in a futile search for me, since for all intents and purposes, the mystery cyclist had disappeared, which made us all laugh.

We exited the autobahn, Rico carefully lowered my bike to the ground while Leni and Moritz lined up my panniers and tent ready to load up.

'Scheisse!'

In his effort to cut the cable ties that held my front wheel, Rico had accidentally punctured my tyre with his penknife. A small, easily rectified mistake.

'Don't worry, I can repair it...'

'We have a repair kit; we will fix it.'

'No...really. You've done enough already.'

'We insist.'

Rico, Leni and Moritz set about taking the tyre off the rim and patching the inner tube and Kathy found a bottle of water for me. All I could do was stand there accepting their incredible generosity.

Once the patch was applied, Rico pumped air into the tyre, but the patch didn't hold.

'Really, guys, you've done enough. I have a spare tube, I'll sort it.'

'No. We won't leave you until you are riding again.'

I fished the tube out of my pannier, and Rico, Leni and Moritz once again removed the tyre to swap tubes. They worked enthusiastically and seemed to enjoy helping an old man. And the old man was genuinely moved by their genuine concern.

Job all done, bike packed, time to say goodbye. Kathy handed me a ten euro note.

'We want you to buy a new tube.'

'I can't take your money, you've done so much for me already.'

'We want you to have it.'

'I just can't...'

'We insist.'

I wasn't going to win this argument...four against one.

'OK. I'll accept it as a donation for the Samaritans.'

How does it happen? What mystical essence causes total strangers to instantly connect? What allows them to completely trust one another without question? Finding a common beingness. Sharing a common thought. I will care for you. I am safe in your hands. I feel comfortable in your presence. I've known you for so long in this moment. When this is over, we will go on to our separate lives. I know, but I will never forget you. Thank you for allowing me to care. Thank you for being there when I needed you. I saw your goodness. And I experienced yours. We shared this time together. You touched my heart. Good-bye. Farewell.

What wonder. What magic. In a random instant on a random spot on the face of this planet, a bond is formed between strangers that cannot, will not, be broken, all because I was illegally cycling on a German autobahn.

But I had to be, to meet them.

Kathy's last words to me were: 'Be blessed.'

And I was, for knowing them.

I watched them drive off until they disappeared. I suddenly felt small and alone, but more so, I felt elated. I began to see my journey, not of distance, not of scenery, not of challenges, not of hardship or lack of comfort, not of achievement. My journey was a series of human encounters. All of them good.

And that inspiring thought stayed with me for all of thirty seconds.

'Scheisse!!!'

I turned around to see a cyclist, about my age, barrelling towards me shaking his fist and shouting. I assumed his nose was out of joint because I was unwittingly blocking part of the cycle path. His reaction was to scream a remorseless string of profanities at me, continuing until he was out of earshot. I was stunned, but all I could do was chuckle. I felt good, I was blessed, and no one could take that away from me.

My subsequent ride into Perleberg was uneventful but pleasant. The only hitch was I inadvertently had my phone on all this time, resulting in a low battery once again. I logged on to Google maps in search of campsites, no results were forthcoming, so my only alternative was to keep my eye out for signs of accommodation of any sort.

Shortly after entering Perleberg, I saw a sign for a hostel. I immediately turned in. I rang the bell, and a voice said that someone would be along shortly to book me in. As I waited, several vans pulled into the courtyard, and men piled out and into the hostel. They appeared to me to be linesmen. I hoped so since the phone signal in Eastern Germany was the worst I've experienced on the entire trip.

Eventually, a woman appeared. She led me to a garage where I could safely store my bike, then after taking payment and getting me onto the internet, she walked me down a long narrow corridor with different music emanating from behind the doors on either side, into a breakfast room, and out the other side into a very old section. We proceeded up a grand centuries-old elaborate staircase. At the top, under an imposing chandelier, was a vast landing with very tall ornate doors with a room number on each one. I thought, 'I'm going to be living a grand life tonight.'

She walked past the grand doors and stopped in front of a petite narrow one, which she unlocked. Behind it was a tiny cubby hole tucked neatly under the eaves, with a single bed, a minute writing desk, minuscule fridge and 7" television. I was not surprised to find that the shower room was equally tiny. I had to laugh inside at the irony of it. It tickled me.

Nonetheless, it was clean, the bed comfortable and above all, very quiet. As far as I could tell, I was the only one in this old section, so I was spared the noise of the linesmen and their music. Upon further investigation, I found a lovely outdoor terrace on the other side of the landing. The table and chairs were perfectly positioned to take advantage of the late afternoon sun.

I hadn't eaten much since breakfast, so I set out in search of dinner. Perleberg is a pleasant town with lovely old architecture and fine cobbled streets. There were several inviting outdoor cafes, but I didn't fancy dining alone in the midst of others enjoying a perfect evening like this together.

I opted instead for a tall cold beer on the river's edge and a chat with a young affable bartender. I then found a supermarket for something simple to take back to my lovely private terrace.

I checked my Instagram and Facebook pages upon my return and was completely overwhelmed with the kind messages of support following my Wet Hell experience. So many people wrote heartfelt messages of encouragement. I was so very moved.

A packet of tortellini cooking on my camp stove and a small bottle of wine in the warm early evening sun was my alfresco indulgence. I wasn't dining alone; I was full of company.

Kathy's words were still loud in my mind.

'Be blessed.'

And I cried.

DAY 31
PERLEBERG – GARTOW

'If you come to a fork in the road, take it.'
-Yogi Berra

Up early. Feeling good. Energised. Raring to go. Quick coffee on the terrace. Pack. Out the door. Early. Good. Bad Bodenteich tonight. Back on track. Breakfast first. C'mon!

Before leaving Perleberg, I stopped at a supermarket for breakfast and a few provisions. I sat under a tree to eat while watching the comings and goings of people starting their day. I checked Google maps to make sure that the route I planned last night was still working. The phone service in Germany was, in my opinion, appalling. I wondered if it might have to do with being in the old East Germany, and adequate infrastructure was still being installed. Perhaps that was what the linesmen staying at the hostel were working on. On the other hand, Germany reunified twenty-eight years ago, ample time to sort things out. I just couldn't understand why the richest nation in Europe had the worst phone signal.

I imagined I would be in Bad Bodenteich in good time with a minimum of fuss since the route looked relatively straightforward. Shortly outside of Perleberg, I turned onto the 189 which would take me across the Elbe River at Wittenberge. From here on, all did not go according to plan. Straight away, motorists began hooting at me. I couldn't understand why. There were no warning signs, and the road was not a dual carriageway, it was just two lanes. I did, however, feel vulnerable riding on the very narrow edge alongside the fast traffic.

I knew I had to get off, and fortunately, there was a road running parallel to the one I was on. Perhaps it was the old road to Wittenberge.

The only thing that separated the two roads was an embankment which I managed to descend by slowly walking my bike diagonally down the slope. I was relieved to be on a traffic-free road, and still within sight of the road I was supposed to be on according to Google.

I soon came to a junction for the main road. I managed to pick up the old road on the other side if it. I thought this was great. Quiet, safe, nice to ride on and heading in the right direction. What's not to like?

I rode at a leisurely pace. All was in control, and I was enjoying the day. I came to the next junction, found the old road on the other side and continued on. Happy days. About two kilometres on, the road came to an abrupt end. There was nothing to travel on, not even a crappy unrideable sandy path. Nothing. I sat there watching the traffic merrily thundering past on the parallel road I wasn't allowed on in the direction I needed to go. I could feel the day and my plans slipping away.

I backtracked to the last junction. The only sign to Wittenberge pointed me onto the forbidden road. I consulted Google maps for an alternative, but my phone could only muster a miserly 2G signal, not enough to download any useful information. In short, I was stuffed. I had no access to any directions that I could rely on.

I cursed Google. I cursed the German phone system. I cursed Apple. (To be fair, Apple's shortcomings didn't have anything to do with my present predicament, but I had plenty of curses left in me, so Apple could damn well bear a few of them.) I remember an episode on 'Faulty Towers' where John Cleese was so irrationally angry, he shook his fist at a flower. And I, on a bridge over the 189, was shaking my fist at my phone. It didn't help solve the situation, but I saw the humour in it.

The dilemma was: do I head east and turn south at the first opportunity, hopefully towards Wittenberge? Or, do I head west in the general direction I needed to go? I chose west.

My plan was to let the sun be my guide, not take any deviations unless I saw a sign to Wittenberge. Sooner or later I would ride into a town or village where I could access the internet. With the courage of my conviction, or least a 'suck-it-and-see' attitude, I set off with the sun at my back, in hopes of finding some sort of direction before the sun was directly overhead, at which point, I would lose my guide.

The ride on the small rural roads was extremely interesting. The roads varied considerably. In some hamlets I rode on ancient cobbled roads. In the middle of open countryside, I rode on a strange surface that was made up of interlocking concrete units that looked like waffles. I assumed it was a remnant from the Communist era. It looked like something that an armoured vehicle would use, for me it was difficult to ride on with narrow cycle tyres. There also were drab concrete barns close by. I definitely had a sense of travelling through cold war East Germany.

Still, there were pleasant picturesque hamlets. I would assume the old cottages survived simply because there was no money at that time to replace them rather than affection for rustic historic buildings. Nonetheless, I was enjoying rural pre-unification Germany as I rode through it.

I eventually found my way (by keeping the sun on my back) onto a main road heading west. I stopped in Lanz to see if my phone could get any reasonable signal, which it didn't. I must have looked lost because a man standing in his garden approached.

'Ich bin…lost.' My obvious command of German was more

honed the more I spoke it.

'Wohin willst do gehen?'

'Bad Bodenteich.'

'Ah…ein moment…'

He went into his house and returned with a small local tourist map. I could see that I was north of the Elbe River.

'Lenzen. Boat.'

'Ferry…?'

'Ja."

'How far…? Kilometres…?"

'Zehn.'

'Ten? OK. Danke.'

He handed me the map with a wave telling me to take it.

'Danke. Danke Shon.'

'Bitte Shon. Goodbye.'

It was close to midday. It had taken me four hours to cover less than fifteen kilometres from Perleberg as the crow flies. I would have to rethink my day, once I crossed the Elbe.

Lenzen is a beautiful ancient town filled with lovely timbered buildings nicely situated on the river. I took the time to ride around and take a few pictures simply because it pleased me.

I met a couple of young cyclists from Hamburg sitting in a cobbled square. They invited me to sit with them and offered me small sweet red berries that they had just purchased locally. Nice. The camaraderie of travelling cyclists.

The ferry crossing the Elbe was positively tiny. There was enough room for eight cars per journey. One man was the captain, pilot, helmsman, deckhand and ticket collector. My one-euro fare treated me to an enjoyable ten-minute unhurried crossing into Lower Saxony.

I wasn't sure how far I could travel, but I was encouraged by the smooth level road because my speed was picking up and I felt I was making good progress. Perhaps Bad Bodenteich was possible.

In less than an hour, I was riding along the north shore of Gartower See, a small lake, where the road took a sharp turn, over a small bridge and into the tidy town of Gartow lying on the south shore. I liked this town; it had a charming laid back feel to it. I found a bakery, bought a sandwich and ice tea, and set off to find a spot on the shore of the lake to rest and enjoy my lunch. On the way, I saw a sign pointing to a campsite.

'Too bad it's only three o'clock. Too early to stop,' I said to myself.

I found a nice shaded spot to sit. I unwrapped my sandwich, took a sip of my ice tea and mused over that sign.

'Why is it too early...?' I said. 'What do you really want to do, Deak? Rest, or sweat?'

I got up, packed my sandwich away and got back on my bike.

Stopping early seemed to go against my work ethic. My conscious mind said, 'You've worked hard, take a break. Relax. You deserve it.' My unconscious mind responded with, 'Chop-chop! Busy-busy! Work-work! Chop-chop! Busy-busy! Work-work!' I sometimes have to literally tell it, 'Piss off!' I thought it would change when I retired. No chance. Or after my stroke. Nope. I should realise after seventy-two years, it is well and truly entrenched, and I'm locked in a permanent fight with it.

If my remonstrations weren't going to subdue it, the cold beer in the little shop at the campsite would. If anything, our unconscious minds are creatures of habit and are programmable with repeated conscious effort. Pavlov's dog springs to mind. Rather than a bell, my unconscious mind has been responding favourably to a cold beer at the end of the day on this trip. 'Woo hoo! Down tools. Let's drink!'

This custom was known as a 'Dust Settler' to Colin (my Lighting Cameraman) and me. No matter where we were in the world, at the end of a day's filming, we'd head straight for the bar at the hotel for a quick cold one before heading for the shower. Usually, my Dust Settler was a white wine, because I'm not much of a beer drinker, except on this journey. Somehow, only a beer will do at the end of a sweaty day's ride.

The designated field for tents was bordered by tall trees. It was spacious and virtually empty. Only five other tents were pitched. I set up under a lovely shade tree. There was another cycling couple there, other than a polite hello, I felt that they wanted to be left on their own. Fair enough.

Later in the early evening, an elderly gentleman rode in on the strangest bike I'd ever seen. It looked like it was made of two different bikes. The two unrelated halves were joined together midway along the crossbar by a rudely welded plate running from the top crossbar to the lower diagonal bar. So, the pedals, seat post and back wheel were from one bike, and the handlebars and front wheel from another. It was, to say the least, a most ungainly looking contraption. His panniers were two wire baskets tied to a homemade wooden rack with rope. He also had a gym bag strapped to his handlebars. He set about erecting his tent, which was a rather large tent of an old design. It looked like it weighed at least ten kilos. Once set up, he crawled inside, zipped it up and that was that.

I read my Kindle into the evening, texted Marnie, wrote a blog for Facebook and Instagram, and for me also, that was that.

DAY 32
GARTOW – BAD BODENTEICH

'Who am I to blow against the wind?'
-Paul Simon

I woke early, I usually do. It was going to be another hot day, so an early start was essential. I wanted to cover as much distance as I could since I didn't get far yesterday. Bad Bodenteich was approximately 45 kilometres away. I was capable of much further. It wasn't really a destination, but a marker reminding me that I was back on my originally planned route, so any distance, further along, would be a bonus.

As I crawled out of my tent, I could see the old gentleman packing his bike. We were the only people awake on the site. He walked his bike over to me on his way out. We talked briefly. His set-up was even more extraordinary close-up. It looked so heavy that I doubted I would have the strength to ride it even for a short distance.

He was a German who travelled around every year on his bike for weeks on end. He was heading north to the German coast. We talked about long distance touring as old guys. He proclaimed that he was seventy-eight! And here he was peddling an ancient steel tank all over Northern Europe. I was in deep admiration. Perhaps there are a few tours left in me.

It was only after he left that it dawned on me that I hadn't thought of taking his picture. I regretted my short-sightedness. My description of him and his bike is really inadequate. I would often picture him in my mind riding out his days across

Europe on his astonishing machine.

The 493 heading west from Gartow was a perfectly straight road to Trebel through a thick forest. I didn't have to ride on it at all, because there was a good smooth path running parallel to the road. Not only did I have the cover of the trees, but I was a good ten metres from the traffic. From Trebel, the road meandered in and out of trees across farmland. The sun was rising quickly along with the heat. There was a stiff south wind, which hindered me somewhat. It was carrying hot air, and it was beginning to be a formidable side wind.

At Luchow, I had to turn south directly into the wind. I still had the luxury of a smooth path, but it was difficult to keep a pace in the wind. There were a few hills to straddle also which didn't help. By the time I reached Salzwedel, I was wet, tired and in need of a break. It wasn't yet midday, and I felt I had done a full day's ride. I haven't experienced a strong headwind for a while, and I had forgotten how quickly it could drain me. I found a quiet café with Wi-Fi for a break and a cold drink. On checking my original route plan from RideWithGPS, I was back on course. From here, it was more or less a straight line to the Hook of Holland, which I figured I could do in less than a week.

My heart quickened a bit thinking that I was so close to home. I felt energised and decided to ride as far as I could for the rest of the day. I thought another sixty kilometres was easily possible.

Back on the road, I was still plagued by the strong side wind. But I still thought a long stint was possible. About an hour later, the wind direction shifted to a westerly direction, meaning I was fighting a straight-on headwind. With this, my thoughts of sixty kilometres changed to: how far can I get before I'm exhausted?

The only saving grace was that even on the small rural road I was travelling on, I had the advantage of a parallel dedicated cycle path. I felt that my energy was draining, but I didn't feel vulnerable. That is until I turned onto a very small road without a path. The traffic consisted of a car or two every five to six minutes. I could cope with that, which is more than I could say for the headwind.

It also didn't help that the hamlets I was passing through, although pretty, lacked any petrol stations or stores for me to get cold drinks. I had ample water on board, but warm water made me even more thirsty.

It seemed that the only thing in my favour is for some reason, my iPhone was staying charged enough to allow Google Maps to give me the occasional direction, although I still got the annoying pop-up window.

Three kilometres outside Bad Bodenteich, the wind had beaten me. I stopped dead in my tracks and slumped under a tree; I had come to the end of my reserve energy. I knew I would have to make a supreme effort to get there. The thought of a cold drink spurred me on.

I stopped at the first petrol station I saw on entering the town. The ice tea was, well, ice cold. It was an instant reviver like a super-drive switch had been thrown inside me. So much so, I felt I was good for another few hours. But, I didn't fancy a few hours of headwinds for so little gain. It wasn't long past lunchtime, but I reluctantly decided to pack it in for the day, overriding the shouts from my unconscious mind: 'Chop-chop! Busy-busy! Work-work!'

Even though Google Maps was working, the German mobile system wasn't. A paltry 2G signal was the best I could get, barely enough to receive a simple text, let alone a full search for accommodation. Again, I had to rely on roadside signs. It wasn't long before I saw a camping sign. I turned off the road onto a smaller road and followed it for two kilometres, over a very wide canal. A bit further on, I found it. My aching legs were very pleased and ready to argue vehemently with my unconscious mind.

A pleasant receptionist with a sunny smile was there to greet me.

'Ey up.'

'Hi there. May I camp for the night?'

'Aye. Where have you come from…?'

'St Petersburg.'

'Flippin heck…you must be knackered.'

By this point, I was a bit confused. Was I in Germany, or northern England? She was obviously German, but she spoke with a Yorkshire accent. It was strange to hear, but intriguing nonetheless.

'First things, first. Do you sell beer?'

'Aye. Follow me.'

We walked across the drive to a small café/store that appeared to be closed. She went inside and came out with a very cold half-litre bottle for the bargain price of one euro.

'I'm going to sit right here in the shade and drink it.'

'I'll join you, I've got nowt to do.'

She made herself a cup of tea and sat with me in the shade.

'Where did you learn English…Middlesborough?'

'No. Here in Germany, I'm married to a Yorkshire man.'

I loved her accent, a curious mix of German and Yorkshire Dales, brightened by her exuberance. It was unique, and it suited her energetic no-nonsense personality.

Angelica and I spent the rest of the day chatting. She was interested in my journey and the Samaritans. We talked about mental health, children, families, Brexit, Germany and life in general. We righted wrongs. We solved society's problems. We railed against injustices in the world. We laughed. It was comfortable, like two close friends who haven't seen each other in years.

By the time she had to leave to collect her children, I had consumed quite a few beers. When I asked to settle my bill, she generously responded with:

'Nay. Don't worry about it.'

She then gave me a souvenir bottle opener from the campsite as her parting gift, a little something to remind me of a lazy summer afternoon in the middle of Germany with an adopted Yorkshire lass.

I found a nice shaded spot and set about pitching my tent and unpacking my bike. There was no Wi-Fi available at this campsite, and I was hungry, so I set off for central Bad Bodenteich in search of food and a decent signal. Eat, blog and text Marnie were my immediate priorities.

Riding my bike when it is unshackled from my bags felt like I was on a racing bike. It was quicker, more agile and, dare I say it, actually fun. I rode alongside the wide canal that led me to town. There were many people walking, cycling and boating on the canal, enjoying the warm low summer sun in the late evening.

I found a supermarket with free Wi-Fi and a place to sit outside with an ice tea. I posted a blog, texted Marnie and bought something for dinner.

A gentle ride back, a small meal, and a shower capped a satisfying day.

DAY 33
BAD BODENTEICH – WINSEN AN DER ALLER

'Oh shit, it's shit.'
-Stephen King, Different Seasons

I was really hoping Angelica would be in the office when I set off. Sadly, she wasn't. I wanted to say goodbye. I wanted to thank her. I wanted her to be a consistency in my life for one more brief moment before I embarked on my new one.

It seemed that each day was a new life for me. The people that peopled my life yesterday will not be the people that people it today. Like all the previous days on this journey, there will be no routine to this day. Nothing will be the same. I will be by myself, but my 'self' will be doing things differently. Waking, packing, washing, teeth brushing, crapping, breakfasting is different every day.

We all need routines. We create routines to have consistency in our lives. Consistency, in many ways, is security. I think it is our way of predicting the future. With consistency, we know what will happen next. My only consistency on the road was there was no consistency.

So I set off on a new life once again. I'm only there for the ride. I let my 'self' deal with whatever comes next while I struggle with my insecurity. I had no idea what would happen, or not happen, once I was on the road.

As I crossed the canal on my way out of Bad Bodenteich, an enormous barge was sailing majestically down the middle of the wide straight canal. I was astounded by its size as it passed under the bridge, bigger than some of the ships I worked on when I was in the Merchant Marine on the Great Lakes. Sadly, it sat low in the water because it was full of coal. My image of Germany, the country of the future with all its wind turbines dotted across its landscape, was shattered. So Germany was still mining and either burning or selling the stuff. I guess the sad thing is, that even with the Paris Accord, no nation has completely stopped using fossil fuels. Most are gradually weaning themselves off, but still earning money from extricating fuel from the earth. It's a slow transition, too slow, way too slow. With consistency, we know what will happen next. Burn coal, oil, etc., the earth will get warmer. Weather will change, coastal cities will flood, there will be widespread drought and famine. That barge allowed me to momentarily consider the future, to know what could happen next, and I thought I must apologise to my granddaughters.

Yet, this smug 'Greenie' on his carbon-neutral bike would be buying several cold drinks in plastic bottles before the day has ended.

Still, I was riding on a lovely cycle path, rather than fighting traffic with my unprotected body. So, I gave a few points back to Germany for providing cyclists, even on rural roads, something which is a rarity in England. I appreciated these paths, and if the drivers would consider that their journeys are easier and faster because we aren't holding them up, they would appreciate them also.

The ride into Celle was easy, trouble-free and enjoyable through the shaded forests. Germany really is a beautiful country, mostly litter free and I imagined that its inhabitants were proud of that. But it wasn't long before my image was shattered again.

Around midday, I stopped at a pretty roadside picnic area in the middle of a forest. There were nice tables arranged under the trees, and it was well enough away from the road where I could have a quiet lunch and rest. Before I got back on the bike, I wandered on a path into the wood for a pee. About twenty metres in, I was confronted with an open sewer. Scattered across the floor of the wood were scores of piles of crap and horrible soiled clumps of toilet paper. There were piles on top of piles. It was a sickening stinking mess inflicted on such a beautiful spot. I wanted to wretch.

When I researched about camping for this trip, I became well aware of the 'leave no trace' policy of responsible campers. Pee will soak into the ground, but for poo, dig a pit, do your business and cover it. I carried a small spade for the few times I have been caught short. I'm willing to bet that the vast majority of the people who deposited these wretched piles live in impeccably clean homes. I don't get it.

My aim was Neinburg, a one hundred kilometre ride, but by the time I got to Celle, I began to feel that I needed to settle for a less ambitious goal. The heat was sapping my strength more than I expected. It seems there is a dichotomy between my mind and my body. I don't feel seventy-two, but often my body does. I couldn't complain, really, I've come this far without too much trouble (except for a couple of tumbles), and considerably few aches and pains. My body was holding up well, and exceeding my expectations.

Celle is a beautiful town. I rode into the main square and was instantly hit with a strong sense of deja vu. I had been here before. I've travelled to Germany many times on various film assignments, it had to have been on one of them. I recognised the café we sat at, I even remembered what I ate; I had a croque masseur, but I couldn't remember who I was with. Very strange, and disconcerting. It was nice to be back, but how did I come to be there so many years ago? And with whom?

I sat at the same café and ordered a croquet masseur. I hoped it would revive my memory. It didn't. But it did revive my energy, so I decided to press on.

I was back on the 214 feeling better, but perplexed. I had two memories of Celle. One fresh and recent, the other detailed but also vague at the same time.

My new found strength didn't last as long as I'd hoped. After about ten kilometres, I stopped at another roadside picnic area for a break. I didn't dare venture into the surrounding wood.

Another five kilometres further, I arrived in Winsen an der Aller and immediately found a campsite on the shore of the Aller river close to the centre of town. It was still early afternoon, but my conscious and unconscious minds weren't arguing this time, they were too busy trying to remember my first visit to Celle.

It was a friendly site, with a bar, restaurant and shop, so I had no need to go into town. I could just unpack and do nothing for the rest of the day, which suited me fine. I found a lovely shaded spot next to a picnic table to pitch my tent in a totally empty vast field.

I had a simple early dinner in the restaurant and enjoyed a conversation with a young British couple. Later, I watched the sunset with a nice glass of wine before turning in.

All in all, it had been an agreeable day, even though it had its shitty moments.

DAY 34
WINSEN AN DER ALLER– REHDEN

*'If you don't know where you're going,
you might end up someplace else.'
-Yogi Berra*

I was determined to be within shouting distance of the Netherlands border. I set my self a one hundred and ten-kilometre goal to Deipholz. All going well, this could possibly be my last night in Germany. The journey was coming to a swift conclusion. I didn't expect it to end so quickly, which was a sad and sobering thought. On the other hand, I knew that each day was sending my overdraught into the stratosphere.

This would be my longest stint thus far, but it looked like an uncomplicated run. I simply had to follow the 214 all the way. Since I would be on cycle paths, it shouldn't be too much of a hardship as far as I was concerned. I reckoned it was achievable. Being on the same road for the entire day, I wouldn't be so reliant on maps, except perhaps, with the exception of riding through Nienburg. I relished a day without the usual frustrations with my iPhone.

I had grown accustomed to riding in Germany. It was mostly stress-free. When I'm on the paths, the danger of eighteen wheeled leviathans riding, frighteningly close is removed. When I'm off the paths or crossing intersections, I have the right of way, and German drivers universally respect my status with patience.

A relaxed ride on a warm summer's morning was boosting

my confidence. As a committed optimist, I could only see a trouble-free day ahead. And the uneventful forty-five kilometres to Nienburg bore this out. Unfortunately, other plans were afoot for me.

In the centre of Neinburg, the 214 came to an abrupt end at a T junction. There were no signs, it just simply disappeared. I didn't see any signs to Diepholz either. I tuned into Google maps who cheerfully instructed me to turn left onto Route 6. I no sooner turned when motorists began hooting at me and shouting out of their windows. No prizes for knowing what that meant. I immediately got off the road and found a path that ran alongside. OK, back on track, that is, until the path stopped about a hundred metres later. I backtracked and found that the path ran under the road. I followed that to find myself in a residential neighbourhood going in a completely different direction on narrow back roads. I was completely stymied.

Once again, I backtracked to the original T junction. I tried to download different directions, but with the useless German 2G signal, it was hopeless. A familiar sight caught my eye, and I thought it might just be a lifesaver. The Golden Arches loomed about fifty metres away. At least, I could get internet access and sort out an alternative route to Diepholz, for the price of an ice tea.

I used the driving route setting on Google Maps, and I ended up on another autobahn, so I did my search with the cycle setting, knowing full well I would either be waist deep in mud, pushing my bike over boulder-sized cobbles, plagued with aerial attacks from kamikaze black fly's hell-bent on my annihilation or a combination of all three. It seemed to be a more favourable alternative than being on another autobahn.

My new route was quite pleasant. Quiet rural roads took me across the Wesser River and deep into rolling country and through picturesque old villages. I climbed steep hills and took so many turns that I had lost my sense of direction. By the sun's reckoning, I was heading north, then west then north again. This route was also draining my phone battery at an alarming rate.

After two hours of concerted effort, I ended up on Route 6 heading back into Nienburg. I was confused, because, I was led to believe that Route 6 was an autobahn, and here I was riding on a cycle path next to it. I didn't know where to go next, and my phone was giving up the ghost. A few loud curses were directed to Apple, to no avail.

I had no battery. I had no maps. I had no idea where I was. I had no clue how to get to where I should go. I stopped at a crossroad, I plugged my battery pack to the dead phone. It wasn't interested. No charge was forthcoming. I sat there mulling over my non-existent options. Without some sort of direction, I was helpless.

There was a restaurant across the road. I had dismissed it because the car park was empty, and it was dark inside. Obviously closed. I thought that maybe there would be an outside power outlet. I approached, peered into the dark window, and there, sitting at the bar was the chef, reading a newspaper. He caught me out of the corner of his eye.

I held up my phone, he motioned for me to go the door. Luckily, he spoke English. I explained my plight, and could I charge my phone. Of course, he directed me to an outlet. I managed about fifteen per cent charge when the restaurant staff came in. The chef began giving orders and I found myself in the midst of a hive of activity for the evening opening. This was obviously a fine dining establishment, and a sweaty cyclist underfoot was not what they needed.

I thanked the chef for his kindness and asked if he knew of a cycle route to Diepholz.

'Yes. You want to go on the 214.'

'I thought cycles are not allowed.'

'You can ride on it, about three kilometres from here. There is a way to get there only local people know.'

Apparently, there is a section of road where the 214 and 6 meet in Nienburg and carries on for five or six kilometres before they split again. That short section of the joined roads is considered an autobahn. He gave me directions, which sent me over farm trails and paths to the resumption of the cycle-friendly 214. I was on my way once again, surely this would be the last. I managed to find a campsite through Google Maps in Hemsloh, about twenty kilometres away, far short of my goal, but I knew I had met my match.

Hemsloh was a tiny hamlet about two kilometres south of the 214. My battery was gone, but I was confident I would find the campsite in such a small place. I didn't see the usual camping signage anywhere as I rode through the village. I passed a farm and saw the farmer working on his tractor.

'Hi. Sprech English...?

'Nein.'

'Ah. OK. Wo ist campingplatz?'

He looked puzzled. He explained in, I had no doubt, impeccable German, which I only caught a couple of words meaning there is no campsite here. He pointed to the main road.

'Danke.'

I rode to the main road, turned left and continued on towards Diepholtz. I had gone two or three kilometres when I saw a road sign saying: 239 RAHDEN 5KM. 239? Rahden? What happened to the 214? Where is Diepholtz? I could only conclude that I thought I was back on the 214 when I left Hemsloh, but I actually turned left on to the 239 heading south.

I had to turn around once again. The thought of riding eight kilometres back to the 214 was too depressing. I had ridden well over one hundred kilometres already, didn't know where I was and it was now late afternoon. I had no idea where I would end up. I began thinking wild camping, but I was riding through open farmland. I couldn't very well conceal my tent. I had no choice but to carry on in hope.

My left leg and buttock were beginning to ache. Because of my stroke, I hadn't been sitting entirely straight in the saddle. Usually, it doesn't bother me, but this is the longest I've ridden in one day. I didn't want to stop; this was a race against time to find a place to stay before dark.

I reached the 214, turned left and felt somewhat relieved that I was back on track and into the small town of Redhen. I found a supermarket for a few provisions and a break from the bike. I had a noticeable limp which righted itself once I was able to stretch.

As I exited the supermarket, I saw a sign for a campsite. I immediately headed down the side road that it indicated. After about two kilometres, there were no other signs. This was worrisome, how far down this road I would have to travel was anybody's guess. I wasn't prepared to go further in pursuit of a mere possibility. I cut my losses and turned around.

Back on the 214, it wasn't long before I saw another camping sign on the opposite side of the road. I decided to follow it for one kilometre, no more. I rode through a neighbourhood on the edge of Redhen and was encouraged to see another sign at a T-junction pointing to the right. In less than a kilometre down a country lane, I found another sign pointing me up a private drive lined by beautiful mature trees, leading into a lovely period farm. I had come to Ferienhof, and the magic began.

Alan Deakins

I rode up to what looked like the reception, but the door was locked.

'They have all gone swimming. I am waiting also.'

I turned to see a young woman sitting in a pergola.

'Right. Well, I guess I'll wait with you.'

'Have you come far?'

'I've done over a hundred kilometres today.'

'I am amazed! Where are you going?'

'Home to England.'

'Where did you come from?'

'Well…I started in St Petersburg…'

'St Petersburg! Now I am *truly* amazed.'

Greta was instantly likeable. I knew I was going to get along well with her. She introduced me to her two-year-old son, Janis, a lovely boy full of two-year-old life, as he should. She, of course, was completely besotted with him, as she should.

'I just adore this little guy.'

'Really, Greta? I would have never guessed.'

She had driven from Berlin to meet others who were already here, and another friend who would soon be arriving by motorcycle. In the meantime, we would just have to wait for the owners to return from swimming so we could be allocated space.

It wasn't long before Tanja arrived on her motorbike dressed in full leather gear, which seemed incongruous in this thirty-degree heat. She was an exuberant straight forward young woman with a broad all-inclusive smile.

A few minutes later, Stephan, an affable friend of Greta and Tanja approached on a bicycle.

'You can just go ahead and set up. I will tell the owners when they return. It will be alright.'

The small campsite was intimate and inviting under the splendid tall trees. There were many other campers dotted about, but there was an air of serenity that relaxed me straight away. Stephan took us to a spot where Greta could fit her small van into, and in front of it was plenty of space for my tent, and to the side, space for Tanja's tent.

'Perfect, now all I need is a beer.'

'You want a beer? Come to my cabin, I will find you a beer. You can set up later.'

We followed Stephan down a meandering path through the trees to a secluded cabin. On the patio, stood a large table full of wine bottles, flowers and food. Around it were six people enjoying the balmy evening together.

'Greta and Tanja are here! And this is Alan, he cycled from St Petersburg. Steffi, can you find a beer for him?'

Everybody seemed genuinely pleased to welcome me to their table. I was invited to stay for dinner, which Stephan had simmering in a Dutch oven buried under the embers in a fire pit for over three hours.

They all made space for me, and when I sat down, I was no longer a guest. I was part of this close group of three families who have been coming to this spot for many summers. I was immersed in their kindness and generosity.

When it was time to eat, many children from toddlers to teenagers descended upon us adding new positive energy to this special summer's evening. All of my aches, pains and frustrations of the day were washed away with good wine, wonderful food and friendly banter under the stars.

Towards the end of the evening, Greta suggested it would be a good idea if I were to stay for another day to which everybody readily agreed. It was gratifying to know that I had made the right decision an hour earlier.

After dinner, Stephan took me to meet Hartmut and Anette, my hosts and owners of Ferienhof, who were most gracious. Of course, I must stay as long as I pleased as their guest.

I pitched my tent in the illumination of Greta's headlights and crawled in for a grateful sleep. Before nodding off, I mused on my day. Horrible, gratifying, frustrating, rewarding, lonely, full of company. Was it me, my ride or the Samaritans that captured everybody's' enthusiasm? I supposed I would never know. But there was one thing I did know, they had all captured my heart.

Alan Deakins

DAY 35
FERIENHOF IN REHDEN – REST

*'People destined to meet will do so,
apparently by chance,
at precisely the right moment.'
-Ralph Waldo Emerson*

Sleeping in is an idea that always appeals to me. But, an early start was always on the cards, even on a rest day. It's my nature. Besides, I enjoy greeting the morning, even if it means crawling out of my tent on all fours, unsteadily rising onto my feet (sometimes with my bike as support if it is close enough), then limping around a bit while I shake out all of the kinks in my ageing muscles that accumulated during the night.

My first coffee was spent observing the first few of my fellow campers surfacing to greet the day. I hadn't thought of breakfast. I had a few bits and bobs in my panniers but not enough for all of us. It wasn't long before Greta emerged from her van. Janis was still asleep, unusual for a toddler, I thought until she told me he was up most of the night. Still, she was cheerful in spite of her lack of sleep. Tanja soon joined us. Over coffee, I said I would go into town to get breakfast.

'No need,' Greta said. 'I found the bread list last night, and I ordered enough for us all.'

Nice. Nothing to do but relax, which is what we all did. At one point, I had to go closer to the farmhouse to get a strong enough Wi-Fi signal to do my blog for the day. I had just finished when I saw an elderly lady slowly making her way across the field with the aid of her walking frame. She headed straight for me.

'Are you English?'

'I am, actually.'

'Oh, how wonderful. I love to speak English, but nobody will talk to me in English.'

'Come sit down, I'll be glad to talk to you.'

She was Ainne, the charming ninety-two-year-old mother of Harmut. She was delighted to have an English speaker to converse with. It seems that she had connections with British soldiers after the war.

'I had a great friend, his name was Ray Cooper. He lived in Long Melford.'

'Long Melford...? Suffolk...?'

'Yes.'

'I live three miles from Long Melford.'

'Oh my, really...?'

'I know Long Melford very well.'

'I visited there, once. It was beautiful. I remember going to the Thomas Gainsborough Museum in Sudbury.'

'My house is a three-minute walk from the museum!'

'There are many wonderful paintings and drawings there.'

'I know. My wife is a volunteer monitor there.'

'Really...?'

'Really.'

It was astounding. I thought, what are the chances of meeting someone in the middle of Germany with such close connections to my home. By all rights, if I hadn't got lost, or hadn't made a wrong turn, I would have wound up in Diepholtz rather than this remote campsite. What are the odds...? Or, on the other hand, was it destiny? If so, then for what purpose?

I spent over an hour with Ainne. She was full of interesting stories and seemed to have a pressing need to share them. I enjoyed listening. I suppose that is part and parcel of being a Samaritan, that's what I do. I'm a listener. Perhaps her family had heard her tales too many times. I was somebody new to share them with, making them fresh once again for her. I hope so. She had a long and interesting life, and her memory was sharp as a pin.

I remembered Thomas Edison's quote, 'the chief function of the body is to carry the brain around.' Her body had become frail through time, but her brain was still young, strong and agile. She told me what life was like during the war. She described an encampment of British soldiers stationed nearby after the war. It was an enchanting hour, and I felt privileged.

I walked back to see what Greta, Janis and Tanja were up to, and to sort out lunch. I was delighted to see Stephan and Steffi had come to visit and to invite us to dinner. How very kind. We had an agreeable chat over a couple of beers.

I headed into town to get lunch and wine for dinner. The afternoon seemed perfect in every way. It was warm, sunny, I had friends and I was happy.

'Hey, Alan!'

Yvonne was cycling back to Ferienhof.

'Hi, Yvonne. Lovely day!'

'See you tonight.'

'I look forward to it.'

I couldn't conceal my smile. I probably had it pasted on my silly face all the way to the supermarket.

'You're a lucky dude, Deak.'

I felt lucky. But was it just a matter of luck? I didn't have an answer. I've experienced coincidences before without questioning whether it was destiny or a mere chance. But on this journey, I felt something special was happening that I couldn't explain.

Was it a coincidence when I took another wrong turn to find Kathy, Rico, Leni and Moritz waiting at that very rest area to rescue me from the Autobahn? Was it a coincidence that Natasha, whose friend was a cycle mechanic, stepped forward in a crowded market to help? Was it by chance I met Waldek and Tanja on the road, or Manny sharing a dinner with me in an old Russian campground? I have met kind people; generous people; people I consider friends. Are they coincidences?

My destiny? Odd happenings? Or perfectly aligned meetings? I supposed I could ponder this conundrum for the rest of my days.

Life happens. Experiences happen. All the lovely people I had met on this journey came into my life simply because they did. That's all I needed to know. I set out on an adventure, I expected things to happen. And they did. Some aggravating, some enlightening, others frightening, then others wonderful and uplifting. But all of these experiences were extraordinary because I was in a life I hadn't been in before.

It is said that wherever you go, you take your baggage with you. You are still you with all your hang-ups, prejudices, fears and history packed inside you. But with this journey, I consciously decided to do something out of my comfort zone, to be open to something new. I expected the unexpected. I forced myself to talk to others, start conversations. I smiled a lot. I made a concerted effort to be open-minded, non-judgemental and friendly…and just to be accepting, whether it was an experience or another human being.

My teacher once told me that if you want whatever you set out to do to be successful, ask yourself three questions: Will it work? Will it hurt anyone? Will it be beautiful?

So far, this trip has answered all three questions to my complete marvelling satisfaction.

Lunch was simple and, of course, relaxed. Soup, bread, cold meats, salad and beer. A perfect meal under the wonderful mature trees that made Ferienhof so special.

Tanja brought her Trangia spirit burner out to heat up the soup. I had one in my pannier but hadn't used it on this trip because I was happy with my Camping gas stove. I did, however, have an ingenious gadget that consisted of two metal plates that made a stable pot holder for the Trangia. I gave it to her as a present.

After lunch, while Janis was napping, Greta and I went for a walk around the site. She confided in me that when she was younger, she wanted to be a filmmaker. But it didn't work out for reasons that are not important for me to disclose. She asked if I would like to see the one and only film she directed.

'Of course, I do.'

It was a lovely film about a chance meeting between a boy and a girl. It explored expectations in their minds of the meeting. It played on their fantasies. It was nicely crafted and showed a confident knowledge of film language and deftness with directing actors. I was impressed. It was so much more accomplished than my first film.

Later on, much to my surprise, we were visited by Ainne. She had painstakingly made her way over to our camp spot. She wanted me to have a postcard of Ferienhof. It was a sweet gesture that took a considerable amount of effort to deliver. We invited her to sit down with us; I doubted she would have had the strength to go back straight away.

She seemed to relish being among people who wanted to have a conversation with her, especially in English, and were interested in her stories. She grew up here. She told us about her and her husband planting the trees together, and how Ferienhof came to be. Fascinating. I walked her back to her cottage; she was tired and I wanted to make sure she made it safely. I was grateful to meet her. She experienced my home town, and I experienced her home.

The day meandered onward. The lowering sun shone through the trees signalling time for pre-dinner drinks. Perfect hour of the day. I poured wine for the three of us before making our way to dinner.

'I have a present for you, Alan.'

Tanja handed me a neckband with the Indian Motorcycles logo printed on it. I was thrilled. Since this trip began, I had an old bandana tied around my neck, it had seen better days. Her gift couldn't have been more perfect. I would wear it with pride, and as a reminder of the friends I had the good fortune to meet.

A short stroll through the trees brought us back to Stephan and Seffi's cabin. A grand table was laid out once again. The families were gathered around enjoying chilled rose wine, a glass of which was promptly thrust into my hand. How very civilised.

Stephan was delighted to see my new neckband. It seemed that Tanja and he designed it for a motorcycle rally they organised together. Stephan showed me several pictures of the event. He also showed me his and Steffi's home and his various motorcycles in his collection. I showed everyone our house in Sudbury, pictures of Zack's restaurant, and Joseph when he received his Doctors Degree. It was lovely sharing our different lives with one another.

The one thing I've found in all my travels around the world, over ninety-nine per cent of the people I've met on six continents have three things in common. They want to be happy. They want to live in peace. And they want a better life for their kids. That's it. They have no hidden agenda; they have no animosity towards others. They just want to get on in life. Am I being idealistic, or hopelessly naive? Perhaps, but it gives me comfort to see that in others.

We dined well into the night, with much food, wine, banter and laughter. But sadly, I had an early start in the morning. It wasn't easy saying good-bye. We hugged, wished each other well and I parted. I felt a pang of sorrow as I stole myself away. I was on my own once again…as I always have been.

DAY 36
REHDEN – LINGEN

'You guys going somewhere or just going?'
-Jack Kerouac

I woke up feeling home. I didn't have far to go, and this life that I hadn't lived before will end. I would soon pick up the life I was familiar with, and then I would know if this journey had changed me in any way.

It was early. I was the only one awake in the entire site. Coffee was the first thing on my agenda, then I packed my tent and panniers. I was anxious to get started, but I wasn't in a hurry. I wouldn't leave without saying good-bye to Greta, Janis and Tanja. It was OK with me, if my wait meant fewer kilometres today, it would be worth it.

The first sound of awakening was a child in a distant tent. A young life was eager to explore a new day. Little by little, a few people began to emerge from their tents and caravans. I brewed a second cup of coffee.

Greta was the first to rise. She walked over and hugged me.

'Have you had breakfast?'

'I was waiting for you guys.'

'Good. Then we shall have breakfast.'

Tanja was soon awake, and we enjoyed our last few minutes together. Janis awoke before it was time to go, so I was able to say good-bye to everyone.

A hug from Greta.

'I will miss you.'

A hug from Tanja.

'Safe journey.'

A smile from Janis.

I rode out of Ferienhof. I didn't look back. I was alone yet again, but eager to see what was around the next bend. And the only person I would be sharing my discoveries with would be me. I had been my travelling companion for over thirty-five days now, and so far, there had been few arguments. I berated myself a couple of times for taking the wrong turns, or for being a wimp in difficult situations. But for the most part, I had been getting along with myself. I was pleased that my spirits were generally up, most of the time. I was gratified that my body had been able to keep up with the demands I placed upon it with hardly an ache, although there were a few painful moments from the falls I suffered.

'You've done all right, Deak. Well done.'

I was following the 214, and if I had been driving a car, I would not have had any problems, but it doesn't work like that in Germany if you're cycling, at least not for someone like me who doesn't know the system. As I approached Diepholtz, I was no longer able to ride on the 214, instead, I had to follow an old road that led me into the centre. This was not a particular hardship, because it was a rather nice town to ride through. I stopped at a petrol station once to ask directions, but I was able to pick up a cycle-friendly 214 on the western edge of town. I was back onto a cycle path heading west…heading home, and that was cool with me. I expected to reach Lingen early afternoon, which would give me plenty of time to find accommodation and enjoy the warm evening. Wrong again.

Not far from Lingen, east of the small town of Thuine, the road became a no cycling zone once again. So very frustrating. In these cases, Google Maps aren't helping, my offline RideWithGPS maps were totally useless, so I was forced to reckon on my own.

The sun told me I was heading west on back roads, and after a time, I began seeing road signs to Lingen, so I followed them. As I approached the eastern edge, I started looking for accommodation. I found a hotel with an outdoor café, so I stopped for an ice tea, a rest and the use of their free Wi-Fi. I managed to locate a campsite (the only campsite in the area) on the opposite side of town.

My capricious iPhone decided to play ball with me and managed to hold a charge while Google maps cheerfully guided me. Why did they decide to work together at this precise time, I hadn't a clue, and I wasn't about to question their acquiescence to my needs. Lingen was sizeable town, and even though it was pleasant to ride through, I felt an urgency to get there for two reasons. I had a pressing feeling that the clock was ticking, and my left leg and buttock was hurting again.

'Don't blame me for your fucking stroke, Deak.'

Kanucamp was discretely nestled is a small forested site on the bank of the Emse river. I was relieved to find it easily and intrigued by the buzz of all the young people running around. Canoes were being loaded on top of cars. Life vests were being piled high. It seemed chaotic, but harmonious in that everyone looked like they knew what they were doing. There was much chatter and laughter. I liked it straight away. The first person to see me was a young lady.

'Hi!'

'Hi there. May I camp for the night?'

'I'm sure that would be OK.'

'Can I get beer here...?'

'There is no problem with beer. You can get plenty of beer.'

Another young man approached.

'Hello. Where have you come from...?'

'St Petersburg.'

'What...?'

'St. Petersburg...I'm on my way home to the UK.'

'Wow, man. How cool. Respect.'

'Can I camp here tonight?'

'Come. I'll show you who to talk to. We are all leaving soon.'

The young man introduced me to another chap who was busy hanging up life vests.

'Yes. You can stay. We will show you where to set up, and where the key is to get in and out, we are closing, we will all be gone soon.'

'And can I buy a few beers...?'

He pointed to a large glass fronted fridge full of beer.

'Help yourself to as much as you want. Keep the empties, we will count them together in the morning. You pay for what you drink. OK?'

Alan Deakins

OK...??!! More than OK. I was amazed at how trusting they were. The first young man walked with me to the small field where I could pitch my tent. It was like walking through an enchanted village on a cobbled street lined with cabins, strange woodland sculptures of dinosaurs and bears, boat stores and wild flowering plants, all hidden under the thick canopy of the lush wood. It was almost as if I had been shrunk down and cast into an elves' village under a bush far away. I was charmed.

The clearing was at the end of the street. There were two other cyclists setting up their tent. Rubin and Janna were a friendly young German couple on holiday. We chatted as we made out respective camps, and it wasn't long before Rubin and I were walking up the cobbled street to the beer fridge for our first cold drink of the day.

We sat in the late afternoon sun enjoying our beers and each others company, which was great. I wasn't keen on spending a night alone after Ferienhof. Janna went off to find where the showers were. She returned a few minutes later.

'Everyone is gone. I've found the showers. There is also a café on the river bank.'

'Let's have a look.'

The café was brilliant. It was open air with large leather sofas under a veranda. I thought it incredible that we had it all to ourselves...another spot of luck...or coincidence...or a perfectly aligned occurrence. In any event, it was comfortable, we raided the beer fridge and settled in.

'Have you guys eaten...? I'm starving.'

'We have.'

'Right. I saw a supermarket across the road, I'm going to nip over there.'

'It won't be open. It's Sunday.'

Alan Deakins

'Did you already check.'

'Everything is closed on Sundays in Germany. Except for petrol stations. And there is one also across the road.'

I was totally unaware of that fact. I thought about it as I found the hidden key, unlocked the gate and rode to the petrol station. In thinking back, I realised that on the previous Sunday, I was at the campsite in Userin. Because it was my rest day, I didn't leave the site, relying on the little store there. When Marnie and I first came to the UK in 1979, all the shops were closed on Sunday. It was a cultural shock for us, coming from Los Angeles, the 24/7/365 society. You could buy anything you wanted anytime in LA. If you wanted a new car at three in the morning, no problem. Now here in Germany, I'm thrown back 38 years in my memory to North London.

The little petrol station had a small selection of unappetising sandwiches. And an equally small selection of tinned food. And a huge selection of chocolates, sweets and crisps. Not a fresh fruit or vegetable in sight. I really fancied something warm, so I chose a tin of sausages and beans.

I heated my dinner on my camp stove in our exclusive café while we continued our chat. Janna was a social worker, and Rubin had just landed a job as a software developer which he would be starting after their tour. He was such a mellow laid back guy, I couldn't tell if he was excited about it or not. Their story of how they met was charming. Their infectious conviviality was exactly what I needed after tearing myself away from Ferienhof.

We did manage to polish off a few beers. Janna found an ice cream treat in the café's freezer, and the sausages and beans were surprisingly good. We had fun.

Before I turned in, I had a hot shower. I wasn't quite ready to sleep, so I returned to the café and sat in the dark for a time. The whole journey was rolling around in my head. I saw the miles, the rain, the black flies, the seagull thief, the wild boar, the tree-lined roads, small shrines to lost loved ones, the towns and villages. I saw the many faces of people I met. I saw smiles. I saw concern. I saw laughter. I saw empathy. I looked into eyes. So many eyes. Would I, could I remember it all? Forty days happened in an instant. And it was all too full for me to contain.

'Wow, Deak. Wow.'

I was well aware that my journey was coming to an end. I wasn't sure I was ready for it. I loved being on the road. I hated being on the road. I was frightened on the road. I was happy on the road. I was lonely on the road. The road. The road. It had become my life. Riding towards that bend in the road.

But now, I was feeling a force, tugging at me. I was being drawn westward, like a compass, I was compelled to point towards my magnetic field...home.

DAY 37
LINGEN – ALMELO, HOLLAND

'Sometimes I just cry at random stuff.'
-Keith Urban

Rubin and I settled our bill, we were a bit surprised at the amount we drank, but none of us seemed the worse for wear. We said our goodbyes and headed our separate ways. Tonight I would be sleeping somewhere in The Netherlands. I didn't think I would get far due to the heat. It was already in the mid-'20s at 08.00. A clear sky without even a wisp of cloud was a sure indicator the day would definitely be scorching.

I felt different today. I didn't know why. I just had a feeling something was about to happen, and that I should pay attention.

I had stopped at a supermarket for breakfast. An egg sandwich and coffee were enough to set me on my way. I was about to rejoin the main road when I hit a patch of gravel in the middle of the intersection. The front wheel instantly spun at a right angle, sending me over the bars with the bike crashing down on top of me. Pain Central immediately informed me that I was hurt this time. My right leg was burning, but I was tangled with the bike, and I couldn't muster immediate strength to lift it off of me.

I was so concerned with my pain and my inability to right myself that I didn't realise my precarious predicament of being flat on my back on a busy crossroad. A white van pulled up alongside, effectively blocking traffic. A young man jumped out and lifted my bike off of me.

'Danke so much. Thanks...'

'Are you OK? Can you get up?'

'I think so.'

He held out his hand, and his strong arm effortlessly lifted me to my feet.

'Steady. Can you stand OK?'

'Yes. I'm...OK...'

'I will take your bike over there, can you go there?'

'Yes. Danke.'

He walked my bike to a safe spot on the other side of the road with me following. He then pulled his van off the road. All the while, the traffic patiently waited.

'I want to be sure you are OK.'

'I'm fine...really.'

'Sure? Nothing broken?

He wasn't about to leave until I assured him that I was OK. I surmised that nothing was broken, so I managed to convince him that he could go with my heartfelt gratitude. Because of the pain, I was quite concerned about my leg, but I really didn't want to look at it or address the extent of the injury just there and then, so I mounted up and continued on my way. At one point, I did look down at it.

'Shit, Deak!'

A nasty looking raised, red, bleeding and oh so very painful abrasion was throbbing away on the inside of my right thigh.

I thought of retrieving my first aid kit from the bottom of

my pannier but didn't really relish the disruption. It was a basic kit, and I couldn't remember if I had anything packed to soothe a large abrasion.

Nordhorn was a few kilometres away, so I thought it could wait until then. The pain steadily lessened as I peddled. By the time I reached Nordhorn, it was bearable, but my leg was a bloody mess. I found a chemist for antiseptic wipes and a cafe for a cold drink.

With a clean leg and a quenched thirst, I felt better, except for the fact that in checking with my RideWithGPS route, I found I had taken another wrong road, and shouldn't be in Nordhorn at all. I had come too far south. Never mind, The Netherlands was small enough to take another route without much effort. I saw Almelo on the map, which looked like a sizable town and decided to head in that direction.

It was a short ride to the border, where I was directed from the German path along the side of the road into cycling heaven. I had entered the highways and byways of the Dutch cycling network. It was extraordinary. There were cyclists travelling in all directions with ease and confidence. Young, old, singles, families, couples. They knew where they were going; it was like second nature to them. Unfortunately, it wasn't for me. I didn't have a clue which way to turn. There were no familiar road signs for me to follow. I stopped to see if I could make any sense of it with Google maps, but before I could turn my phone on, I was approached by a gentleman.

'Hello. Where do you want to go?'

'Hi there. Almelo.'

'I am going in that direction; you can ride with me for a while.'

'That's very kind of you.'

We rode for about 3 kilometres together. When it came time for him to turn, he pointed along the path.

'Just go straight...you will get to Almelo.'

It seemed easy enough. The path I was riding on ran alongside a tranquil straight canal. There were no cars, nor roads in sight. The only traffic to contend with was the flow of fellow cyclists. Calm, relaxed and worry-free. And oh so very quiet. I loved it.

Every so often I would see a bench or picnic table nicely positioned in the shade. They were obviously very popular as most of them were occupied by other cyclists. I finally found a vacant bench, which was welcomed. I needed a break, and I wanted to have a look at my leg. It was still quite swollen, it looked better thanks to my cleaning it with the antiseptic wipes, and, although still throbbing, felt better also.

Being an exceedingly hot day, the sight of a picturesque café with shaded tables on the edge of the canal was too much to resist. I sat with an ice tea watching the cyclists riding by. It was an idyllic scene, and I felt I could easily be permanently contented by this serenity if it wasn't for the fact that I'm not one for contentment. That bend in the road always has been, and probably always will be, just too enticing.

I reached Almelo just after midday. The ride, although pleasant in many ways (mainly due to the wonderful cycle network) was extremely hot. The temperature, under a cloudless sky, had reached thirty-one degrees. And although I only covered fifty kilometres, I was ready to call it a day. I found a McDonalds for a cold drink, Wi-Fi and cool air-conditioning.

My thoughts turned to the Hook of Holland ferry. I got onto their website to their schedule. There were two sailings a day. The day crossing would land in Harwich around 21.00 which was not ideal. It would be impossible to sort out accommodation or to carry on to home in the dark. The night crossing would land at 06.00 which would be perfect. Unfortunately, that crossing was fully booked for weeks. That was a dilemma. I would worry about it later.

I searched for campsites. Google didn't offer many, but one stood out as easy to get to. I was all for getting settled as quickly as possible, and sit in the shade for the remainder of the day.

'What the hell, Deak. You took the wrong road, you're in the wrong town. What else could possibly go wrong?'

Westerholt seemed a nice enough site as I entered. The reception was behind the bar in the modest restaurant. The young friendly receptionist explained that the majority of the people on this site are permanent residents. Since tent space was limited, she suggested I go to Section S at the very back of the site to find a spot for my tent.

There was a group of eight or nine people sitting in the shade as I entered section S. All eyes were upon me.

'Hey...!'

'Hi there.'

'English...?'

'I am, actually.'

'Where from...?'

'Well...I started in St Petersburg...'

'St Petersburg...??!!'

'Afraid so...'

'You need a beer!!'

They invited me to sit down. And I didn't leave that chair for the next two hours. They were a welcoming, open, inclusive bunch, and by the time it took me to drink half a beer I felt a part of this jovial group. I was one of them, sharing banter, drinking more beers and laughing. Other neighbours joined us, we talked about everything, my ride, Trump, Brexit, Holland, life, the Samaritans. Especially the Samaritans. They were genuinely interested in my explanation of how Samaritans work, how we listen and the power of listening. They were touched that I was riding in support of our branch. So, the conversation got serious for a moment…then we had another beer, and we were all laughing again. I was having a wonderful afternoon.

A couple, Rene and Ingrid turned to me.

'We want you to come for dinner. Will you?'

'I would be delighted! Thank you so much.'

'It will be simple, just pork belly.'

"Fantastic. I love pork belly.'

Rene showed me a secluded spot to set up my tent very near to their cabin. After a quick shower, I joined them and their two children, Joell and Niek for a relaxed and comfortable dinner. They made me feel special. The pork belly was absolutely delicious.

After dinner, we sat in their lovely front garden. I had an interesting conversation with Joell, an engaging young woman who was determined to travel to America to pursue her passion for fashion design. I had no doubt that with her intelligence, and ease of conversing with new people in her life, she would realise her goal. I liked her very much.

Then the surprises happened. Ingrid had surreptitiously posted about me on Facebook, and soon we had visitors. Mandy and her young son arrived with a donation. I was speechless. I didn't expect such generosity.

Then Jolanda arrived with her daughter Bo. When Bo walked

through the gate, I was drawn to her sweet open-faced vulnerability. She seemed a shy young woman, even though she looked straight into my eyes. Jolanda explained that she didn't speak English. No matter. Bo walked straight up to me and held out her arm for me to see. It was covered in scars, obviously from self-harm. I took her hand and stroked her wounds with my other hand.

'Oh, my dear. How are you?'

She then held out her other hand to me. In it were two coasters that she had made, and a €10 note. I was stunned. It was such a simple honest gesture, that reached inside of me and touched my core. I burst into tears. I cried. I couldn't stop. I noticed that Joell and Ingrid were crying, maybe the others were also, I don't know. I was so unprepared for a young unpretentious tormented person, who struggles with terrible haunting relentless voices in her head, to give to me, to be so openly generous. I wished I had something to give in return.

Many donations have been made to Samaritans Bury St Edmunds as a result of my ride. Each one has meant a great deal to me. But this one touched me so deeply I was utterly lost for words. Over the years, I have taken calls from people who have voices inside their heads, telling them they are worthless, telling them to harm themselves, telling them to kill themselves. These malicious voices are real and are almost impossible to shake off. It is a horrible pernicious debilitating circumstance to be afflicted with.

Bo sat next to me for a while. I could see that everybody there cared for her very much. She was understood and supported with love. She finally got up to leave. Jolanda explained that the voices were too loud for her. A final hug and she was gone. She is stoically fighting a difficult battle. I wish her well.

Another friend, Michel, stopped by. He was very helpful in mapping out the best route for me to take to catch the ferry at the Hook of Holland. We were relaxing into another beer when Jolanda returned with a huge packed lunch for my journey. Such kindness and generosity was a wonderful humbling surprise. I was lost for words once again.

Ingrid, Joell and Niek bade me farewell, as they were returning home, leaving Rene alone at the cottage. I would miss them. Their company and kindness were so much a part of this most astonishing day. I stayed with Rene and Michel for one more beer listening to Willy Nelson songs, before turning in. Rene announced that he would be cooking me breakfast in the morning. These wonderful people just couldn't stop giving.

My day had been surprising, eventful, emotionally charged and deeply affecting. I didn't think I could ever forget it. Ever.

My tent was just a few metres away, so I was able to fall asleep to the strains of Willy Nelson, accompanied by Rene and Michel.

DAY 38
ALMELO – ZWEEWOLDE

'You'll never catch a nudist with his pants down.'
-David Letterman

I woke early to write my blog about my extraordinary day. I was half way through when Rene appeared with my breakfast. I didn't want to eat alone, so we returned to his cabin and sat together, he with his coffee, and me with my delicious bacon and eggs. Rene made every effort to see to it that I was satisfied. More bacon? Another egg? Yogurt? He impressed me as a kind-hearted gentle man. I enjoyed sitting with him, talking about the brilliant day yesterday, and the unforeseen day ahead. We were both aware that we needed to get on with this day and that saying good-bye would be difficult, but inevitable.

I packed my bike, and returned to Rene's cabin. He brought out Jolanda's wonderful huge packed lunch, which, I suspected, would keep me going for the rest of my journey. I managed to fit it into my panniers with a bit or re-packing. Then, another surprise, another tender emotionally charged gesture. Rene held out a beautiful orange rugby shirt.

'Orange for Holland. To remember us.'

'How could I forget you all.'

I embraced him. I think he might have been surprised, but I wanted to give him a bit of me, to show him that his thoughtfulness, and generosity, and indeed the whole family's kindness was appreciated beyond words.

As I rode out onto the main road, I could feel the strings of home pulling on me, but I could also feel the strings of so many wonderful people across Northern Europe tugging at me from behind as well.

'You gotta come back, Deak.'

So many feelings were swirling around inside me until I saw that bend in the road. I leaned on my pedals, and headed for it.

Cycling in Holland is a pleasure. Even where there are no specific cycle paths, there are wide lanes painted on the road, and motorists patiently wait until it is safe to pass. The whole experience is calm and reassuring. I've lost track of the number of scary moments with UK motorists. Some have attempted to pass me on blind curves, only to be met by oncoming traffic, at which point, they swerve, forcing me off the road. I've had motorists pass me dangerously close, because they insist on squeezing past while traffic is coming the other way. Or motorists that stomp on the accelerator as they pass to make their distain known to me. All because my presence has inconvenienced them. They are willing to put my life in danger to save a few seconds in theirs. As a cyclist, I find a large percentage of UK motorists, ignorant, rude and dangerous to cyclists.

My final journey on the Continent would take me through Rijessen, Deventner, Apeldoorn, Amersfoort, Utrecht, Rotterdam and finally to the Hook of Holland. It seemed a straightforward journey. I figured that I would have one more night, probably around Utrecht, and sail on the day ferry. Michel's detailed directions were accurate enough to replace the hit and miss maps on my unpredictable iPhone.

Because I was resigned to crossing the Channel on the day boat, I felt I had time to slow my pace and enjoy the scenery. At Deventner, I crossed a bridge high above the Ijssel River which gave me a splendid view of the town on the river's edge. A large yacht passed underneath with several young people sunning themselves on the decks. The thought of Western Europe at peace for seventy-five years entered my mind. How fortunate we are.

I stopped at a roadside picnic table west of Deventner to enjoy a bit of Jolanda's lovely lunch. I've had dozens of sandwiches from cafes, markets and petrol stations since St Perersburg, but I enjoyed Jolanda's more than all the others.

A bit further on, I passed an extraordinary exhibit of three identical dancing fat men statues measuring about four metres high. With outstretched arms, they kicked their left legs high, as if thy were frozen in a nude chorus line. They were whimsical, outrageous and humorous. The laughing Buddha sprang to mind. Like them, I felt like dancing. I was in an exceptionally good mood.

My ride to Apeldoorn was as expected on the dedicated cycleways, except for the fact there were many more cyclists out and about than any other country I rode through. The only problem I was having was dealing with the intense sun. Marnie had been telling me about the heat wave that gripped Britain, and it was obvious that it was also gripping Holland, a short distance across the North Sea. Drinking too much water made me thirstier. For some reason, a cold ice tea seemed to quench my thirst for longer. For that, I was stopping frequently at petrol stations, or markets. I was blowing the budget at one euro a time.

Apeldoorn seemed a very nice town. When I got a bit turned around, I stopped at a bicycle shop for friendly directions. At this rate, I figured I would be near Utrecht by mid afternoon. I would look for campsites then. Everything was going smoothly.

About an hour later, a young man pulled up beside me.

'Hoi...'

'Hi there.'

'I like your mirror.'

'Really?'

'I looked in all the bike shops in Amsterdam for one like that. Where did you get yours?'

'Actually, I got this one in Estonia, but I've seen them on Amazon.'

'I didn't think of that. Good idea.'

He explained that he was planning of a bike tour to Athens. And I told him that I was coming to the end of mine.

'How much further to Utrecht...?'

'Utrecht? We're not heading to Utrecht. We're going north.'

'North...?'

'Yep. Zweewolde is about 20 kilometres.'

'I'm on the wrong road. I'll have to stop and check my maps.'

The wrong road. Again. I seemed to have a habit of ending up on the wrong road. A quick check on Google Maps showed that I was way far off the mark. There was no way that I could make Utrecht by the end of the day. My only alternative was to look for campsites, have a rest, and continue on a new route in the morning. That would mean my spending another night in Holland, not really a hardship.

The two nearest campsites that Google offered up were Natuurcamping and Flevo-nature. I reckoned their names meant one of three things, either they were both camping in nature (which seemed logical since I've seen lots of campsites with nature in their title), or they were both naturist campsites, or finally one or the other was naturist.

Flevo was a bit closer, so I ended up going there. The receptionist was welcoming, gave me directions to the section where tents could be set up, and a key for the unlimited hot showers. Happy days.

As I rode into the site it took a nanosecond for me to realise I had indeed entered a full blown, get-your-kit-off-and-do-everything-naked campsite. People were walking about, playing tennis, cycling, sunning themselves, you name it...all in the buff. I wasn't quite sure I was prepared for this.

'What the hell, Deak. Can't be much different than a nude beach.'

As I rode through the camp looking for the tent section, I started to become self conscious...I was the only one with clothes on, which brought a thought to mind: perhaps people were undressing me with their eyes. Ha! An old man...hardly.

Old Hippie on a Bike

Once I found a spot for my tent, I immediately stripped off before setting up. Straight away, I felt more relaxed. I began to blend in by donning my naked costume.

After pitching my tent, I sat there for a while thinking, "Now what?' I was certainly in an unexpected situation, but in it I was, so I might as well check it out. Because it was such a large site, exploring it by bike would have been an option if I were ready to ride naked. I wasn't overly confident of arranging my accoutrements on the saddle for a comfortable ride, so I slipped into my Birkenstocks, and set off on foot with my wallet and phone in hand, since I had no pockets.

I headed for the centre of the park. The swimming pool was very large, I sat on the edge for a few minutes. The water was inviting, but at the moment, numerous teenagers were having a raucously good time jumping in and out and generally having teenage fun. I decided to come back later with my towel when it was calmer.

A beer was certainly in order, and the market was just around the corner. It was mildly disconcerting as I entered, I've never been shopping in the nude before, and it took a few minutes' adjustment to get used to being in a store full of naked people nonchalantly browsing as shoppers do the world over. The aisles were narrow, and I thought 'how does one get past without accidently brushing up against each other?' But people moved out of the way as I approached like in any shop. I guess our personal bubble radar works with or without clothes.

Silly clichés managed to find their way into my mind. Don't squeeze the melons. What would happen to man-bits if their owners shopped too long in the freezer section? And of course, the obvious sausage department puerility popped up. Oh dear. In spite of my infantile humour, I found a cold beer and a bag of crisps to take back to my tent. When it came my turn at the checkout, I was acutely aware of the juxtaposition between the young cashier sitting behind the cash register in her bright newly pressed uniform, and me standing before her in my well worn wrinkled seventy-two-year-old birthday suit. But I realised it didn't seem to matter to me. I was becoming less and less self conscious.

When I first started walking around, I felt strangely vulnerable being totally au naturel, even though I considered myself a veteran of Parnu Beach. To me, a nude beach was totally different than a nude society. This was a little town, there was a network of small roads filled with people moving about on foot, bicycles, motor scooters and skateboards. Minor streets were arranged in neighbourhoods of numerous pristine cottages, where people were relaxing on their front porches, gardening or chatting with their neighbours over the fence. It was a manicured small community, much like Seahaven Island in the Jim Carrey film *The Truman Show*...except in this town, all of the inhabitants were stark naked...from toddler to ancient pensioner, and every age in between. A naked microcosm of humanity.

And my goodness, humanity was on unabashed display here. I couldn't help but muse on how astonishing the human body is in its infinite variations of shapes and sizes. On a normal street, people can look somewhat similar simply because they dress according to the style of the day, and that determines the look of everybody to a degree. But take their clothes away and, every one is completely different... as unique as a fingerprint. Tall, short, slim, plump, corpulent, muscular, soft, angular, round firm, sagging. Walking, skipping, running, limping waddling, jiggling, bouncing, swaying. It was all exhibited here. And no one seemed embarrassed.

I observed, among other things, a one-legged man walking along on his highly polished titanium prosthetic, a young woman in a wheelchair, a man standing outside his cottage with a catheter fitted and his urine bag strapped to his leg.

These were sights I didn't expect. But why would this community be any different than a clothed one?

It reminded me that we don't have a choice on the machine each of us is allocated to carry our brain around, we just have get on with what we've been given the best we can.

Even in nudity, though, some people are prone to fashion. I noticed I was one of the very few men who wasn't clean shaven... and I'm not talking about my beard. OK, I admit it. I looked. I would defy anyone who says they exclusively maintain eye contact in a nudist colony.

I had the last of Jolanda's lovely sandwiches with my beer and crisps. I tried laying in the sun, and even though it felt good on my back, I'm not one for lounging about. Besides, most of my body hasn't seen the sun in months, except for my short visit to Parnu Beach. My tan was a cyclist's tan, consisting of very dark arms, legs and face, and a pale white everywhere else. My naked costume was indeed different than the completely tanned locals.

I walked back to the pool. Most of the youngsters were still there, but were either sitting on the edge, or chatting in groups in the pool, which gave us oldies room to paddle about. I swam a couple of slow lengths, then just lazily treaded water for awhile.

The outdoor bar and restaurant were next to the pool, so I didn't have far to go for something chilled. I found a lounge chair and leaned back to let my hair dry while I enjoyed a dry white wine. It was a lovely afternoon, and I was relaxed and comfortable in my surroundings. My old sagging battered body, that decidedly leaned to the left thanks to my stroke was still carrying my brain around without too much difficulty. I reflected on what it had been through on this trip; it had endured many physically challenging times and suffered nasty falls that should have broken bones, yet here it was, stronger, with no real pains, sporting a bizarre tan, warming itself in the late afternoon sun.

People began filling the restaurant. I don't know why, but I half expected them to be dressed for dinner. The thought of sitting alone in a throng of naked people wasn't the least bit appealing. I couldn't think of anything more forlorn. In fact, my stay here thus far had been a completely lone experience. In every campsite on the journey, with the exception of the first one in Estonia, I talked to somebody. The past few were absolutely brilliant. But here, I felt alone and isolated. Did our nakedness prevent us from talking to one another? Perhaps naturists aren't so innocent, open and free as they claim. Maybe nudity is really a barrier. All I knew, I would be dining alone back at my tent.

'Just you and me again, Deak. Let's go to the market. Don't squeeze the melons, and stay away from the freezer section.'

The vast majority of my meals on this trip have been solitary, but somehow this one felt particularly bleak. But it was OK, I would be away in the morning. Closer to home. One more night until I catch the ferry…just one more.

DAY 39
ZWEEWOLDE – HARWICH, ENGLAND

*'Time is slipping away,
and I am chasing it, chasing it.'*
-Dev Anand

It wasn't quite 6.00, but already the heat was rising with the sun. I knew that it would be a scorching day. I reckoned it would be a short day's ride, I just needed to get to within twenty to thirty kilometres of the Hook of Holland for the night, then have a short ride to the midday ferry. That was the plan, anyway.

I didn't need to be in a hurry. I had time on my side. I brewed a coffee and enjoyed the warm fresh morning.

I donned my Birkenstocks and headed for a long warm shower. On the way back, I stopped off at the market for breakfast and a proper coffee. I sat at a picnic table and consulted Google maps to sort out a route for the day. It looked like I could reach Leiden without too much effort, which would give me a short run to the ferry the next day. I plotted a route using Google's cycle option…judging from my past experiences, I thought I might live to regret it, especially since the route would take me through forests rather than roads. I pictured myself once again pushing my bike through sand and rocks. But, it was a direct route to the coast.

I returned to the tent to pack everything. As I took down the tent, a neighbour ambled over to see what I was up to. He was a pleasant German chap who was curious about my travels. I wanted to ask him, 'So what prevents everybody here from talking to each other? Is it because we're all naked?' I didn't. It was just nice to have chat for a few minutes.

I had to admit, this wasn't my favourite campsite by any stretch of the imagination. Would I stay at a naturist site again? I wouldn't be against it, but I certainly wouldn't go out of my way to get to one.

I finished packing, got dressed and headed off at the complete mercy of Google Maps.

At first, Google led me down a rural road into the forest. It wasn't long before I was directed onto a dirt path. 'Here we go again.' Less than a kilometre later, I turned onto a paved path about a metre wide, signposted: Almere Haven. Perfect! I followed this path, which crossed several other paths heading off in different directions, each signposted. Even in a remote wood, the Dutch accommodate cyclists. Brilliant.

I eventually came out onto the road travelling along the north shores of Lakes Eemmeer and Gooimeer to Almere Haven. The cycle path was directly on the shore, giving me an outstanding view of all the boating activity as I rode along. After spending weeks travelling inland, it was wonderful to be on a coast. It would have been ideal, except for one thing, there was a strong prevailing westerly wind off of the North Sea, meaning I was pushing against a brisk head wind. There were many wind turbines along the route, all of them working, and all of them facing west. It was lovely to see their huge elegant blades turning in the summer sky, but I was paying a price for this simple pleasure. My legs were tiring. I had to make frequent stops. I was making slow progress, but I was in no hurry.

I reached Almere Haven, a lovely little town on the edge of the lake. The waterfront in the centre of town is quite picturesque, lined with several outdoor cafes. I was tempted to stop, but they seemed a bit too elegant for a sweaty cyclist. Further on, there was a little café off the side of the path, which was part of a windsurfing club. It was rustic, and inviting.

A rich cappuccino along with a homemade cake was a perfect snack. I was able to plug my phone in for a top-up charge, as well use their Wi-FI. I decided to check the availability of the night ferry once again. Damn. Still fully booked. I was beginning to worry a bit. Crossing during the day would be easy, but landing at night would be a huge hassle.

'You don't get if you don't ask, Deak.'

What the hell... a phone call to Stena Line couldn't hurt. I talked to a pleasant Dutch chap who informed me that the crossing was indeed fully booked. I explained why I was keen for the night crossing, and that I had been cycling from St

Petersburg for charity.

'That is amazing. I will make a call, stay with me.'

'Thanks.'

Two minutes later: 'I have managed to find a cabin for you on tonight's ferry. Do you want me to book it for you?'.

'Really...? That would be amazing.'

'OK. Boarding starts at seven o'clock tonight. Final boarding is at nine. You must be there before then.'

'I've got some cycling to do. Thank you so much.'

'Good luck.'

I was so excited. I would be on tonight's boat. I checked my maps. Google estimated it would take four to five hours to cycle the one hundred and eight kilometres. I reckoned that estimation was for a normally fit person on an average day. Being a seventy-two-year-old granddad, cycling in thirty-degree heat, with fifteen kilos of weight on my bike, there was no way I could match that pace.

I so wanted to make the seven o'clock boarding so that I could have a shower, dinner, relax a bit then have a good sleep for the duration of the crossing.

'All you can do is what you can do, Deak. Just fucking get a move on.'

My first hurdle was the considerable Holllandse Bridge that spanned the strait between two lakes: Gooimeer and Ijmeer. The incline to the apex was quite steep, and in my earnestness to cover as much distance as possible, I pushed myself to the limit. When I got to the top, I was breathless, profusely sweating and my heart was racing. And even though the ride down the other side was effortless, I was still shattered from the initial climb when I reached the bottom. This didn't bode well for the rest of the journey. I would have to pace myself better, especially with the rising heat. It was just midday, and already the temperature was in the mid-twenties.

Once across the bridge, the cycle highways were more crowded than I've been accustomed to, I assumed it was because I wasn't far from Amsterdam, the most densely populated area of Holland. It was particularly frustrating that even though I was in a hurry and pushing myself, just about everybody was passing me, making me painfully aware of my feeble limitations. Still, I pedalled as hard as my old body would allow.

At the entrance of the town of Muiden, all the cyclists had to take to the narrow cobbled streets. The cobble was smooth, and bikes had the right of way over cars. How very civilised. I stopped at a small cafe for a cold drink. When I enquired how far it was to Hook of Holland, I was informed eighty-five kilometres. I was worried as I got back on my bike.

'Shit. Almost two hours, and all you did was fifteen kilometres. You might not even get there in time for the sailing.'

Muiden was a beautiful town with narrow streets, and ancient buildings. With so many cyclists, and compliant slow moving cars, I reckoned it would be a delightful place to live. The Vecht River runs through Muiden, and in the centre, there is a swing bridge to allow boats to pass through. Unfortunately, the barriers were down, and it was the turn of cyclists to acquiesce to the river traffic. As much as I was impatient, the sheer scene of the river, the boats quietly passing, the outdoor cafes on either side full of people enjoying the sun captured me. I took it all in, and for twenty minutes, I was travelling again, rather than making tracks to get to somewhere. It was utterly beautiful, and I promised myself that I would return. I almost forgot that I was on a mission, until the bridge swung back and the barriers lifted.

Alan Deakins

I was back at it giving it everything I had, while others casually passed me, even little old ladies. I felt deflated. Granted, many people were riding electric bikes (which were obviously very popular in Holland), but still, most were ordinary cyclists like me. I placated myself by thinking: 'Yeah, but they aren't seventy-two, and don't have fifteen kilos on their bike.' It didn't help, I could feel the night crossing slipping away.

Astonishingly, Google maps, and my iPhone were working. I tried to keep the phone off as much as possible to conserve the battery, and to let it charge via the solar panel, and Google maps was exceedingly accurate in cycle mode, which was a good thing, really, because my route took me through south Amsterdam where there was a vast network of hundreds of cycle paths. In spite of the fact they were all well marked, without local knowledge, I would have easily been turned around. Even with the maps, I took a wrong turning on several occasions, forcing me to back track and lose time.

At one point, I stopped at a market for a cold drink and sandwich, as I sat on a bench eating, I saw a train enter the station across the street. 'There's an idea.' And for the next few minutes, I gave serious consideration to getting on a train to complete the journey.

I finally dismissed the notion for several reasons, namely: I had no idea what train to catch, and checking out schedules would eat up valuable time. The journey might involve more than one change, and wielding a bike around with fifteen kilos on the back from platform to platform would be more difficult than just riding the distance. But the real overriding reason was the fact that I said I would complete the journey under my own steam. A promise is a promise; I couldn't back out on the last day. I jumped back on and doubled down on my effort.

My route from Amsterdam basically followed the A4, and the

Old Hippie on a Bike

N444 bypassing Leiden, every bit of it on cycle paths. Although my run was free from traffic, the heat of the day was taking its toll. I was making frequent stops for drinks. It would have been easy enough if I wasn't up against a deadline.

At one point, I followed a sign, rather than Google maps, when I realised my mistake, I attempted to turn around. My haste, the heat and my weak legs got the better of me at that moment, and I crumpled, landing flat on my back, with my bike, once again, on top of me. I laid there with my eyes closed to shut out the bright sun, to do a quick diagnostic check of all my bones and because it was more comfortable than riding. I sensed a shadow on my face. I opened my eyes to see a woman standing over me.

'Are you all right?'

'I don't know.'

She lifted my bike so I could stand.

'Yeah...I'm...OK. I was in a hurry.'

'You must rest.'

'I will when I get on the ferry.'

'I will hold your bicycle. Drink some water...better?'

'I guess so.'

She handed me a banana from her basket.

'Now...eat this...it is very hot. You must take care of yourself.'

'I'm booked on tonight's ferry.'

'You will get there. How do you feel?'

'Better for having met you.'

And I was better. Much better. Was it the water, the five-minute break, the banana or her kindness that renewed my energy?

North of The Hague, I was directed to take a path that led west, rather than the southerly direction I had been following. The Hague was just a few kilometres south, surely it was best to take the shortest route. I was too tired to argue, so I relented and followed Google. Soon I was riding up and down steep hills which was quickly sapping my strength.

'SHIT. Why did I listen…?'

It became obvious when the North Sea came into view. I would be following the coast to the Hook. The sea was beautiful as the lowering sun reflected off of its gentle waves. And it seemed that thousands of Dutch cyclists agreed. The wide smooth beaches were filled with people enjoying the perfect day, and the parking bays were overflowing with their bikes.

The scene was so stunning, that I had to stop when I saw an empty bench on the top of a dune. I wanted to give my legs a rest for the final push, but most of all, I wanted to have a final look at the beautiful continent that I had traversed.

'Damn, Deak. You did it. You're gonna miss it.'

I would get to the ferry well before the sailing, but I would be late for the first boarding. That would be OK…at least I would be on that boat, and I had the pleasure of the North Sea on my right for remaining five kilometres.

As I entered The Hook of Holland, the sight of the Stena Britannica towering over everything else was exciting. I would wake up in Britain, and be home for lunch. I entered the vehicle gates, rode up to a ticket window and handed my passport to the young lady.

'Ah yes, Mr. Deakins. We have a cabin waiting for you.'

A quick payment with my debit card, an electronic key thrust into my sweaty hand and I was off to board. I could hardly contain my exhilaration. As I approached the boat, I was delighted to see the queue of cars and lorries still on the quay, obviously boarding hadn't started yet. I made my way to the front, and joined several other cyclists.

I talked with a nice Dutch cyclist who was about to explore the UK for a month. I told him about my journey.

'So where will you go on your next trip?'

'I don't know if I have another one in me.'

'You will go again.'

'I'm not so sure. I'm seventy-two.'

'So what? I am seventy-six. You have more trips in you.'

We were given the go ahead to board. I joined the others in riding up the ramp into the belly of the huge ferry. The young seaman in me was reawakened. The sounds inside a steel ship were immediately recalled. It felt familiar, even though this was a ferry, not an old freighter. I've been on numerous ferries as a car driving passenger, but riding a bike into one is awe inspiring. My sense of scale was totally different. I followed the others to a cycle bay, where there were racks and straps to secure our bikes for the crossing. I took my panniers, and front bag with me to the upper deck where my cabin was located. It was two hours away from casting off, so I had plenty of time to shower, and find a cold beer.

My cabin was a study in how to extract the most from a tiny space. It was perfectly adequate in every way. There were two bunk beds, another narrow bed, which was more of a sofa, a vanity unit, and small toilet/shower room. It was sparkling clean, and pressed crisp sheets adorned the lower bunk bed. I was happy. Very happy. I immediately hopped into the shower to wash the day away. I unpacked my only button shirt, zipped the legs onto my shorts and looking as presentable as a cyclist can, headed topside.

The aft deck was outside and crowded with travellers enjoying the evening sun. There is always an expectant atmosphere before a sailing, it is a good feeling. Even as a merchant seaman (working - not holidaying), I loved the feeling as we got underway to the next port.

I ambled up to the bar and ordered a beer. I took it to the upper deck, found a bench and sat. Simply sat. I didn't know how I felt. It's not that I felt empty, or full. It's just there was nothing I needed to add to what I was experiencing just then, except for the cold beer and the gentle North Sea breeze. That was enough. I sat there until, my perception changed. The scene across the channel seemed to be moving ever so slightly. I instantly knew that we had cast off, and were slowly pulling away from the dock. To most, this slight movement would be imperceptible, to me it was the start of the voyage. Ships really don't start a journey; they gently ease into it.

It silently slipped away into the night.

I remember my first voyage on the Samuel Mather as a deckhand. I was given an hour to stow my things before reporting on deck to the First Watchman who set me to work tightening the bolts that secured the hatches. I worked for over an hour before I realised that we had slipped out of the harbour. I was stunned to see the lights on the shore moving along, while I stood on this (what I perceived) immovable deck. It took living on board for a period of time before I got a feeling for the ship...the slight vibration of the engine working away in the bowels, and the faint sounds that a steel ship makes as it travels.

I stayed topside as we left the Hook and headed out into the North Sea. Suddenly, I was starving. I made my way below to find some food. Fish and chips seemed appropriate, along with a chilled chardonnay. Afterwards, I had a stroll around the top deck taking in the North Sea air. Tomorrow I will be home. Home. Home.

In my cosy cabin, I settled between the crisp clean sheets. I lay there in the pitch black feeling the boat like I did fifty years ago when I rode the waves in an old steam ship, reflecting on how I just rode close to three thousand kilometres on an old bike in an old body.

DAY 40
HARWICH - SUDBURY

'Home again, home again, jiggity-jig.'
-Anon

A shudder, and a low boom from within the ship woke me.

'Fantastic!'

A few minutes later, an announcement came through the room's speaker confirming what I already knew. We had landed, and disembarking would commence in an hour's time.

'Right. Time for breakfast.'

A full English breakfast was on offer for £16, which I thought a way too steep for me, so I opted for a croissant, yogurt and coffee from the bar…cost…£10! I nearly fell over. My budget had been blown for quite some time, even so, I hated being so blatantly gouged.

Breakfast wasn't really my first priority. My main interest was to be on the car deck as soon as access was granted, and to be on my way home. I ate quickly, returned to my cabin and readied myself for the final push. I could feel the excitement rising in me. I was a greyhound in the starting gate. Let me go…I need to run, run, run!

By the time I packed, the announcement came that the car decks were open. Naturally, everyone was in a hurry. I had to join a queue at the main staircase, but it didn't take long to reach the deck. I met the other cyclists who were busy untying their bikes and loading up. We wished each other good luck and made our way along the gangway to the top of the ramp, where we mounted up and rode down the ramp onto land and merged with the cars towards the immigration windows.

I love the new customer friendly interrogation chat that UK Immigration officers now engage in, all done in a nonchalant conversational way, as they are scanning and looking through your passport and their computer screens.

'Good morning, Sir.'

'Hi there.'

'Well, Mr. Deakins. Did you have a nice holiday?'

'I did, thanks.'

'Did you travel far...?'

'I guess so. I started in St Petersburg.'

'My, my...that is a long way. It must have been a very interesting trip. And what countries would you travel through to get here...?'

'Let's see...Estonia, Latvia, Lithuania, Kaliningrad, Poland, Germany and Holland, of course, and now home.'

'And where is home, Mr. Deakins...?'

'Sudbury...about forty miles...do you need the exact address...?'

'No. That won't be necessary. Welcome home.'

OK. I was free! The starting gate opened, and I was off and running...at a considerably slower pace than just about any moving thing within a five-mile radius. Still, it was slightly quicker than I had been most of the trip, because I was so close to home.

I have driven back and forth to Harwich several times. I knew the way. I had intended to cycle the A120 out of Harwich to Wix (about seven miles) at which point I would take the back roads to Dedham, Stratford St Mary, Higham, Nayland and Sudbury. It seemed a good plan, except for the fact I hadn't considered the volume of traffic from the ferry combined with rush hour traffic leaving Harwich, the appalling state of the road, the complete lack of any safe room for a cyclist and the rude impatience of UK drivers.

At first, I was pleased to see wide pavements alongside the road as I made my way from the quay. I felt good, my thoughts were of home. It would be a good easy short run. Wonderful.

All that changed as I turned onto the A120. The pavement ended abruptly, and I rode into a cyclist's nightmare. A high curb lined the side of the road, less than a metre from that was the white perimeter line. Between these two was a filthy trough filled with litter, broken drain covers and dirt. I had to straddle the white line to keep my pedals from catching on the curb, which would cause me to fall. Behind me were huge lorries, vans, cars and motorcycles impatiently waiting for a break in the oncoming traffic to pass me.

I was feeling enormous pressure. All I could do was keep my head down, avoiding the abysmal broken road surface and keeping my left pedal clear of the dangerously close curb, and ignoring everything else. When a lorry did manage to pass me, it would be frighteningly close, due to the narrow road, and the merciless oncoming vehicles. On a few occasions, they would have to pull back into their lane unexpectedly forcing me swerve perilously into the cluttered gutter.

A few of the car drivers' patience began to wear thin, so some of them didn't wait for a break in the oncoming traffic, they just forced their way past, giving me a few centimetres space, instead of the metre and a half that the law requires them to do. Sadly, they were invariably British.

'Shit! Oh shit! Oh SHIT!!!'

For the first time on this entire journey, I feared for my life. I was truly terrified. And there was nothing I could do about it. There was no place to stop, no space to pull over. I was at the mercy of people who were willing to dice with my life to save a few seconds in theirs. And all I could do is stay on that white line...don't veer off the fucking line. My hands began to ache from gripping the handlebars so tightly. I broke into a sweat, not from exertion, but rather a cold sweat of fear.

I came across a tiny patch where thankfully, I could safely pull off the road. I had to check Google Maps to find a way out of this. My hands were shaking so badly; I couldn't use the touch screen. I found a place to sit behind a hedge. I closed my eyes and tried to shut out the thundering traffic next to me. Not a chance.

'C'mon, Deak. There's a way out. There's gotta be a way.'

Google maps showed a route through back roads to Dedham, which was fantastic, except that I would have to travel on this road for another kilometre.

'SHIT! Well...you gotta do it...'

I got back on the bike and looked for a space in the traffic to straddle the white line once again...but there were no gaps big enough for me to safely join the road. I sat and waited. Finally, there was a small gap, between the car that just passed me, and the huge approaching juggernaut.

'Fuck it!!'

I help up my hand with conviction, the lorry flashed its lights, I took that to mean he understood, so I began riding. He followed me for about half a kilometre until he found a big enough gap in the oncoming traffic for him to pass me with a wide margin. Once safely in front of me, he flashed his blinkers. I waved my thanks. He was from Belgium.

Another half kilometre, and I had to cross the road for the turning. I knew I just had to do it in spite of everybody on the road and not be intimidated. I held out my right arm, turned into the middle of the road and stopped. The lorry behind me also stopped, and waited for a gap for me to cross. Finally, an oncoming car flashed his lights, and I crossed onto a sleepy country road. Relax.

Relax hell. It seemed this was a rat run for the rush hour commuters off to work trying to beat the traffic of the disgorging ferry and a slow ancient cyclist. I was well aware of how fast people travel on these narrow lanes, as if they are the only ones travelling on them. I have learned from experience from riding the lanes around Sudbury what to expect and how to fend for myself. I sometimes wonder if UK drivers lose all sensibility when confronted with a cyclist, or are some of them just permanently clueless.

I stopped in a petrol station in the village of Lawford, for something more substantial than a croissant and yogurt. The cashier told me of a quieter way to Dedham. This road, although a bit hilly was a welcome relief from the constant onslaught of cars. Once in Dedham, I was in familiar territory. I knew of all the back roads to Sudbury.

Through Stratford St Mary, up Gun Hill past the La Tollbooth Restaurant, where Zack got his first Head Chef position, on to Higham, up the long hill to Stoke by Nayland. Closer, closer. I am so close to home.

Onto the A134 Colchester to Sudbury road, a narrow fast, very cycle unfriendly road. I didn't fancy risking life and limb again, so I turned off as soon as I could to Assington, and took the back roads to Great Cornard...less than two miles to go.

I felt quite emotional as I entered Sudbury. Although I would have one more day's travel to the Samaritan's Centre in Bury St Edmunds, Sudbury was home, so essentially, my journey was coming to an end. I would be exiting the forty-day life I had lived, and re-entering the life I've always known.

Turn onto Eastern Road, then onto Station Road. I was quietly slipping in. No one took notice, no head turned as I passed. Just another inhabitant of Sudbury cycling along. Left onto Friars Street. Another hundred metres to our drive. I dismount push my faithful bike into the courtyard, and close the gate.

I'm home. I'm home. Home.

DAY 41
SUDBURY – BURY ST EDMUNDS

*'Don't cry because it is over.
Smile because it happened.'
-Dr Seuss*

It was six days before I made the final leg to the Samaritans in Bury St Edmunds.

There were a few reasons for the delay. First, I thought I would need recuperation time, which really wasn't necessary. I felt fine, my body had coped well.

Second, Gordon wanted to organise a reception at the Samaritans.

And last, and most importantly, our second granddaughter, Evelyn, made her appearance into the world.

There is nothing more wonderful than holding a new-born in in your arms. New and pure. I couldn't help thinking of the tragic death I witnessed on the road from St Petersburg to Estonia. Life is amazing in how it is resolutely renewing itself at every opportunity.

Charlotte and Evelyn are wondrous, joyous additions to our lives, and I'm so gratefully glad to be their 'Grampy'.

Alan Deakins

The thirty-two kilometre ride to Bury St Edmunds was on quiet country roads. I thought of making this last ride easy, by not fully loading my bike, but decided against it because I felt it would be cheating. Also, I thought people would like to see my bike in full travel mode. I had ridden this route before, so I knew what to expect. No nasty surprises. I remembered it as a lovely country jaunt.

Part of me was looking forward to it, another part was dreading the fact that in a few hours it would all be over. In all honesty, I wasn't sure if I was prepared for that.

But, once again, I was on my bike riding on a mostly shaded country road on a balmy day...the final leg of the entire journey.

As I rode through Long Melford, I caught a reflection of myself in a shop window. I looked glum.

'For fuck's sake, Deak. Cheer up.'

Exactly. Cheer up. It was a beautiful day. I was off to see friends and colleagues. I helped raise funds to keep Samaritans Bury St Edmunds alive, and if I made good time, I would have a beer with my son. What's not to look forward to?

I had given myself plenty of time for my final push, judging from the last time I had done this route, it was an effortless pleasure. The one thing that I didn't factor in on this particular run was I was considerably fitter now. I passed through the pleasant undulating countryside much quicker than I estimated. I arrived at the edge of Bury St Edmunds well over an hour early for my scheduled 'arrival'. Terrific!

Zack's restaurant, 1921 Angel Hill was less than three hundred metres from the Samaritans Centre. Since I was so early, there was nothing for me to do than to make that serendipitous stop for a cold beer. I knew I would be stopping, but Zack didn't.

There is a window between the kitchen and the restaurant, and when he saw me enter, he rushed out to greet me with his usual hug.

'I've come for a beer.'

Jamie, the head waiter, placed a cold one on the bar for me. Zack and I had a quick chat. As usual he was frantically busy, and on top of that, exceedingly tired thanks to Evelyn who had a penchant of being boisterously awake in the wee hours. He returned to the kitchen to prepare for lunch, and I sat at the bar with my beer.

I looked out of the window at my bike. It had been remarkably reliable on the journey. It never let me down. Even with a broken back hub, it held on until I was able to ride to a cycle shop for repairs. Don Quixote had Rochinante, Roy Rogers had Trigger, and I had: Bike. OK, even though I didn't have a pet name for it, I had grown extremely fond of it.

'Another small one…?'

'I've got time, Jamie. Why not?'

The whole journey was washing through me. The good times, the bad times, the unexpected times. The welcomed times. The happy times. The frightening times. The lonely times. I saw faces. Generous faces. Kind faces. Happy faces. Concerned faces. Sad faces. So many wonderful people filled my days, gave me company when I was alone, came to my aid when I was vulnerable, laughed with me, cried with me, and helped me on my way. All because I was a fellow human being on the face of this planet. I loved it. I didn't want it to end.

I looked at my watch. No matter what I wanted, the time had arrived.

I walked into the kitchen to embrace my son.

'I'm off.'

'OK. I hope there's a crowd waiting for you.'

'Thanks.'

I didn't say more. I couldn't. I would have burst into tears.

The last three hundred metres was a chance to regain my composure, which was easy enough to do since I needed all my faculties to ride in the busy Bury St Edmunds traffic.

I turned off Northgate Street into the Northgate Business Park, around the bend, and there were several of my fellow Samaritans waiting for me with welcome banners and a bottle of bubbly.

Marnie was there, along with our neighbours John and Jude, and our friend, Barbara. I was particularly pleased to see Joe, a young waiter at Zack's restaurant. There was also a reporter from the East Anglian Times, so I reckoned I would get my fifteen minutes' fame.

Joe was kind enough to help me load my bike into the car, then Marnie drove us home.

It was done. It was finished. That life I had lived for forty days was over. It happened. I was grateful it happened. I was glad it happened. But equally, I was grateful and glad to be home with those I loved, in a neighbourhood filled with good friends. Soon I would be back on the lines at the Samaritans.

Alan Deakins

Now this life, the life that I've come back to, is happening.

AT THE END OF IT ALL...

*'If an ass goes travelling,
he will not come home a horse.'
-Thomas Fuller*

Months have passed, and I'm still full of my journey.

It raised over £6000 for Samaritans of Bury St Edmunds and West Suffolk. Donations came in from all over the world from people I haven't seen for over forty years, people I encountered on the road, people who heard about it from friends and people I never met who stumbled across my journey online. I was truly amazed and humbled. My heartfelt gratitude goes out to every one.

Equally important, I feel my journey has raised awareness of the essential work The Samaritans do to help people who can't cope in their lives, which is also gratifying.

I feel extraordinarily privileged to be a Samaritans listener, and to be back on the line.

Did I come back an ass, or a horse?

I disagree with Thomas Fuller.

Alan Deakins

This journey, my journey, my forty-day life has had a profound effect on me. How could I return as the same person?

I made it thanks to a seventy-two-year-old cussedness. My equally aged brain carrying machine complied with few aches or pains. And the memories of the extraordinary people I met along the way are deeply imbedded within me.

I'm still an ass, but I am fuller. I am richer. I am another step closer to being complete.

And for the most part, I'm satisfied with that.

But every so often, a memory wanders into my mind of the time I was waiting to board the ferry home. And the voice of the Dutch cyclist quietly reminds me:

'You have more trips in you.'

Old Hippie on a Bike

CYCLING ON A BUDGET – OR NOT

*'If you budget carefully
and watch your expenditures,
you can get by on a couple billion dollars.'
-Ted Turner*

DAY-TO-DAY SURVIVAL

I started on this trip woefully underfunded. I hadn't fully considered how much it would cost me. Since my initial plan was to wild camp all the way, I figured it would be cheap travel. I also figured that with careful shopping, I could get by on less than £5 a day for sustenance.

I hadn't considered three things.

First, wild camping isn't for everybody, I'm one of them. As much as I like my own company, being with only me twenty-fours a day is excruciatingly tedious and lonely. I found fighting traffic all day then doing hand-to-hand combat with mosquitos all night particularly wearing. Also the distinct lack of toilet or washing facilities made travelling distinctly uncomfortable. As well as feeling dirty, I'm sure I probably assaulted others' sense of smell as I approached. All of this made the trip more of a tiresome chore rather than an adventure.

Also, there were times when I was just too tired, or the weather too inclement, or there wasn't any suitable hiding spot to securely camp in reasonable comfort. At these times, a room was necessary.

As it turned out, of the forty nights I was away, twenty-two were under canvas, four of which were wild camping.

Secondly, I didn't realise that my appetite would grow so much. I became an eating machine. My body was in need of constant fuel. With only a small camp stove, my options of making meals were quite limited, so I ate a lot sandwiches, convenience meals, and expensive snacks such as nuts. Of course, I would shop in markets as much as possible for fresh food, but there were times when I only had access to a petrol station, which is more expensive. And understandably, there were times when a café or restaurant was the preferred option simply to make the journey more enjoyable.

Lastly, I hadn't counted on the number of times I would stop for refreshment. I visited just about every petrol station along my route. The weather for the most part was hot, so cold drinks were frequently necessary. If it was raining, hot drinks were needed. And almost always, a break from the tedium of the road and another human to say hello to was most welcome. I found that warm water, although hydrating, didn't cut my thirst, whereas, a cold drink and a bit of a break would revive me more. For that reason, I spent more than £5 a day that I hadn't budgeted for.

In hindsight, if I had wanted to make drastic savings, I would have wild camped the entire way, exclusively eaten simple meals cooked on my camp stove, avoided costly snacks and consumed only water. But if I had to to all that, I'd rather have not made the trip.

If I do decide on another tour, I will factor in my preferences for travelling, and save enough accordingly to pay for them before I set off.

It's difficult travelling with worries of what you will face financially when you get home.

GEAR – WINNERS AND LOSERS

I realised that the success of my trip would largely depend on the gear I decided on. Being on a budget, I had to weigh up price vs performance of all the items that would accompany me on the journey.

While top end gear would have been preferable, such as Ortleib pannier bags, I set out to find similar products that would effectively perform as well at a smaller price.

I was a complete novice in equipping myself. I read several blogs, and viewed countless YouTube videos for advice, all of which made me more confused. What works for some doesn't work for others, perhaps because of price, preference or availability. The best outcome of my research was to figure out what items were necessary for the journey, and what I should reasonable expect from them within my budget.

In choosing my gear, I honed my priorities down to a short list:

- Price.
- Availability.
- Quality.
- Performance.
- Weight.

I figured if something was inexpensive, but poor quality, then it wouldn't last. Or if something was good but would take months to ship from China, it wasn't worth the gamble. If something was high quality, but much heavier than more expensive rivals, perhaps it would slow me down. On and on. I tried to find acceptable compromises that would enhance my trip without breaking the bank.

What I ended up with was a travelling kit that suited me personally and was comparatively inexpensive. Most of it worked satisfactorily, some of it didn't. Herewith is my list of Winners and Losers.

WINNERS:

Dawes Sonoran Hybrid Bike.

To be fair, I didn't go out to source this with the express intent of riding it on this particular trip. I already had it for over a year before deciding to tour. After a lot of riding, I adapted to it, thanks to a few modifications. It was at least fifteen years old, so not the lightest machine by any stretch of the imagination, but it was sound, sturdy, cheap and readily available. I had paid £80 for it on eBay. I also trusted it.

It proved to be a comfortable, reliable and agile bike. I grew quite fond of it. And it proved to me that you don't have to spend thousands on a touring machine.

Brooks Flyer Saddle.

The one thing I gleaned from all the blogs and videos is that the saddle is one of the most important items.

The original padded Dawes saddle was comfortable for about five miles, then discomfort increased with each succeeding mile. I tried several other saddles with little success, until I heeded most peoples' advice: get a Brooks.

I decided on a carved Brooks Flyer. Carved meant that there was a cut-out in the centre of the saddle that supposedly relieved pressure on the prostrate. It was also sprung, which would help smooth out rough terrain.

Starting retail price was in excess of £100, but by frequenting eBay, I managed to find a second hand Flyer for £46. It was one of the best purchases I made. For the most part, I was comfortable except for very sweaty days, or when my left side bothered me because I had a habit of sitting off-centre, but that is due to the effects of my stroke, not the design of the saddle.

Overall, this was an excellent purchase.

Schwalbe Tyres.

Tyres can make of break a tour. They account for reliability, comfort and safety. A lot of cyclists insist on belt and braces by buying the heaviest and sturdiest tyres along with puncture proof tubes. Others opt for extremely expensive tubeless tyres and rims for peace of mind.

My Dawes came with fairly worn Schwalbes, which seemed the brand of choice for most cyclists, so I was inclined to stick with the brand. It seemed that the most puncture proof Schwalbe was the Marathon Plus, which, unsurprisingly, was the most expensive. They were also the heaviest by a long way.

I had heard good things about the Marathon Supreme on bike forums, at half the weight. I wanted the widest tyre available that would fit my rims for comfort. I found an end of stock pair of 700cX42 tyres on eBay at half price. I was shocked at how thin and flimsy they seemed when they arrived. At first I thought they might be counterfeit, so I took them to a local cyclist who was a wheel specialist. He assured me that they were genuine, and that he used them on local trails and rough terrain without a problem.

I decided to go with them, but at the last minute I found a used Schwalbe 700cX42 All Motion tyre on eBay. This tyre was a bit sturdier without excessive weight. I rode the entire 3,000 kilometres with the Marathon Supreme on the front and the All Motion on the back. They proved comfortable and reliable. The only puncture I got was when Rico accidentally poked the Supreme in Germany.

My £3 Halford's Basic inner tubes also performed well without any issues.

Panniers.

The Gold Standard of pannier bags are roll top German Ortleibs. I couldn't afford the £100-120 price tag. I diligently searched eBay for a second hand pair with no luck. So I opted for a pair of similarly designed, made in China Ross Bros bags at £46. The quality was impressive.

They performed well for the entire trip, keeping my things perfectly dry, except for the heavy downpour in Germany. I opened one to get my waterproof jacket, and didn't close it properly resulting in extremely wet contents. My fault, not the bag's.

Tent.

I looked at scores of tents. The three main factors in my final choice were room, weight and price. I read many reviews on Amazon, eBay and various forums.

I needed a tent that I could sit up in, and was big enough to accommodate me, my two panniers and my handlebar bag. I also wanted it to be lightweight. All the preferred tents that met my criteria were very expensive. I really couldn't justify £200 plus for one.

I finally decided on the Yellowstone Alpine tent at £27 from an online camping store. All the reviews I read singled out two points where it tended to rip, and that the woefully weak fibreglass pole would eventually break. I glued nylon webbing patches on the two weak points, and purchased aircraft aluminium tent poles on eBay for £8 which I had a friendly mechanic at my local garage cut to the exact lengths of the original segments that came with the tent. Resulting is a very sturdy tent that weighed 1.7 kilos for £35.

The tent performed well. It was strong, weather proof and roomy. It was a bit of a chore to roll up each morning, but a small price to pay for such good performance.

Sleeping bag and mattress.

I knew that the night temperatures would probably get warmer as I progressed southwest through the summer. I thought one 3 season bag would be overkill, expensive and heavy.

I had heard good things about SnugPak bags, and upon further research of their products, I decided on their Jungle Bag, at 800g and a Jungle Blanket at also 800g. I figured when it was cold, I could sleep with the blanket inside the bag, and on warmer nights use one or the other. I managed to find second hand bag and blanket on separate eBay auctions for less than £25 each. I ended up with a compact, comfortable and versatile sleep system that served me well for the entire journey, there were a couple of nights where the addition of a fleece was necessary, but all in all I was happy.

I also found a lightweight mattress by NatureHike on Amazon that inflated with a separate bag, so I didn't have to blow it up with my own breath. It weighed in at 750g, and was a bit pricy at £35, but totally worth it considering the convenience of inflating it with the included bag every night.

Generic 3 Panel Solar Charger.

Zack knew I was amassing bike stuff for the journey, so he kindly asked what I wanted for my birthday. A solar panel, please. He found a good 20W folding panel on eBay that worked admirably well. Rain, shine or overcast, I could count on a charge. It was willing to charge my iPhone, and my iPhone was willing to accept a charge for the first part of the trip. (See Losers).

Merino Wool T-Shirts.

I managed to find three T-shirts online as an end of stock sale.

They were approximately £12 each. Merino wool is noted for its anti-bacterial properties, namely you don't pong as readily as with other materials. They are also quick drying.

I was more than impressed with them. When I had access to a shower, I would take the one I was wearing in with me, and wear the other while the showered one was drying. This system worked well.

Top marks for them.

Kerimor convertible trousers.

These were simple lightweight polyester trousers with ample pockets and zip off legs that converted into shorts. I found two pairs in my local Sports Direct store for £19 each. That was all I needed for the trip.

They were comfortable, quick drying and very light.

Camp Stove.

I found a micro-light stove on Amazon that required a camping gas bottle. It was unbranded but only £7 with next day delivery. I also ordered a small gas cartridge. I tried it out the next day, and was pleased with its performance. I bought a gas canister for it in Russia that lasted the entire journey. It was trouble free with daily use.

Leatherman Multi-Tool

My sister-in-law was once employed at Leatherman in Oregon. One Christmas, over thirty years ago, she gave me a medium sized Leatherman that boasted the usual array of blades plus sturdy plyers. It was perfect for my needs and still useable after all this time. Leatherman quality is unbeatable and I think it is worth the extra money over cheap knock-offs.

Birkenstock Arizona Plastic Sandals.

Joseph gave me a standard pair of Birkenstocks for Christmas two years ago. I loved their fit and comfort. I wanted to take them with me, but they were heavy, and the leather tops were not suited for showers. I found a used pair of plastic "Birks" on eBay for £15 of the same design.

At less than 300g they were the perfect lightweight travelling sandal. I had a substantial pair of Karimor walking/cycling shoes, but I found that the warmer the weather got, the more I wore my "Birks" on and off the bike. Highly recommended.

LOSERS:

Lycra padded shorts.

I read so much about padded shorts and peoples' obsession with their chamois (the padded crutch area). I've also seen, ad nauseam, guys strutting around in their lycras displaying more than I cared to see.

I learned early on that the chamois was not for me. I was distinctly uncomfortable with the padding bunching up in my nether region and finding its way into crevices I didn't want it to be in. I cut the padding out, and rode with only the lycra shorts under my Karimor shorts, I didn't need to display the lunch box. It was much more comfortable for me. On the journey, however, I found that I was sweating profusely in the hot weather. The lycra became unbearable. One one particularly hot day, I ducked behind a bush, took them off and rode commando in just my Karimor shorts.

I threw the two pairs of licra shorts I had in the first bin I came to and never looked back.

LowePro Classified 140 Camera Bag.

I chose this bag because it was compact, easily mountable onto my front rack and padded to protect my cameras, iPad and Kindle. It also had the benefit of a waterproof cover that stowed away in the bottom.

It worked well until I was caught in that terrible downpour in Germany. Even with the cover, everything inside was soaked. My Panasonic GM1 camera was ruined. Luckily, I had sent my iPad and GoPro cameras home otherwise they would have suffered the same fate.

This bag let me down (in the words of Donald Trump) "bigly."

Ride with GPS.

This programme was useful in creating a route for the entire journey. I was also impressed that I could download it to follow offline with the GPS in my iPhone.

I assumed it would work like an ordinary satnav, where it would offer up an alternative if I wandered off course. It didn't. It would make a annoying noise until I found my own way back on course. I found this extremely frustrating. I ended up only using the route I had mapped out as a guide, and relying on Google maps, paper maps, and the sun to keep me in a general direction.

This is not remotely a satnav app. Frustrating and annoying.

iPhone 6s.

My O2 contract was completed with my iPhone a few months before the trip, so I didn't have to fork out for a new device. It was working well, kept a good charge and to my mind ideal to take along for maps, GPS, blogging, calls and texting. What more did I need for no added expense?

And it did what I expected it to do. When it was attached to my solar panel, I had a constant screen and unlimited access to Google Maps. All was rosy, until I upgraded my IOS at the insistent badgering from Apple. From then on, it refused to charge reliably via the solar panel, while it was turned on. When it was plugged into the panel, a window would constantly pop up saying that the device (my panel) was not compatible. I missed crucial directions due to this new madding occurrence. I began to curse Apple. I hated my phone.

I learned that the new IOS had a security setting that didn't allow non-approved devices access. I couldn't turn this setting off, and I couldn't return to the older IOS. I was in the middle of the Baltics, where the hell would I find an Apple approved solar panel…? Even if I could, would I be able to afford it?

It seems to me that Apple is anally retentive about security. It is my phone, my privacy, why couldn't I set the level of security I wanted.

Apple left me high and dry.

I hated my phone and Apple by the end of the journey, and promptly bought an Android Huawei P20 Pro on my return. It works perfectly with my solar panel, thank you very much.

TWO PENNIES WORTH

'Advice is a form of nostalgia.'
-Mary Schmich

*'I don't think I could give advice
to my younger self
because she probably wouldn't listen.'*
-Annie Leibovitz

I hope it is clear by now that I don't consider myself an enthusiastic cyclist. I've completed one journey, which was not an arduous record breaking undertaking, nor was I the oldest to do a long tour. Perhaps I could claim some sort of record for doing it after having a stroke, but I doubt it.

Which begs the question: am I really qualified to offer advice, or am I still a novice? I will leave that to you.

I was hoping to pass on practical how-to advice as an older cyclist, but to tell the truth, I didn't feel particularly old. Even if I could offer it, I'm sure there is someone in a forum or YouTube video that could advise more eloquently than I can.

I will, however, share some insights about my approach to cycle touring and about what was going on inside me while on my journey. Think of these thoughts as reflections of my personal learning curve, rather than advice. I can't tell you what is right for you. I can only relate what was right for me. Except for my thoughts on helmets.

WEAR A HELMET. I met so many cyclists in the UK and on my tour that don't wear helmets. They are, in my opinion, utterly stupid. The attitude 'Nothing will happen to me,' is naïve. I'm sure that poor Lada driver in Russia thought the same thing before his demise.

Last year, I was riding on a trail near home away from any traffic. Without warning, a dog ran out from the underbrush and straight under my front wheel, sending me over the handlebars. The first thing to hit the rock hard ground was my head. My helmet was badly dented, and I had a headache for hours afterwards. I'm convinced my helmet saved me from a serious injury, possibly from losing my life.

Need more? Joseph, my younger son, is a Clinical Psychologist who works with brain injured people, he could tell you of lives ruined from head injuries that might have been prevented with proper protection.

So please, DON'T BE STUPID…WEAR A FUCKING HELMET!

LOOK AFTER YOUR ASS. I'm thoroughly convinced that your mental attitude is directly linked to your bum on a cycle tour. Comfort in the saddle is everything. If your backside hurts, your tour will be a misery. Find the saddle that is right for you. Spend time with it, make sure you can spend hours on it. If it needs breaking in, do it before you set off, not on the trip.

Sort out your wardrobe, if a chamois is the thing that makes you comfortable then go for it. If it doesn't, then go without it in spite what other cyclists advise. It's your bum, you will know what's needed to make you comfortable.

LOVE YOUR GEAR…BUT DON'T BE AFRAID TO GET RID OF STUFF. Choosing gear to do the job is important. But keep in mind, you will be living with it for quite a while and your enjoyment of your tour will largely depend on it. I chose my tent not only for weight and price, but also because I enjoyed being in it. I grew terribly fond of my bike. I liked the look of my Gortex jacket. I loved the feel of my SnugPak sleeping bag and quilt. To me, it was important to be emotionally, as well as practically, attracted to the items that travelled with me.

But, when I realised that my iPad and GoPro cameras were a burden, I didn't hesitate to ship them home. I also sent my Gortex trousers and waterproof socks in the same package because I got along fine without them. I binned my uncomfortable lycra shorts.

AGE IS IRRELEVENT. If you feel up to it, and you think your body is capable, then why not? Don't miss the chance to do a tour simply because you think you're too old. When I was travelling, I met people older than me on longer tours. If you want to do it, consider it, think it through and make your decision based on your desire and determination. If you decide not to, don't let your age be the reason.

KNOW YOUR LIMITS...THEN PUSH YOURSELF. I am not a marathon cyclist. I am not Tour de France material. I am not a speed cyclist, nor a mountain biker. I travel at the speed that suits me for as long as I'm comfortable. Which is one reason I ride alone. I fear I would hold up the group if I joined a cycling club.

When I first started riding, two miles would have me winded, and my legs feeling rubbery. I worked my way up to fifteen miles a day. I forced myself to ride longer between breaks. It soon became apparent to me that I could influence my body to do more without doing it damage by willing it to go along with my plans.

This became necessary many times on the journey where simply stopping wasn't an option.

TRAIN YOUR MIND...YOUR BODY WILL FOLLOW. I'm often asked, 'How hard did you train?' Actually, I did very little physical training. I rode daily, but only for ten to fifteen miles (sixteen to twenty-four kilometres). I knew I would have to do at least double that every day on my tour. I made the decision that I would, and promised to myself.

On my daily rides before the journey, I imagined I was somewhere between St Petersburg and Bury St Edmunds. I already had an idea of what the roads were like because I rode the entire route on Google Maps (except for Germany) via the street view facility. That really helped me to acclimatise my mind to the journey.

My body doesn't make decisions. Its job is to carry the decision maker around. Of course, I was constantly monitoring my physical situation, but by the time I had to come to a decision to do the trip, my body was no longer a factor in the final consideration.

My mind was going…and my body would just have to carry it.

HONE YOUR SPIRIT. It's impossible to be an eternal optimist, especially on a bike tour. It helped me to remind myself daily that I was doing something different and extraordinary in my life.

'Look at you, Deak. You're actually riding in Russia!!'

I would frequently pat myself on the back, tell myself, 'Well done, Deak,' out loud.

GROW TO LIKE YOUR OWN COMPANY. Be prepared to be alone most of the time. It is the nature of long distance cycling. I soon realised that I was my companion, I was the one who would have to entertain me and converse with me most of the time.

I would talk to me, carry on a conversation with me, sing out loud…sometimes shout at drivers, or mutter at their antics under my breath. I did whatever was needed to make a monologue feel like a dialogue.

And for the most part, I got along with myself.

FEEL SORRY FOR YOURSELF. If you fall or sustain an injury, nobody's going kiss it better. Nobody will stroke you and say, 'There, there, there.' It will be up to you to recognise that you need a bit of TLC to carry on.

LOOK AFTER YOURSELF. Your personal safety and security is paramount, which takes constant vigilance and awareness of the situations you are in, and doing whatever is necessary to stay out of harm's way, like WEARING A HELMET. You also need to see to your daily needs like nourishment, rest, cleanliness and good health habits like sunscreen and vitamins. In short, keep an eye on yourself and the environment you are in.

STAY IN TOUCH. Communication is so easy with mobile phones just about anywhere in the world. Share your progress with friends and loved ones. Let them know you are safe. Do a blog, if that interests you. Answer any and all texts. It will help you feel less lonely.

EXPECT THE UNEXPECTED. This is a phrase that is unfortunately becoming increasingly trite. I call it the bend in the road. Every day, something would happen. Be prepared to be surprised, and appreciate whatever comes your way.

I'll never forget that bizarre night in Latvia with the model boat racers. It was totally mad, but makes me chuckle whenever I think about it.

There are times when expecting the unexpected is easier said than done. It took a long time for me to appreciate the horrendous rain in East Germany. That was the closest I came to quitting, but I pushed myself, felt sorry for myself, gave myself a pat on the back to make it better and carried on.

Around every bend in the road is a potential adventure. Be open to it.

BE CURIOUS. When I was in Riga, and the passer-by handed me a coupon for a free coffee, my first reaction was 'scam'. In surrendering to my curiosity, however, I was rewarded with a lovely snack and a thoroughly pleasant experience.

FORCE YOURSELF TO TALK TO OTHERS. I'm a shy person. I'm happy to respond to a stranger if he or she approaches me, but I find it incredibly difficult to walk up to a stranger and strike up a conversation.

Once I was on the road, I found that people responded favourably when I said hello, or asked a question, or even waved.

There was only one time where a German couple in my first campground didn't respond to my attempt to talk. I didn't take it personally. And it didn't stop me from trying with the next person I encountered.

Even a two-minute chat with a petrol station cashier can be rewarding.

There is no doubt in my mind that this journey is forever with me because of the people I met along the way.

WHEN IN ROME. I've been around the world several times as a filmmaker. I always considered myself a guest wherever I found myself. I would do my best to act in the way the locals did. I respected everybody, and didn't hurt anyone. I would regard local customs. I endeavoured to be courteous.

I also ate whatever food was put in front of me, and showed my appreciation.

I remember filming in an Omani seaside village ten years ago. The village elders were sitting under a palm-fringed veranda next to the sea. I wanted to film them, and asked my guide to inquire if that would be possible. The elders agreed. After I filmed, I took the field monitor over to them and played the footage back. After watching, the chief elder turned to me and said: 'I knew it would be good, because I could see that you are a good man.'

It's not rocket science. Simply get along. My cycle journey was no different.

Also there were times when I found myself in a different environment, like my stumbling upon on a nude beach and a naturist campsite. I had the choice to leave, but I thought, 'Why not? I'll just adapt and see what comes of it.' So I took my clothes off. The beach experience was good; the campsite was 'interesting' for lack of a better word. But, hey, I experienced something new. And that's what it's all about.

If you manage to complete a cycle tour without leaving your comfort zone, then you really didn't travel.

DON'T BE AFRAID TO MAKE A FOOL OF YOURSELF. Many times I felt the gaze of the locals when I rode through rural villages. I was the circus that came to town. My reaction was to smile, wave and say, 'Hi there!' Most times I would receive a smile in return.

Then there was that simple moment in Holland when Bo placed her coasters and a donation into my hand. I didn't try to contain my emotions. I openly cried in front of everyone. It didn't matter to me if I looked like a blubbering fool. I was deeply moved and needed to express it.

It ended up being a powerful moment for all of us.

DOCUMENT YOUR TRIP. Take a journal, take a camera…or if space and weight is a concern, take just a smartphone. Write about what you've experienced. Take lots of photos. Don't be afraid to ask local people to be in your selfies. Blog. You will be creating memories. But without some sort of documenting, you will soon forget them.

And finally, one final thought.

Alan Deakins

Wherever you are on your journey: **DON'T WORRY**.

THE SAMARITANS

*'Sometimes all a person wants
is an empathetic ear,
all he or she needs is to talk it out.'*
-Roy T. Bennett

*'Just the act of listening
means more than you can imagine.'*
-Bob Nelson

In the early 1950's, a young vicar in the Church of England, Chad Varah, performed his first funeral service for a fourteen-year-old girl who took her own life. She killed herself because she feared she had contracted an STD, when in fact, she was having her first period. She was too embarrassed and frightened to talk to anyone about it. This senseless loss of an innocent life deeply moved him, and the thought of her stayed with him.

A few years later, in 1953, he launched an emergency phone service called '999 for the Suicidal'. His vision was to provide a safe space so people could talk and be listened to without judgement.

It was the Daily Mirror who coined the term 'Telephone Good Samaritans'. And although Samaritans is not a religious organisation, the name has stuck and become synonymous with the idea of people being there for others who feel suicidal, or are struggling to cope in their lives.

Today, Samaritans consists of 201 self-funding branches

by over 15,000 volunteer listeners throughout the Kingdom, available 24 hours a day, every day.

Calls are free, anytime from any phone:

116 123

Email anytime:

jo@samaritans.org

To Find out more, or to find a branch near you:

www.samaritans.org

Printed in Poland
by Amazon Fulfillment
Poland Sp. z o.o., Wrocław